Editors Talk about Editing

Mass
Communication
and
Journalism

Lee B. Becker
GENERAL EDITOR

Vol. 11

The Mass Communication and Journalism series
is part of the Peter Lang Media and Communication list.
Every volume is peer reviewed and meets
the highest quality standards for content and production.

PETER LANG
New York • Bern • Frankfurt • Berlin
Brussels • Vienna • Oxford • Warsaw

SUSAN L. GREENBERG

Editors Talk about Editing

INSIGHTS FOR READERS, WRITERS AND PUBLISHERS

PETER LANG
New York • Bern • Frankfurt • Berlin
Brussels • Vienna • Oxford • Warsaw

Library of Congress Cataloging-in-Publication Data
Greenberg, Susan L.
Editors talk about editing: insights for readers, writers and publishers /
Susan L. Greenberg.
pages cm. — (Mass communication and journalism; vol. 11)
Includes bibliographical references and index.
1. Editors. 2. Book editors—United States—Interviews.
3. Periodical editors—United States—Interviews. 4. Newspaper editors—
United States—Interviews. 5. Publishers and publishing—United States.
I. Greenberg, Susan. II. Title.
PN149.8.G84   070.5'1—dc23   2014048954
ISBN 978-1-4331-2004-6 (hardcover)
ISBN 978-1-4331-2003-9 (paperback)
ISBN 978-1-4539-1523-3 (e-book)
ISSN 2153-2761

Bibliographic information published by **Die Deutsche Nationalbibliothek**.
Die Deutsche Nationalbibliothek lists this publication in the "Deutsche
Nationalbibliografie"; detailed bibliographic data are available
on the Internet at http://dnb.d-nb.de/.

The paper in this book meets the guidelines for permanence and durability
of the Committee on Production Guidelines for Book Longevity
of the Council of Library Resources.

© 2015 Peter Lang Publishing, Inc., New York
29 Broadway, 18th floor, New York, NY 10006
www.peterlang.com

Printed in the United States of America

My thanks to Iain Stevenson and Claire Warwick at UCL's Department of Information Studies; colleagues at the University of Roehampton; David Abrahamson at Northwestern University; Robert Boynton at New York University; my editor at Peter Lang, Mary Savigar; and the people interviewed here, who made time in their busy schedules.

Contents

Introduction   1

Part 1: Identity   17

Chapter 1   19
Johnny Grimond, *The Economist*

Chapter 2   33
Adam Moss, *New York* magazine

Part 2: Attention   43

Chapter 3   45
Ileene Smith, Farrar, Straus and Giroux

Chapter 4   53
Jerome McGann, University of Virginia

Part 3: Legacy   73

Chapter 5   75
Mary Hockaday, BBC Multimedia Newsroom

Chapter 6   83
John McIntyre, *The Baltimore Sun*

Chapter 7   91
Philip Campbell, *Nature*

Part 4: Devolution 101

Chapter 8 103
    LOUISE DOUGHTY, Novelist

Chapter 9 113
    CAROLE BLAKE, Literary Agent, Blake Friedmann

Chapter 10 127
    CONSTANCE HALE, Book Editor

Part 5: Digital 141

Chapter 11 143
    PETER BINFIELD, *PeerJ*

Chapter 12 157
    PHOEBE AYERS, Wikimedia Foundation

Chapter 13 171
    EVAN RATLIFF, Atavist

Conclusion 185

Appendix 193

References 195

Further Reading 203

Index 209

Introduction

Editing takes place behind the scenes, and is called by many different names. There is not all that much information about what happens during editing— what it is, exactly, that people *do*. Many people are unaware of the full range of possible editorial interventions, and therefore remain unaware of the difference editing can make, for good or ill. Like other work that happens behind the scenes, editing is often noticed only when it is done badly, or not done at all.

When one does find information about editing practice, the activities it describes are bafflingly varied. 'What an editor does all day and why he does it is usually a mystery to an author and just as much of a mystery to most of the people inside a publishing house,' writes Clarkson Potter, an editor-turned-publisher (1990: 82–83).

The result is that editing, as a subject in its own right, is not talked about very often—not even by the people who do it. Editors are by and large reluctant to draw attention to their own work, perceiving it as something that could harm the text's relationship with both author and reader. The reluctance is captured in the comments of veteran book editor Thomas McCormack, who wrote that editors 'are always in the "backroom" [and] that's where we should be' (1988: 95).

The collection of interviews presented here is an attempt to fill some of the gaps and silences. The interviews came about as part of a larger research project, a PhD that analyses editing in a comparative way. Not all of that work is covered here. In particular, a mapping of editing theory and practice through time, in the past and in the digital present, is the subject of another book to come.

Why editing?

Why bother to fill this particular gap in our knowledge, in the first place? And does anyone care?

I start by admitting my own bias, because I am writing from personal experience; first as a writer and editor in journalism and publishing and now, from the vantage point of a second career, as a teacher on a writing programme. I hope that my perspective has been transformed by viewing the topic through the lens of scholarship.

I have also discovered that curiosity about editing *is* shared by others, especially if they have ever tried to wrangle sense out of a text for other people's benefit. The huge expansion of social media and self-publishing has brought this experience home to an audience extending well beyond the world of professional editors, and has stimulated discussion about the ways in which we mediate texts. It also speaks to writers seeking an audience who have learned that pre-submission editing, of a high enough quality, will help their work find a publisher; and to the many people now teaching and studying different forms of media practice, for example at universities and colleges.

Why interviews?

Why fill the gap, specifically, with a book of interviews? Anyone wishing to know how writers approach their work suffers no lack of choice. A large and growing literature describes and explains the author's experience of the writing process, in memoirs, 'how-to' guides, essays and interviews.[1] But when it comes to editors and editing, the torrent turns into a trickle. It is rare to find accounts of editing as an everyday activity, or interviews with the people who work on the production of texts.

In scholarly works, with some exceptions,[2] editing as a specific subject can become lost within more broadly defined studies, and so potential new areas of research are lost to view. A review of scholarship about magazines notes, for example, that editing 'has not been viewed as a body, its parts having been published at wide intervals in a disparate range of publications and made relatively inaccessible due to poor cataloguing and indexing' (Jolliffe 1995: 52). The comment was published 20 years ago, but the landscape has not changed much since then.

In history, a study of editing in Victorian Britain asks: 'How does one begin to quantify and speculate on the variety of functions [that] editors of periodicals served in nineteenth-century Britain? So often we refer to someone as "editing" a magazine, without much thought about what such duties entail' (Finkelstein and Patten 2006: 148). In bibliography, there are rich pickings about the theory and practice of scholarly editing.[3] But by and large, the debate takes place in isolation from conversations about non-scholarly editing.

Descriptions of everyday editing practice can be found in 'how-to' guides; examples include Saller (2009); Lerner (2002); Norton (2009); and Zinsser (2001). However, these accounts, while useful, have a closely defined, normative purpose; they are written to provide advice and instruction, to suit a particular time and place. Occasional works of journalism make editing their subject,[4] along with a handful of memoirs such as Diana Athill's *Stet* (2000) or, from earlier times, Harold Latham's *My Life in Publishing* (1965). Gerald Gross's essay collection (1993) provides a platform for editors to write more reflectively on their own experience, but it remains an outlier.[5]

As far as I can tell, no book-length collection of interviews with editing practitioners has been published before; certainly not one that presents the encounters in a way that deliberately sets out to encourage comparison and analysis. This book therefore covers entirely new ground, by offering deep descriptions of experience from a wide range of practitioners. The aim is to throw light on how editing problems are defined and negotiated in the contemporary publishing world, and offer original source material on what people do—and think they do—when they are editing. I hope that it is also done in a way that offers a basis for future comparative explorations.

A working definition

Because of its invisibility, it is important to define the subject. According to the *Oxford English Dictionary*, the noun editing (OED 1989a) is defined as 'The action of edit (v)'. This, in turn, is defined as 'To be or act as the editor (n)' (OED 1989b), and the noun editor is defined as 'one who edits' (OED 1989c). All terms derive from the Latin noun editor, someone who puts forth or gives out—the 'e' indicates outwards movement. The earliest noted use of 'editing' as an English noun is dated 1840, but 'edition' has a first mention in 1551. This is defined as '1. The action of putting forth, or making public; publication' but also, more broadly, '2.a. The action of producing, or bringing into existence; hence, birth, creation (of orders of knighthood etc), extraction, origin. Obs' (OED 1989d).

By nature, however, dictionary definitions have a circular quality, and only tell us so much. I therefore developed a working definition for the wider research project to serve as a testable, organising hypothesis; a generic benchmark for comparative analysis.

The very short version of this working definition runs as follows: editing is a decision-making process, usually within the framework of a professional practice, which aims to select, shape and link content. The aim of editing practice is to help deliver the meaning and significance of the work to its audience; the process thus involves a relationship between author, editor and text, with the editor representing the as-yet absent reader.

For the benefit of this book's readers, the definition can be expanded as follows:

Process

Editing is part of a process, in the obvious sense that a text moves through a production cycle. But it also has its own decision-making process, and is part of a wider sense-making process. An awareness of process avoids pitting style versus substance: they are both needed. A decision-making process involves reference to a standard, which can be an implicit part of the culture or expressed in formal rules. Standards are only partly ethical: they are also an attempt to bring meaning and aesthetic beauty to a work.

Selection

Editorial selection goes by many job titles: 'content strategy' or 'curating' are recent examples. Selection involves decisions about what gets published, and what is left out. It is selection that features in the image of editor as 'gatekeeper'. But even when the gatekeeper is abolished, decisions are still made, although they may be automated or widely distributed.

In the popular imagination, the editor is a passive creature, busy telling people 'No'. An author dreams up a text and sends it to the gatekeeper, where it joins the pile of work sent by other authors; the gatekeeper then chooses from this fully imagined and achieved work. In the mind of an editor, however, selection is an active business that involves discovery; the *inventio* of rhetoric.[6] This can take the form of building lists, anthologies and series, assembling a particular set of contributors, and defining *types* of content. The editor may develop ideas from scratch and give them to someone else for development, or help a writer determine the shape of an idea.

Shaping

Editing gives a text its final shape, helping to bring it into existence. In rhetoric, this corresponds to *dispositio* (structure) and *elocutio* (style). These choices used to be the sole province of the professional; they are now experienced by a much wider public. A common assumption is that shaping decisions are made by the author alone and editing is limited to the correction of mistakes. But in practice it is difficult to draw a line between the two, even for the lightest of edits. The shaping of language includes an engagement with the text's voice; the way it sounds on the page. For texts put together by groups of people—for example, magazines, websites, works of reference, or films—a distinctive collective voice is needed, and it is the people doing the editing who create that effect.

Linking

A text does not appear in a vacuum. The interventions needed to move a text from private to public status are often taken for granted but each one calls for a set of decisions, and the material conditions of a text's production can influence its potential meaning. Conditions include the impact of the design, the title and other paratexts; public perceptions of the publisher or author; and the way it links to other texts—for example, is it part of a series? At the front of a publication or the back? Discovered randomly or a main destination? In digital media, the linking is literal and provides a key measure of value. Linking also includes metadata at the back end, and social media links pointing to a text at the front. Some online publishers, working to specific ethical standards, provide extra information about a text's history, including attribution and the rationale of post-publication amendments.

Relationships

The process does not take place in a vacuum either. All outcomes depend on the nature of the relationship between editor, author and the content itself. The author's intentions matter to the editor, but the priority is to the text, to make it as good as it can be. To do this, the editor is asking questions about the process of creation which are similar to those asked by the author, but with the distance of a third party. It is a triangular relationship.

The working definition outlined above was provided to all interviewees, and some of the conversations published here use it as a reference point. As a result of the encounters a further evolution in the definition has taken place.

The interviews suggest that editing can be described as a state of mind that enables the practitioner to see a text *as if it is not yet finished*.

Why these people?

To the extent that people know what editors do, they tend to picture them in very specific worlds. The image we conjure up for a book editor, for example, is very distinct from that of a newspaper sub.[7] We are already familiar with how those worlds differ. The aim of this book, therefore, is to draw out the ways in which different kinds of editing may be the *same* as well as distinctive. The working hypothesis is that even when editors are working on different writing genres, using different technologies, the problems they encounter and the way they attempt to resolve them contain many shared, generic features. It also takes into account that not all those performing acts of editing are called 'editor', and not all will describe themselves as one.

The people interviewed for this book are therefore chosen deliberately to represent a wide range of editing practice. The nature of their shared concerns emerges in conversation, along with the differences. To help develop the argument, the interviews have been grouped thematically, under five headings—the role of editors in creating a collective identity; the quality of attention they bring to bear; the practices and influence of legacy media; an awareness of how editing can devolve to new positions; and the journey into digital experimentation.

All of the people interviewed here are known by their peers for excelling in an aspect of editing and publishing; some are also known to a wider public, but the behind-the-scenes nature of the work makes that rare. Nine of the interviews were conducted in face-to-face meetings; another three took place by some form of telephone, and one was carried out as an email exchange. Meetings took place in London and New York, with the exception of one meeting at a university campus. Encounters lasted an average of one hour; a few ran longer. In some cases, answers to follow-up questions were gathered later by email.

Can a reliable picture of an entire subject emerge from 13 interviews? With quantitative methods such as the questionnaire, validity depends on a large sample. But in qualitative research, smaller 'purposeful sampling' of 'information-rich cases' is accepted as an important way of learning 'a great deal about issues of central importance to the purpose of the research' (Pickard 2013: 183). Steps are taken to strengthen validity, for example by establishing a chain of evidence—in this case, via digital recordings of interviews and notes taken before, during and after the encounter.[8]

When knowledge of an interviewee's identity is not essential, qualitative research may be anonymised to protect privacy. In this case, identification helps address the invisibility of editing and match the attention given to (named) authors. At the same time, the risks that interviewees might face from public exposure are reduced by the fact that they are more than commonly familiar with 'the production of written texts for broad audiences' (Wilmsen 2001: 77).

Nevertheless, to ensure fairness, care was taken to obtain informed consent and all interviewees were given the explicit right to stop the interview, or leave a question unanswered. They were also given a chance to view the transcript; an undertaking was made on my part to correct factual errors and listen sympathetically to requests for change, but 'ownership' of the recording and transcripts, and all final editorial decisions, have remained with me.

A note about frameworks

A full evaluation of interpretive frameworks relevant to editing is the subject of another book, but it is worth outlining briefly some conceptual models.

The first comes via Robert Darnton (1990), who argues that research about any single element of publishing practice can only be understood as part of a broader social system, a 'communications circuit' that takes a text from the author to its reader and back again. The circuit is not immutable: the role of participants, their position in the circuit and the nature of the relationships between them change over time.[9] The thinking behind Darnton's model has influenced the decision taken here to follow 'acts of editing' wherever they go on the circuit, and whatever they are called.

The second is Pierre Bourdieu's 'field of cultural production' (1993). Bourdieu proposes that within specific circumstances, different cultural groups create their own social universe in which they compete for power and influence, 'struggling to gain cultural capital that can be translated into more material rewards' (Finkelstein and McCleery 2005: 22). In that context, editors are among the cast of characters that drive the narrative of struggle.

Analysis of cultural production is sometimes framed in the language of social constructivism,[10] an approach that—simply put—highlights the contingency of human behaviour and warns against making assumptions about the neutrality of social institutions. In the field of communications, it provides an alternative to overly mechanistic models of 'transmitters' and 'receivers': in social constructivist enquiry, the transmitter is not neutral and technologies are seen as expressions of a particular social order (Hamilton and Heflin 2011: 1052).[11]

In the case of editing, the prevailing social constructivist metaphor is that of 'gatekeeping'. The term was first coined by Kurt Lewin (1951) to explain aspects of organisational psychology and was later applied to the news industry, for example to understand editorial decision-making processes (Clayman and Reisner 1998; White 1950; Donohew 1967). It gained new life in debates about new media channels, perceived as allowing individuals to bypass the gatekeeping of 'mainstream media'.

As an organising metaphor, gatekeeping survives because it is useful. Using Bourdieu's model, for example, it appears in Jane Tompkins' study (1985) of the changing reputations of two nineteenth-century American authors, as a way of understanding how different actors in the field of cultural production wield their influence. But it can struggle to fit all sizes. A rare example of the gatekeeping model applied to book publishing agrees that such a 'highly decentralised' industry (Coser 1975: 16) has an ability to make 'idiosyncratic decisions' that escape generalisation (1975: 18). In a broad survey of contemporary publishing, 'gatekeeper' is described as something that 'greatly oversimplifies the complex forms of interaction and negotiation between authors, agents and publishers that shape the creative process' (Thompson, 2010: 17).

Gatekeeping's usefulness can also be limited simply by becoming an orthodoxy, based on the kind of assumptions about social groups that constructivism was designed to challenge. In studies of new media, for example, it is rare to find editing described positively.[12] A common trope is to locate gatekeeping uniquely within media considered 'traditional'. By contrast, the ability to bypass professional editors—for example using social media—is taken as a marker of democracy and anti-elitism (for example, see Bruns 2005; Bardoel and Deuze 2001).[13]

The difficulty thus created is that too much is assumed, rather than examined. One assumption, that gatekeeping exists in only one place, potentially closes off discoveries about how it can mutate in form, moving to new positions in the communications circuit.[14] Another, that editing can serve as a metonym for vested interests, valorises *ulterior* motives over *ultimate* ones[15]—in this case, the impulse to make a text as good as it can be. This has the potential to add to the invisibility of practitioners by reducing them to ciphers, and deny us access to the circumstantial detail of experience that comes with recognition of their agency.

An additional difficulty with any framework that achieves the status of orthodoxy is that it can create circular thought that is closed to challenge. Hence, in the case of publishing, one comes across studies that dismiss in advance contrary views from professionals such as editors on the grounds that they are too close to their own industry to appreciate the implications of change. The result, intended or not, is an *a priori* rejection of expertise, which is excluded from debate on the grounds that the experts know too much.[16]

Social constructivism is helpful in understanding media practice as a social phenomenon, and it informs the interview methodology used for this book. But the usefulness of the 'gatekeeping' metaphor, and the wider constructivist framework, depends on remaining part of a heterodox mix. By definition, a single approach cannot ask all the questions that arise about a complex human practice. A mix of approaches, or the use of an explicitly non-totalising framework, also allows both researcher and subject to appreciate the limitations of what they know.

More about methodology

A definition helps to make the practice of editing more visible; a deep description helps even more. The semi-structured interview is a good way to achieve this.

At one end of the spectrum, interviews can be unstructured 'purposeful conversations' led by the interviewee. At the other end, human responses are collected via the highly structured researcher-administered questionnaire. In the middle lies the semi-structured interview, a form of field work in which the discussion is guided—but not ruled—by a common set of questions. It is a mix that provides both adaptability and consistency.

In the social sciences, the semi-structured interview is considered appropriate when the aim is to access 'descriptive, in-depth data that is specific to the individual and when the nature of the data is too complicated to be asked and answered easily' (Pickard 2013: 196). Interviews 'allow people to respond on their own terms and within their own linguistic parameters, providing them and the interviewer with the opportunity to clarify meanings and shared understanding' (2013: 196). The interview as a method also 'permits the respondent to move back and forth in time—to reconstruct the past, interpret the present, and predict the future, all without leaving a comfortable armchair' (Lincoln and Guba 1985: 273). All of these concerns arise here.

Interviews in the book cover the same themes, approached from multiple angles, but the selection of questions from the full set and their precise wording are varied to suit each encounter. In all cases, the aim is to throw light on the research 'problem'. Interviewees are asked, for example, if it is possible to identify the effect of editing or an absence of editing on a text; whether editing skills, principles and culture can be passed on to others in a consistent way; and whether any insights arising from editing might apply to other, similarly invisible forms of human mediation. The full set of questions is available in the appendix.

In an in-depth interview, as in any form of immersive research, the level of engagement is intense. This can create a feeling of affinity that mitigates professional distance. A larger concern relates to the need to acknowledge the ways in which a researcher's subjectivity might impinge on the discovery process. In my own case, it is not possible to remove all elements of identification that arise from long years of personal experience—nor should it be. A shared background can also make a positive difference, for example by providing insights into a little-known field and by helping to establish trust. The aim of the encounters presented here is therefore to create a forum for free discussion and maintain a balance of closeness and distance, while remaining aware of my own possible weaknesses.

Underlying the choices outlined above lies a deeper, more theoretical debate. In classic terms, the quantitative model is framed as a 'positivist' approach to observable events that are perceived as measurable, and the qualitative approach is understood within a social constructivist frame that sees meaning as socially constructed through language. To identify the meaning thus constructed, it becomes important 'to understand those being studied from their perspective, from their point of view' (Gorman and Clayton 2005: 3).

The narrative approach is sometimes discussed using the language of 'performance', as a way of explaining how the subject of an interview chooses stories that appeal to a particular audience (Thomson 2011: 88). The concept of performance can also be applied to the interviewer, to describe both the interview encounter itself and the writer's 'persona' on the page (Keeble 2014).

Oral history is a rich source of guidance for interview technique. Historians have built up a body of practice around the public use of spoken evidence from named individuals. This includes ethical precautions to prevent harm to interviewees (Quinlan 2011: 27–8) and a sensitivity to 'time' as a dimension that can influence meaning, both in terms of the life stages of the interviewee and his or her place in the chronological events of the external world. Although the present book is not a work of history as such, each interview is inevitably an act of remembering that situates personal experience within a much larger picture.

Memory is famously complex and oral historians, along with other writers using personal narratives, have generated 'ever more sophisticated understandings of the social and psychological processes of memory and remembering' (Thomson 2011: 88). To support the reliability of sources, the oral historian is enjoined to 'listen to how interviewees describe and explain their own memories and remembering' because 'memory work is not the exclusive preserve of the researcher [and] most people can offer profound insight about...their past experience and its meaning and significance in the present' (2011: 91).

The phrase 'shared authority' is used to describe the particular type of remembering that goes on in an oral history relationship. At best, the interview becomes

> a dynamic, dialogic relationship that encourages active remembering and meaning making. The interviewee may start by performing fixed or rehearsed stories, but in the process of remembering, and with the careful encouragement and gentle probing of the interviewer, more complex and unexpected memories may emerge (2011: 88).

In the shared authority approach, the emphasis on collaboration is extended to the post-interview editing process. The conventions of oral history encourage giving interviewees—the 'narrators' of the story—a chance 'to reflect further and to recollect and to think purposefully about what kind of statement they want to make for the historical record' (Wilmsen 2001: 67). This is partly to avoid 'an overemphasis on the interview as the magical moment when meaning is produced' and, more generally, to include in the process the 'social relations of oral history production' (2001: 65). It is interesting, given the subject of this book, that collaborative work at this stage is seen as 'key to the production of meaning during editing' (2001: 72).

A more practical reason for such an approach to editing is also cited: that 'some degree of editing is necessary to produce a transcript that conveys the meaning clearly' (2001: 71). This, in turn, involves decisions about how to adapt speech to the printed page, including

> how to adjust punctuation to assure that the text accurately reflects the narrator's meaning, which false starts to delete, if any, how many crutch words to retain in the transcript to portray the idiosyncrasies of the narrator's speech without them becoming distracting to the reader, whether to complete or change incomplete and ungrammatical sentences, whether to ask the narrator to elaborate on a given topic, how to divide the transcript into sections to help future readers easily find portions of the interview that may be of particular interest to them, and many other points peculiar to the transcript under consideration (2001: 70).

In best oral history practice, therefore, a balance is sought between verbatim 'faithfulness' to the words spoken in the moment, and clarity for the reader. Such work involves selection, structuring and précis:

[E]xtremely lengthy excerpts from...interviews are not practical from the point of view of publishers' word limits or readers' patience. Wherever the particular choice of words, nuance, or a causal dynamic and its complexities are at issue, it is generally most persuasive to rest the argument on narrators' actual words, but summary, paraphrase, and categorization of narrators' stories...are all necessary' (Maynes et al. 2008: 144–145).

In sum, researchers handling verbatim records discover what every writer, reporter, editor, printer, or web producer knows from daily practice in publishing: that language is opaque, successful human communication is difficult, meaning flies through one's fingers and expression requires skill and care.

In the social science literature, this difficulty is usually framed in social constructivist terms, relating to the 'social relations' of the interview process. However, it would be wrong to see constructivism as the only approach that engages with the expression of individual human subjectivity through language. An analysis of the alternatives is the subject of future study.

Collaboration or confrontation?

The priority given in naturalistic research to consultation with interview sources is one of the key differences between scholarship and journalism practice.

The convention in oral history is that interviewing is a collaborative act 'in which both players make equally important contributions' (Quinlan 2011: 26). Collaboration is also important in the everyday work of media production, as the stories here show. And for the interviews in this book, too, a collaborative approach is justified. In another context, one can imagine a sharper debate with the individuals and organisations appearing in these pages, and some tensions remain in the encounters—as they must. But there are already many studies that analyse media practice at the level of wider trends and forces, alert to its contradictions; the priority in this study is to listen to voices that do not often speak loudly on their own account, and through juxtaposition, put them in dialogue with each other.

Nevertheless, it is not safe to assume that *all* interview encounters, in all circumstances, can be collaborative. Within journalism and other forms of publishing, the sheer pressure of events can mean that collaboration—between editor and author, and between author and subject—is an ideal that cannot always be followed. In practice it exists on a spectrum, ranging from ultimate control by the interviewee or author, to total control by the publisher.

Journalism has also developed its own ethical conventions to address the 'public interest' dimensions of the genre. In particular, to maintain a pact of trust with the reader, it must allow for the possibility of confrontation with a source. Conventions exist for consultation with the source, but the routine sharing of interview transcripts is treated with caution as something that might undermine editorial independence.

Journalists are among the 'question-asking professions' (Quinlan 2011: 26) and oral historians acknowledge that 'some similarities between journalistic approaches to interviewing and oral history approaches are worth noting' (2011: 25). The journalist, as much as the social scientist, may consider not only information given but also the way in which it is delivered—body language, pauses and silences that indicate possible motives (Rabinowitz 1977).

Narrative journalism in particular often involves the use of 'immersive' forms of discovery involving intensive engagement with people, places and events through personal witness, as well as in-depth verification of documents, for example when used for the dramatic reconstruction of events. All this requires the author to negotiate complex ethical and aesthetic tensions (Greenberg and Wheelwright 2014). In particular, questions arise about the 'phenomenological origins' of the work (Hartsock 2000; Sims 2009), stances towards subjectivity (Greenberg 2011), and the editing of verbatim speech (Forde 2008).

Even when different language is used, therefore, direct parallels in methodology exist between oral history and non-academic forms of discovery. But it is worth underlining that the lessons of experience do not travel in only one direction, from scholarship to more general writing practice. We can also speculate how naturalistic inquiry in the academy might learn from the best practices of journalism, for example on managing potential conflict in the reporting of human speech.

Not 'just' an interview

The importance given by oral historians to collaboration with sources is significant here for another reason: it recognises that the making of an interview text—as with *any* text—involves a complex process of transformation.

This is a useful corrective to the assumption sometimes made about interviews, that the transcription is given, and that the words on the page are in the sole ownership of the speaker. In reality, the process is a highly mediated one, and there is nothing obvious or given about it.

Just as a text is never just a text, an interview is never *just* an interview. The interviewer is constantly engaged in producing meaning through the framing of the topic; the selection of the interviewee; the wording of questions; the tone of the encounter; and the nature and timing of responses.

And then, there is the editing. As noted above, even the most basic interview transcript demands a series of decisions about how to re-enact a conversation on the page. When that text is published for a wider public, yet another round of decisions must be made about how to balance fidelity and clarity, to find what is 'right' and true in the encounter and to apply skill to language use. Nor are the decisions ever made by the editor alone: the people whose words are being re-enacted have their own responses to seeing their words in the raw.

In the case of this book, editing was carried out with four main concerns:

- Ethics: the removal of passages designated 'off the record' by the interviewee.
- Clarity: the use of square brackets for paraphrased passages and ellipses that help to link utterances separated by a short digression;
- Salience: the removal of utterances relevant only to the practicalities of the encounter, such as greetings and explanations, and removal of repetitive verbal tics such as 'you know', as the minutiae of oral style are not directly relevant to the aims of this project.
- Time: with a book, the editing must anticipate a long lead time from interview to publication. In places, therefore, references have been added to make the timeframe clear.

The central concern of the book, and the larger research project that gave it life, is to test assumptions about editing. Such assumptions are often expressed in binaries that pit against each other the raw and the cooked, creative and critical, authentic and processed. The working hypothesis is that such binaries obscure rather than enlighten our understanding of editing practice. This idea is explored and expanded by the varied voices re-enacted here.

The discussion about method and ethics summarised in this introduction serves to remind us of the almost comic *meta-ness* of a text about editing. The core subject of the book is the making of a text, and it is being explored through the making of a text—what Tennis calls 'writing as a technique' (2008: 106). The transcripts of discussions about editing have been edited by the interviewer and reviewed by the interviewees, so that editors are reviewing the editing done to a discussion about editing. In one case (McGann) the interviewee talks not just about his own editorial practice but his own work on the theorisation of editing. It is a game of three-dimensional chess.

Patterns of conversation

In the original research project, the interviews were structured in a wholly thematic way.[17] For this book, an explicit choice was made to present them in narrative form, to convey a sense of conversation between two people. The thematic potential is still present, but it is up to the reader whether or not to give that attention. For those interested in this aspect of the work, some key themes are identified in the conclusion, but they can be summarised here: 'Naming and metaphors'; 'Defining editorial principles'; 'Giving value to practice'; and 'Responding to digital challenges'.

In the pages that follow, the interviewees themselves have the chance to put some of these themes and insights in their own words.

Notes

1. Examples include Hemingway 2010 (memoir), King 2000 (how-to), Conroy 2000 (essays), Boynton 2005; Vida 2005; Gourevitch 2009 (interviews).
2. Surveys of contemporary publishing include Bradley 2008 and Thompson 2010.
3. See for example Simon and Fyfe 1994; Cohen 1991.
4. See MacFarquhar 1991; Morrison 2005; Edemariam 2006.
5. There are some breakthrough moments: at the time of writing, the story of the legendary book editor Max Perkins (Berg 1978) and his relationship with author Thomas Wolfe was being made into a Hollywood film.
6. For background on rhetoric, see Crowley and Hawhee 2012; Burke 1969.
7. In the UK, 'sub-editor', or 'copy editor' in the US.
8. Other measures recommended for qualitative research include cross-validation of personal testimony from a variety of sources; the establishment of logical connections between data and conclusions; the deliberate inclusion of contradictory data; preparedness to entertain alternative explanations; awareness of the limitations of both data and generalisability; and self-reflection on the part of the researcher 'to allow for their own perceived prejudices and biases' (Gorman and Clayton 2005: 25).
9. An updated version of the communications circuit has been developed by Murray and Squires (2013).
10. An approach first outlined in the 1960s by Berger and Luckmann (1990).
11. Morozov, for example, warns against 'essentialism' in the analysis of socio-technical systems and refers to social constructivism to justify putting 'the internet' in permanent scare quotes (2013a, b).
12. In one rare example, gatekeeping is described as a 'potential force of cohesion in a period of rapidly accelerating social fragmentation' (Singer 1998).
13. This emerges in the tone and vocabulary. In Bruns, for example, people with whom the author disagrees are described as 'insincere' (2005: 71) and showing an 'ugly face' (2005: 72). People with whom he agrees are said to be 'critiquing and counterbalancing the hegemonic interests which control much of the mainstream media oligopoly'

(2005: 309). McIntyre (2014) sometimes confronts anti-editing animus in his blog at *The Baltimore Sun*.

14. Morozov argues that mediation has not disappeared but has increased, through the actions of metadata. Using the outsourcing of a comments section for spam analysis as an example, he says: 'Something that didn't used to have mediators now has dozens… Amazon says it is fighting gatekeepers so that people can go self-publish. But [it] is the ultimate gatekeeper' (2013b).

15. The distinction between 'ulterior' and 'ultimate' motives is articulated by Burke (1969).

16. The 'vested interest' argument is used by Clay Shirky when he argues that professional publishing is now 'a bottleneck, not a service' (2008: 57) because it no longer solves a problem. Later, Shirky allows that 'editing' and 'fact-checking' can be exempted from the diagnosis of redundancy, as two necessary 'parent professions' of writing (Shirky 2012).

17. In addition to standard textual edits, the transcripts were put through manual coding using qualitative analysis software. Although this is not strictly necessary, it does provide an additional lens through which to view the conversations, helping to highlight thematic patterns.

Part 1: Identity

Editors help to create a collective identity, beyond the voices of individual contributors. Historically, the magazine is the form that has brought this role to the forefront. This section therefore includes two major figures in contemporary magazine editing, on both sides of the Atlantic: Johnny Grimond at *The Economist*, and Adam Moss at *New York*.

Chapter 1

JOHNNY GRIMOND

Writer at Large, The Economist[1]
Interview: Wednesday, June 13, 2012
Holland Park, London

The meeting recorded here took place just a few weeks after Johnny Grimond's retirement from *The Economist*, his professional home since 1969. Some of that time was spent as foreign editor, and during the interview it became clear that Grimond had edited my own work in the 1990s, during a stint as a Prague correspondent.

The Economist is an apt case study for this book, because its 'tightly edited and closely argued' style[2] is widely recognised as a key to its success. It is an example of a consistent collective voice and a model of publishing in which *not* getting rid of the middleman has made a positive difference. Until his retirement, Grimond played a key role in defining that voice.

The publication's style guide, long edited by Grimond, explains the creed:

'*The Economist* has a single editorial outlook, and it is anonymous. But it is the work of many people, both in London and abroad. If the prose of our Tokyo correspondent is indistinguishable from the prose of our Nairobi correspondent, readers will feel…robbed of variety [and] wonder whether these two people exist…The moral for good editors is that they should respect good writing. That is mainly what this style guide is designed to promote.'[3]

The discussion that follows adds some three-dimensional detail to this picture, throwing light on how an editing culture is created and maintained, how skills are shared, and how technology can pose new challenges for the transfer of practice.

SG *When you took the job, what level was it? Were any qualifications required?*

JG No. I had a degree in PPE[4] from Oxford [which] was relevant to *The Economist*. But as you know, it's not a profession in the proper sense of the word, in that there are no qualifications required to be a journalist. The one qualification [needed] for a national newspaper, in those days, was being a member of the National Union of Journalists, but that was not necessary at *The Economist* so I didn't even have that.

I didn't intend to be a journalist. I fell into it by accident. I wanted to be an economist, or I thought I did. I applied for a job and was told that if I really wanted to be an economist I should go back to university and do a second degree. But one of the people interviewing me, a former editor of *The Economist*, said that since I'd done a bit of journalism, why don't I go there? I'd travelled in the United States after leaving university, in the latter part of 1968. And in order to live there I'd done a bit of freelance journalism. [The interviewer] introduced me to his successor Alastair Burnet, who offered me a three-month summer job; what might now be called an internship. And one way or another, I have been there ever since.

SG *What different roles did you have, while you were there?*

JG I started out with the specific responsibility of writing about Africa. I had virtually no qualifications for that, [only] slightly more than the person who'd been doing it before, who knew very little and had a reluctance to go there—a phobia of flying, almost. I had spent what would now be called my gap year in Africa…And without the intention of being a journalist, let alone displacing anybody else, through a series of accidents I found myself writing about Africa. I went on to do other things after that. I wrote about the European Community when Britain joined, went to the United States for a year on a fellowship, then came back and edited the Britain section. I edited the US section—American Survey, as it was then called—for about ten years in the eighties. Then I became the foreign editor for about 13 years. About ten years ago—2002, possibly 2003—I became something called a writer at large.

In practical terms, what happens at *The Economist* is that pretty much everybody is a jack of all trades. You have a subject area or region, but everybody is expected to write and edit, and sub-edit, and do everything from the very beginning of the journalistic process. [That means you] commission articles, sub them when they come in, and read other people's subbing work, because the nature of editing at *The Economist* is that every piece goes through several people. And then, [you] oversee the pieces right up to the moment they go to the printers. In the days when we were set in hot metal, we used to go off to the typesetters on a Thursday, the day *The Economist* is printed. Reading the proofs, reading and correcting, many times—first of all in-galley, and then in-page— putting in captions, writing headlines, proofreading and all the time polishing, or attempting to polish, until the very last moment. *The Economist* is the work of many hands every week.

The division of labour that existed on other papers didn't apply at *The Economist* and it remains a fairly small staff. Everyone was expected to do everything and that included writing the captions, choosing pictures with the picture editor, commissioning charts, making sure the heading on the chart is appropriate…That was great fun. It meant that you weren't confined to one particular activity which you might or might not enjoy, and you were doing a bit of everything. That was something most people enjoyed, but inevitably, some people were better at one thing than at others.

SG *Do you have the reader in mind when you're working, and if so, in what way?*

JG It's a very difficult question to answer. You have the reader in mind to the extent that there is someone whom we shall call the reader and we want that person to read what you're writing, or what you're editing. And with the reader in mind, you should feel under an obligation to ensure that the article that you're working on is intelligible, interesting, well written, accurate— all these things. The article should have a structure; it should have, broadly speaking, a beginning, a middle and an end, and the reader should want to read on.

I think that's a good test of any article; you imagine there is somebody who has picked up the magazine and it falls open at a certain page; and they see Swaziland as a fly title and they say, 'I have no interest in Swaziland'. But then the headline catches their eye and so they find themselves reading the first sentence. And the first sentence draws them in a bit, and after a paragraph they're hooked. I don't pretend that you can do this with every single story in every single issue.

I'm a great admirer of *The New Yorker* in its current phase. Very frequently I find myself opening it, seeing an article and saying, 'I have no interest in this whatsoever' and yet I end up reading the whole thing—and they're much longer articles than most in *The Economist*. I think that's the mark of good journalism, or good writing.

You have a duty to the reader to make things as interesting, as accurate, as well written, as you possibly can. But I don't write things to *please* the reader. Well, even that has to be qualified, because you do say to yourself sometimes, when you're subbing an article, 'the reader needs to know more about this;

what we're giving is inadequate', or more often, too much. But in general I don't say, 'our readers don't want to know about Swaziland'. I think that's a mistake. What you say is, 'I think this is rather interesting and readers would find it interesting even if they think they wouldn't'. So in that sense, I think it's a mistake to prejudge your readers' interests and curiosities.

It may be different if you work for a different kind of publication. If you were writing, for instance, for a newsletter on the petroleum industry, people are reading you because they really have to find out what's going on in their industry. Very few people really *have* to read *The Economist*. There may be some diplomats who feel it necessary [but] most people read it because they enjoy it, and they enjoy being informed, and they enjoy coverage of the news that perhaps other papers don't give them. They enjoy agreeing or being annoyed sometimes, but it's not essential for them, and the reason they read it is as a form of entertainment. I hope it's a superior form of entertainment.

We do try and cover the week's news and put it in a context and make sense of it, [but] we don't say to ourselves, 'Oh we *must* cover that'. We think, if you're not interested in this, too bad—you're missing out on something and let's see if we can't get you to read this story.

Sometimes, what you learn is unrelated directly to what you're reading about, but it's applicable to other things, so you never know what people will get from it. The serendipitous discovery of reading newspapers, of any kind, is a big part of their charm to me. One reason I don't like getting my news online is that I know that if I want to find out what's going on in Syria I can turn to Syria in any paper, but what I don't know is the unknown unknown. You've turned the page, and here's a story on something that you had no knowledge about, you didn't know that it would be there, but there it is, and it's interesting.

SG *Is judgment important?*

JG Yes, *The Economist* is unashamed of its approach to journalism. There is a leader section at the front which is outright editorial and the rest is presented as analysis. There is a lot of raw reporting in there, but it's usually combined with analysis and putting events into context, and so there is a lot of comment throughout. You can criticise it on several grounds; some would no doubt say it's biased reporting. A lot of it is opinionated, but it's not masquerading as completely impartial, a God's-eye view of events.

The Economist has a point of view, and always has done. It was founded in the 1840s to make the case for free trade against protection. [It was a time when] there was a great debate about the Corn Laws and free trade in Britain and it is a liberal paper, in the old-fashioned sense. Nearly everyone who picks it up realises very soon that it has a point of view. You may like it or you may dislike it, but I think it's more honest than the attempted division of newspaper writing into comment and reporting.

The truth is, you can write a story which is ostensibly completely objective, but the very choice of remarks you choose to publish, and the order in which you use them—who gets the last word, and whether you get some nitwit to offer the contrary view—can leave in the reader's mind a completely different sense of how this event played out, from another equally—on the face of it—objective account. You or I could set it as an exercise—choose an event, write it in a completely objective way, and you would quite easily get people giving accounts that present a very different picture of what happened.

The very selection of what you're going to write about is important: what you put on the cover in a given week. Or if you're a broadcaster, what's going to lead the news. I happen to know that yesterday at the BBC World Service there was a discussion about whether they should lead on a UN-sourced story about putting children on Syrian tanks as human shields and the torture of children, or whether they should lead on a judgment in Australia about Lindy Chamberlain, whose child was eaten by a dingo 25 years ago. Well, they led on the dingo. I think journalists kid themselves if they think that it is possible to [be] completely unbiased. We're all biased by our background, by our education, by our outlook—and in some ways it's a good thing to recognise that.

SG The Economist *expresses an opinion, yes, but the choices are not arbitrary— it is documented in some way...*

JG Yes, and you analyse something very badly if you choose to ignore aspects that don't suit your case; if you present only half the story, or choose to ignore the counter argument. I think you can be opinionated but fair, and if it's done properly, you will leave the reader with the possibility of coming to a different conclusion from yours. Certainly in any editing I've done, I hope I've always wanted to see the other side of the story and acknowledged it, even if it's not elaborated fully.

SG *One could say that is where the reader comes into mind, because you're having an argument with yourself in your own head: you are reading the article and saying, 'Well, if I wasn't me, what would I think about this?'*

JG I think there is an analogy there with judges who obviously hold views but nonetheless conduct a trial in a way that can achieve justice. In a very small way, I think journalists should be trying to do the same thing. They have a duty to try to get to what is going on but they should acknowledge that they do this with limited information. On the *Today* programme this morning, Peter Hennessy was talking about contemporary history and acknowledged that you're very constrained, writing history about the present day: there are a lot of documents available, but you don't have the benefit of context, seeing things from a distance. You can still do it, so long as you acknowledge your limitations.

SG *You have explained that editors are not a separate group at* The Economist, *so perhaps this question doesn't apply. But can I just check: have you ever felt as an editor that your work is invisible or unrecognised in any way?*

JG I think it *is* an unrecognised art, if you want to call it that. Its importance is recognised within *The Economist* because I think editing is the secret of *The Economist*'s success. What it has done so effectively is to take the same sort of copy as you find from any journalist anywhere, and turn it into something just a little bit different and, I hope, better. The key to that is in the editing process, having editors. I think this jack-of-all-trades aspect is also important, because editors know what it's like to write a story and—if they're good editors—they know how to ruin a story as well. If they're very good editors they can change a story hugely with just a few tweaks. The best editors at *The Economist* have been capable of altering the entire thrust of a leader, for instance, with the addition or deletion of just a few words.

But certainly, editing is crucial to the print edition of *The Economist* and for that reason, it is well recognised that it's one of the most important things you do. The people who have both power and responsibility at *The Economist* are the section editors, and they're the ones who do most of the raw editing.

SG *The Economist is noted for having its own voice, as distinct from the voice of each individual writer. I'm curious about how the collective voice is achieved.*

JG Not surprisingly, it has several components. One is the magazine's history. It comes from a nineteenth-century liberal, free trade background [and this] colours the general outlook.

I think it's fair to say that *The Economist* is, and always has been, liberal on social issues and that is extended to things like decolonisation as well. *The Economist* has generally taken a stance that is liberal with a small 'l', and sometimes, especially in the nineteenth century, with a capital 'L'. Even in the twentieth century, after the Second World War for instance, it shared the Liberal Party's support for the independence of African colonies, Britain's membership of the European common market and an enlightened attitude to immigration, at a time when both Labour and the Conservatives were opposed. But in the twentieth century *The Economist* has often been associated with conservatism, and not surprisingly—although perhaps vigorous pro-Americanism would better describe the outlook. When I joined it was chiefly famous for its views on Vietnam. It was credited with making the case for American policy in Vietnam more cogently than anyone else, including possibly the American administration of the day.

Anonymity [is another factor]. It's easier to have a collective voice if you don't have individual names above the articles because—and here we go back to editing—it means the editor has greater licence to alter copy. So if we have a Marxist or an extreme right-winger writing a piece, that was possible because of the editing; people's copy would not go straight into the paper with passages or sentences that jarred with the tone.

It would be dull if the whole thing read as though it had come out of a sausage machine. So I hope there is a variety; it would be ridiculous to say that there should only be one style. Everything should be clear, intelligible, accurate, interesting and readable—but beyond that, I don't think every paragraph should have three sentences, or whatever. There should be a variety of writing within the constraints, and those constraints aren't very limiting. Presumably, most publications would insist on similar criteria.

I'm not saying that views *constitute* the tone. But the fact that it's anonymous makes people believe that there is a form of *Economist* writing that is consistent throughout, and it is true to some degree. Not entirely for ideological reasons; it's because we try to cram into one issue a whole week's news, and we cover a lot of things. We cover the world, and we cover a lot of topics in business and finance in greater detail than many other publications—certainly more than other news weeklies. [And most business publications] wouldn't have so much in the way of politics, books, arts and science and so on.

So, there is a lot in *The Economist,* and in order to cover them all, there is a premium on conciseness. I think tight writing, combined with clarity, is one of the keys to *The Economist's* success. If everything is so compressed you have to read it three times to understand what's being said, that's not good. But if you cut the waffle and get to the point quickly, and you make it clearly and give people the nub of what they want, you're doing pretty well. It's much more difficult to write an article of 600 words than 1,000 words. It's a good exercise to ask people to write the same piece at different lengths, and find whether you get any more out of a longer piece.

Sometimes you do. One of the changes that's taken place during my time is that we now carry two or three longer articles—three-page articles, usually on the cover story or related to it. It was felt, I think rightly, that our leaders came forth with thundering opinions...but did not always provide the

supporting material. And on some topics it is good to have a handsome helping of that, to give the feeling that the view is based on some degree of fact.

SG *Does* The Economist *use freelances?*

JG We do use freelances, mostly abroad. We depend on freelances for a lot of
copy. [This] takes us back to where we started; this is where the importance
of editing comes in. If you are a freelance, you write a story for *The Economist*
in the same way as you would for [any publication]. If you're in a foreign
posting, you're really busy, things are going on and you can't spend too long
saying, 'How do I phrase this?' You get your story done and get on with it.
And that's where the editing comes in. If it's well done, the tone or the voice
can be achieved without too much trouble by someone sitting in St James's
Street. But if they get it wrong, if you're a freelance, it can drive you mad.

SG *We've talked about voice and tone in a general way. There is also an aesthetic
to this. How would you describe the aesthetic of the editing?*

JG It's another characteristic of *The Economist* that there is some wit in it,
largely conveyed through headings and captions. That is one aspect of the
aesthetic. Readers definitely do like a nice turn of phrase, and even a joke
now and again. Probably three out of four jokes should be crossed out, because they work when they're good and they become tiresome if they're not
good—and by good, I'm setting the standard quite high. I think the same
goes for a lot of other things that journalists do, like using swear words or
obscenities. They should find their way into print very seldom. Not because
we're shocked by reading 'fuck', but the words lose their value if every issue
has a swear word.

There are ways of writing in which you want conversational everyday language, but I don't think you want contractions in every sentence; I think it's
worth writing out 'it is not' rather than 'it isn't' because the mind makes the
contraction for you and it becomes too chatty if it's all like that.

I think the aesthetic is to keep things plain, almost austere. We went to
colour relatively late. Alastair Burnet, the editor who employed me, was the
person who made the covers witty. Before that, in the fifties, the first leader
was on the cover; there was no cover worth speaking of. Then it evolved [but]
it was a pretty austere publication even in the seventies. It was printed on
coarse newsprint with an airmail edition for America.

When we went to glossy paper, letters came in saying, 'We loved reading the old toilet paper that *The Economist* was printed on'. They didn't last
long, those letters—any change is always greeted with some resistance. But
even then, there was an austerity to the layout, the use of photographs and

illustrations. To this day, people sometimes ask, 'Are there pictures in *The Economist*, or is it all words?' They're obviously not close readers but nonetheless, it shows that the wider public still think of *The Economist* as being quite hard-going.

The writing was designed to be in keeping with the design; it wasn't immensely jazzy, and you didn't have the variety you can have in a serious daily newspaper, like a very funny columnist. But at the same time it was also designed to be readable, so that people who made the effort to pick it up and start reading would find that it was pleasurable to do so. Part of that pleasure was derived from getting what they wanted in an economical way.

So the aesthetic is about concision, clarity, and of course, nice writing. It's very hard to say what constitutes good writing but we recognise it when we see it. Anne Wroe, [who] generally writes the obituary, is an example of someone who just has it, and is also a very good editor. She is taking on my role as the style person there.

So good writing is terribly important, and people expect it. They notice when we make a mistake. They write in and invariably say, 'One of the reasons I read *The Economist* is because I enjoy the writing, and I am shocked that you should say "whom" when you mean "who", or vice versa'. I won't say everyone reads it because it's well written, but it's a factor and it's appreciated.

You set the tone to some degree through these headings and captions, because when people pick up [an issue] and flip through it, that's the first thing you see. They're drawn in, or possibly repelled, by these headings and captions. And if they're witty or well put, that's successful. I think people weary of stale expressions [like] 'southern discomfort', 'the empire strikes back', or 'unlevel playing field'. *The Economist*, when it appeals to the intelligence of the reader, is at its most successful when the reader says, 'Aha, that's nicely put' or, 'I see that allusion'.

There is an element of snobbery in the advertising campaigns which sometimes makes me squirm, but they play on that a certain amount.

SG *It's a type of attention to language that is sometimes what is meant by describing something as 'literary'. In that sense,* The Economist *is literary.*

JG I think that's right, but with a lack of pretension. We always try to change foreign phrases dropped into a piece: if there's an English phrase that does the job of a Latin phrase, take it out for heaven's sake.

SG *The old George Orwell rule—'use' instead of 'utilise'.*[5]

JG Exactly. That's very much my bible, and [Sir Ernest] Gowers' *Plain Words* (Gowers 1987). It's wonderful when people use words well, and it's important to have an ear for what you're writing, but much of the greatest English literature is written in very simple ways. And of course jargon and technical terms are off-putting. 'Try not to annoy your reader' is a good rule, and you can annoy the reader by being too clever, or by making too many in-jokes, being pretentious or simply by using language that he doesn't understand. Why should you struggle to read something if it's full of technical terms, or badly written?

SG *It raises the question, how do people learn the art of editing? You've described in general terms how it happens at* The Economist. *What should one do to develop this skill, this kind of attention?*

JG I think that's a very difficult question to answer. There has never been any formal training at *The Economist,* and the way in which people have learned or not learned is by observation—and this has become much harder. In the days when you had a typewriter, you typed your story on a piece of paper and handed it to somebody who made changes with a pen, and then handed it back to you and said, 'Is this okay?' You could see exactly what had been done; and if it was well done, it was a revelation. Working with a good editor, it was a wonderful way of learning. And if you didn't like something you could also go and say, 'You've done an injustice to what I'm trying to say here; can we come to some agreement?' So it had many merits.

Now, we have all got screens. You send your piece to someone who picks it up on his screen, or her screen, and subs it. And then you are asked, 'Is it okay?' and it's actually very difficult to see. It becomes much harder to see why things have been changed and how they've been changed. Somehow, the opportunity disappears, in spite of new technology being a time-saving activity, to read it closely and discuss it with the editor, who's always busy moving onto the next thing. That's not a good reason, but it nonetheless seems to be true. The fact is, it's much harder to see what's happened to your story. Indeed, if it's been really well edited, you won't even know: you will just think, 'Oh, that's how I wrote it, is it? Reads rather well'. And that is a real drawback, I think.

SG *Yes, good editing is meant to be invisible.*

JG It should, be, you're right. And of course, I won't for a moment say that all editing is good. There are bad editors who make things worse, no question. And even people who make very modest changes can deaden or flatten something. John Gross, who used to edit the *Times Literary Supplement,* [once described] how a contributor could write a piece and it would hardly be changed at all, but just a few words had been altered and the general effect was to flatten the whole piece and deflate it just a little bit. So, I'm not saying that all editing is for the good, but nonetheless a well-edited piece is what you're there for, and it can be done. But it's a difficult thing to learn.

The only solution to this problem I've described, with computer typesetting, is that you take a printout and you do some textual analysis, and you compare what you wrote with what it [looked like before].

SG *Or you use 'track changes'...*

JG You can do that in Word and so on, but we have a [content management] system which makes comparison difficult. It may be possible, but it doesn't really happen.

The only other way is to have someone who will metaphorically put an arm around your shoulder and say, 'Look, I think your pieces would be more successful if you did something differently; if you worked out what it is you're really trying to say'. Or, 'Don't clear your throat in the first paragraph; get straight into the story'. Very often, even relatively trivial advice such as a preference for 'use' rather than 'utilise' requires someone going through a piece you've written and saying, 'This is how I think you could improve your work; it would be a better piece if you did this'.

To some extent, the stylebook that I produced makes these points. But one can read these bits of advice, and not see how they apply to your own copy...it makes a difference having someone point something out, allowing you to see that one way of putting it works better than another way.

And euphony, as well: does it sound nice to the ear? 'Eastern Europe' is a perfectly nice phrase [but] 'Eastern European' isn't such a nice phrase, and it is helpful if someone points that out to you and says, 'Instead of saying "Eastern Europeans", why don't you say "East European"—it just sounds better'. And saying to people, 'Read your copy through: when you've written a sentence or paragraph, stop and read it and ask yourself, is there a better word I could have used? Could I have used fewer words?'

You need to ask yourself these 'Orwellian' questions. They're the luxury you have on a weekly; [a luxury] that your reader expects you to have. They're paying quite a lot for *The Economist* and they expect it to be well written, and these are the little things that can make a difference.

SG *Does this process of coaching, mentoring take place?*

JG *The Economist* runs very much to a rhythm. On Monday morning at 10.30 every department has a meeting, followed 45 minutes later by a general editorial meeting. This has been immutable over the last 50 years, if not longer. And at those meetings you draw up a list of what you think is going to appear in your sections, and each part of the paper comes together to see whether they're overlapping, or contradicting, or fitting together. And to decide what goes on the cover, and what leaders will be written. Of course, that list changes through the week, but nonetheless that's where you'll begin.

On Monday afternoon, journalists who are writing articles or leaders start doing their work. They make calls, they do interviews, they do their reading, they try and work out what they're going to say. In the old days, section editors sent telegrams and telexes to correspondents saying, 'Can you tell us what's going on, and can you answer the following questions?' Now it is done by email. Some of that will have already [taken place] over the weekend, or the previous week. And there is planning, for example what would be a good week to write about the energy crisis.

Tuesday's more of the same, but some copy may start coming in. Wednesday is the day on which most of *The Economist* gets edited. Correspondents send in their stories. If you are, say, the Argentine correspondent, you send your piece to the editor of the Americas section, who reads it with several things in mind, accuracy being one of them. Another is to make sure it hangs together and makes sense and isn't obviously self-contradictory—a shortcoming which is surprisingly easily committed. And also the humdrum tasks of sub-editing, like making sure of punctuation. In the case of Spanish, we try to put in all the right accents and diacritical marks. Some people think we should do [that] for every other language in the world [but] we can't quite bring ourselves to do it.

Then someone will send that subbed copy back to the correspondent to make sure the correspondent's happy with it; that errors haven't been introduced, or something important hasn't been crossed out. At the same time it will go to the foreign editor, who will read it and ask questions and say, 'I don't understand this'. And then it will go to the editor-in-chief—in practice, the editor delegates to a night editor who is nearly always a senior figure of some kind—who does it again. And in the meantime, the section editor has lined up any charts or maps or pictures.

As far as the actual editing process is concerned, there will be at least three people who have read it by Wednesday night.

On Thursday morning, people arrive at 7.30am or even earlier. They start reading page proofs, and go through the whole thing again. Very often it will be a fresh set of eyes—deliberately. All the section editors read everything again in proof, but it will be someone with a different area of expertise, and he will say or she will say, 'I don't understand this' or, 'Are you sure this is the way we spell it?'

What goes up online over the course of the week doesn't go through these iterations, and I think it shows. And of course online, you have no constraints about space, so people can babble on.

SG *It sounds like a form of peer review.*

JG It is. That's exactly what it is. And it's all done within a short space of time. And on the whole, I think it works.

Notes

1. For official purposes, and as a matter of tradition, *The Economist* is registered as a newspaper.
2. The phrase is used in an *Economist* blog post reporting on a digital media conference. The correspondent predicts the 'nuclear fission' of breaking news, but argues that this can be resisted by the more luxury editorial products: 'For a publication like *The Economist* the basic unit of journalism is unlikely to change, because it perfectly suits the thing we produce: a once-a-week round-up of the world's main events, tightly edited and closely argued' (Babbage 2011).
3. See print edition (*Economist* 2014) and online version <http://www.economist.com/style-guide/editing> accessed August 14, 2014.
4. The abbreviation stands for Philosophy, Politics and Economics.
5. A reference to 'Politics and the English Language' (Orwell 2013).

Chapter 2

ADAM MOSS

Editor-in-chief, New York *magazine*
Interview: Wednesday, November 14, 2012
Manhattan, New York

Adam Moss is described by media critic David Carr as 'one of the best editors working in a hybrid age' (Carr 2010). Before joining *New York* in 2004, he edited *The New York Times Magazine*, and was assistant managing editor for features at the newspaper. Earlier he spent six years as editor of *Esquire* and was the founder of *7 Days*, a magazine covering New York arts and culture.

New York has won many awards, most recently for 'general excellence, print and digital' given by the US-based National Magazine Awards in 2014. The previous year, it won Print Magazine of the Year and Cover of the Year, for a cover about Hurricane Sandy in November 2012 [Fig. 1. Storm]. The magazine has also significantly expanded its online and mobile presence.

Since the interview, the magazine announced that its print version was moving from weekly to biweekly frequency, explaining the aim of the change as 'combining the timeliness of a weekly with the heft of a monthly' (*New York* 2014).

Figure 1. Storm

SG *What do you call what you do? Do you think of yourself as editor?*

AM I do. That is my title. Of course, what it means has changed drastically over the years, because I've had different jobs and because times have changed. What I do for most of my day as an editor resembles not very much what I did when I was an editor, say, 20 years ago at *Esquire*. For one thing, I'm the editor-in-chief of *New York*, but *New York* itself is both a [print] magazine and a [group] of digital publications...Those are just as important to my job and to this company as the magazine.

A lot of what I do during the day is to try to understand our publications—and possible publications, because we're starting things all the time. I try to think of ways to convey information, tell stories, entertain, illuminate; all of the things that an editor tries to do, but in many different forms and using many different platforms, technologies and media.

SG *There is a recent news story saying you publish new content on your web pages every six minutes...*

AM ...Which is actually an outdated number: it's probably been shaved by about two minutes. We publish a lot of content here. And there was a time, not long ago, where what I would do most of the day is take one story and try to make it its best self. I don't do that at all anymore. What I really do is look at the big picture and try to make decisions about it and also, frankly, to manage. When you get to a position where you're accountable, you're dependent on others to do the work you used to do. A lot of it is about trying to understand their issues, making it easier for them to do good work.

SG *In my working definition, I talk about selecting, shaping and linking. Mostly, when people think of editing, they think of the shaping side of it, possibly selecting.*

AM Both of those things are still very important parts of what I do, the selecting especially. I have different roles for different parts of the magazine. For the print [edition] I'm much more active in the shaping. I determine the line-up. I approve story ideas for the most part; others do that [too], but I am the ultimate filter in terms of what gets out to the world. Whereas on the web side of things, we're publishing [a much larger and ever-growing quantity] of content a day. I don't even know what we're publishing until after it's published, for the most part. There, my role is much more [as] guide. I have been active in selecting the people who write or edit the material, and figuring out what our voice should be: our identity, our purpose in the world. I have a collaborative role in shaping the decisions that influence those things, although not an active 'yes this, no that' role.

SG *You mention 'voice', which interests me. Is voice a key part of editing a magazine, whether print or digital?*

AM I think voice is essential for a magazine; for newspapers and [some] books too. You're creating an environment, you're creating almost a *being*, and you want it to be vivid and you want it to have an identity, a distinct quality. On a website you want the voice to be fairly uniform. We hire writers who have a similar perspective because that's what it is. Come to *Vulture*, our culture side, and there is a certain way of looking at culture that *Vulture* inhabits. That's basically carried forward by the writers and editors.

The magazine itself does have a certain way of looking at the world, but it's less rigorously enforced, more cacophonous. It's always had a less imposing house voice than some other magazines. If you read *The New Yorker*, for instance, all the writers write differently, but because of a very intensive editing process, there's a kind of sound that comes out of everything in *The New Yorker*. Less so for us here. And from its birth *New York* magazine has been defined as a place where the writer's voice would take precedence over the house voice. In the first years you had Tom Wolfe, who has such a strong voice, sitting side by side with Pete Hamill, who also has a strong voice but it's nothing like Tom Wolfe's voice. That still pertains.

SG *How would you describe the magazine's voice and identity?*

AM Well, it's changed over the years, but in the time I've been here I would describe it as knowing, sceptical, generous, amusing, a little brash without—I hope—being obnoxious.

SG *While I was waiting to see you, I looked at the framed covers on the wall and that came across. Especially the cover about the scandal which broke over Eliot Spitzer, the Governor of New York from 2007 to 2008. Even without knowing all the details, it didn't take me more than a second to figure out what type of story it was* [Fig 2. Spitzer].

AM That's good. That means we've succeeded. That cover was put together in a day. That cover defines the magazine pretty well.

SG *How much of that voice—knowing, sceptical, generous, amusing, brash—is about the fact it is a magazine in New York City?*

AM A lot. Our subject is not New York. It used to be, but it's not anymore. Our subject is anything. We write about national politics, some would say obsessively. We write about the culture capitals of Hollywood, London...but we write about all of it through a perspective which is urban cosmopolitan; or more particularly, New Yorkish.

Figure 2. Spitzer

SG *How do you achieve that? Is this all down to who you hire in the first place? Is there training? Constant discussion?*

AM Yes, I think there's constant discussion. There is no formal training, at all. I think these two things are true: one, it is about who you hire. Two, through the process of making something, there's a great deal of conscious conversation. Then there's a third thing, which is unconscious; something happens in an organisation where it learns to conform to a shared purpose, even if it is never articulated. People model their work after other people's work. New writers come in and they see what you publish and they will write in that manner, if they're paying attention. Sometimes it happens too much and you want more deviation, but in general the effect is positive. Even without trying, you cohere.

SG *I've asked everyone to describe a day in detail, because people often don't know what editors actually do.*

AM Okay, I'll try and describe my day as it happens now [although that is liable to change]. I read a lot—newspapers, blogs—and come in armed with bits of knowledge and curiosity about things. First thing that happens in the morning is a 15-minute conversation among all the print editors about the last 24 hours. We have this meeting every day, and it's a free-wheeling but very fast meet.

Then there's a separate conversation with the editor of the front of the magazine, the 'Intelligentsia' section, in which he tells me what he has planned for this week, and we talk about what we should do and shouldn't do. Today, that meeting yielded quickly to another conversation about two manuscripts I read last night. I gave comments to the editors about what I thought was working and not working.

After that, it was about two covers coming up; some decisions had to be made, and there was a very fast 'do we want to do this or do we want to do that' conversation. That meeting led to another one in which I looked at the magazine's pacing, for the first time this week, and the beginnings of layouts, and how advertising intersected with editorial, where there was a problem and where it was fine.

And then [for] most of my morning, I sat down for a very long conversation with the editorial director of the website, and we discussed two particular hiring situations. We discussed some existing personnel, how they were doing and what we could do to help them. He alerted me to one person who might be leaving and we discussed how we should address that. And then we got into a very abstract conversation, about how much we should be selecting editorial for traffic reasons and whether trying to game editorial for traffic reasons was even productive, let alone spiritually a good idea. We talked about that for a long time—that was a huge conversation today. Then I got lunch: during the lunch hour I watched the [US] president's press conference. Then I read a manuscript.

As soon as this interview's over I will be looking at a lot of art design stuff, and discussing a specific project that we're doing in January [2013]. Then I will have a conversation with the managing editor about money. I will sit down with the design director and we'll work on this week's cover for a while. That's about it.

Oh, I forgot; I wrote a cover line. Everyone writes cover lines—they sort of compete through email—so I did my bit.

SG *That type of work is so much fun, fitting the right words into tight spaces. When Twitter happened, with its 140-character limit, I thought, 'Oh, it's like writing headlines'.*

AM It is.

SG *What is your main concern when you're editing, and how is that concern resolved?*

AM I have two main concerns. Is it interesting? Which is also to say, what ideas are we throwing into the world? The second part is, is it clear? If there is anything that is true across all of my work, I would say that I try to be vigilant about clarity, because that's where people have the most trouble.

SG *Which people? Contributors or…?*

AM Everyone. Writers, editors, my business colleagues, myself—clarity's the hardest thing. You have so many things going on at one time, and you have to be ruthless about making sure that what you're saying to the reader, what you're saying to each other, is clear.

SG *Is that because it's journalism, or does it apply to anything that is being published?*

AM I think that anything people publish needs to be clear, but especially in journalism, especially here—this is a big general interest magazine, we're taking on so many things at once, and we're trying to learn fast about all those things, so that we are informed when we publish. We have very few experts here. And then, on top of the information we're bringing forward, we're trying to have insights about it. Each individual thing and how they connect to each other. That's very hard and there's a great deal of clutter in all that intake. And then you have to sort through the clutter and come out with something clear.

The Spitzer cover is a good example, because that cover was crystal clear, but it was a very complicated event; things were coming at us very fast. The cover of a magazine is the hardest thing; one has to be ruthless about clarity.

Another example where I thought we did that successfully was the November 12 [2012] cover after Storm Sandy, which blacked out half of the city. We wanted to talk about 'have' and 'have not', and this cover illustrated it with perfect vividness. It got picked up [by other media] because it cut through; there wasn't anything muddy about it.

SG *What's specific about editing this magazine rather than any other? You mentioned that it was set up with the aim of letting writers have their own voices.*

AM It was a magazine that was especially infatuated with newness. I mean, all journalists care very much about what is new, but *New York* was fanatical about that. I think that was also part of its connection to the city, which is a place that moves on very quickly. The pace of things here is fast; it's an ADD (attention deficit disorder) environment and always has been, in the modern era. And so the magazine itself was especially ferocious about new trends, new ideas, new people. Also, it is a general interest magazine, even though it has the trappings of a regional magazine.

SG *But when you said it* was *especially ferocious, is that different now?*

AM I personally think the magazine's deeper now than it has been for years. At this moment, it happens to have a specially good writing staff. It's more thoughtful, essayistic, than it's been during other eras. So, there's a lot more thinking on the page that happens than in previous eras. Which makes it, I suppose, a little slower, a little more deliberative but really, for the most part, it moves fast. If you contrast it with *The New Yorker* in particular: *The New Yorker* takes months and months to do stories, most of the magazine has absolutely nothing to do with the specific moment in which it's published. That's not knocking it or anything—it's just definitional. That's really not the case for us.

SG *You said you don't get to spend so much time to engage with individual writers.*

AM I love doing it when I can.

SG *Are there moments when you're aware of the difference between writing and editing, or between editing your own work and editing someone else's?*

AM I'm terrible at editing my own work. There's lot of difference between writing and editing. I'll just frame it this way: when I talk to younger people who are trying to make a decision about whether to be an editor or a writer, I ask them to think about it as a matter of temperament. Editing is collaborative; you're doing a million things at once. In that sense, it is something of a superficial activity, because you can't go deep on anything. Writing for a magazine, you choose a subject and you go and burrow, you go deep and you're by yourself a lot of the time. [It's] solitude vs. group, focus vs. breadth. If you can decide where you're most comfortable, that's a good [way to decide] about where you'd be happier.

SG *Have you come up against resistance to your editing, or criticism of it?*

AM Oh yes, all the time. It's always an argument, and you *have* the argument. If you're in a job like mine, you can win the argument all the time if you want, because you decide what gets published or not. But if you do your job well, you're not going to settle matters that way very often; you're going to allow a conversation to happen and see what the best idea is.

That has to do with the larger conversation among editors about what to put on the cover, or what stories to cover. And it has to do with individual arguments with writers, where you feel strongly their stories should be about *x* and they feel strongly their stories should be about *y*. For the most part, you cannot talk a writer entirely into your idea; they have to feel that the idea is theirs, otherwise they're going to do a crappy job. So you have to persuade them as opposed to make them.

SG *Would you say that it is difficult to teach editing?*

AM I don't know. I teach all the time—it's part of the job, right? In a formal setting, there's a lot of people now in the academy who teach journalism.

SG *Not so much teaching about editing, though.*

AM I don't even know if you can teach journalism. When I was coming up, nobody went to journalism school and so my bias is certainly towards 'better to learn through experience than in a school setting'. But a lot of people I meet, and work with, and hire, have been students in journalism schools, and have profited very much from that. Editing, I don't know. I think basically, editing you have to *do*.

SG *Can you give an example where an absence of editing, or bad editing, has led to something going wrong?*

AM Well sure! I can't give you a specific incident, but bad editing is when you overly impose your own idea on the writer and the story becomes a mishmash as a consequence. Bad editing is when you haven't thought something through enough. Bad editing is when you overly trust a writer or don't trust a writer at all; bad editing is bad judgment, which we have all the time.

Part 2: Attention

This section looks through the lens of editors who work with the relative luxury of time; Ileene Smith at the literary publishing house Farrar, Straus and Giroux, and Jerome McGann, a leading theorist and practitioner of scholarly editing at the University of Virginia. Their experience highlights the attention brought to bear by a skilled editor, and the difference this can make to the way a text is perceived. In the process, it also highlights the complex nature of textual relationships.

Chapter 3

ILEENE SMITH

Vice-president and executive editor,
Farrar, Straus and Giroux
Interview: Friday, November 9, 2012
Manhattan, New York

Ileene Smith joined the literary publisher Farrar, Straus, and Giroux (FSG)[1] in February 2012. In that role she acquires and edits authors on both the FSG and Hill & Wang lists. Her first acquisition for FSG was a biography of the publishing 'matriarch' Blanche Knopf.

Before that, Smith was 'executive editor at large' for general interest books at Yale University Press, a senior editor at Random House, and executive editor at Summit Books. She is the recipient of the PEN Roger Klein Award, the Tony Godwin Memorial Award, and a Jerusalem Fellowship.

Smith's career illustrates, among many other things, the potential creativity of 'linking', the third element identified in this book's definition of editing. In this case, it involves building groups of associated authors on a publisher's list. The interview captures the intensity of feeling that dedicated editors have about what they do, and the joy of understanding a text in all its dimensions.

SG *What drew you to this kind of work? How did it enter your head to work in publishing?*

IS I started at Simon & Schuster in 1979, reading the slushpile. I was doing it part-time to earn money, to further my musical education. But I fell in love with the culture of the publishing house and decided to cast my lot. I went from Simon & Schuster that year to Atheneum Books, where I was assistant to the editor-in-chief. Because it was a small house, I had a very quick opportunity to acquire [titles] and do many things that wouldn't have been possible in the larger houses.

After about a year and a half, I was nominated for something called the Tony Godwin Award.[2] It seemed improbable to me, because I hadn't done much at that point. I spent a month at Penguin UK, in London's World's End at that time. And I spent a month at Jonathan Cape, when it was in Bedford Square. Tom Maschler was at Cape and Liz Calder and Peter Mayer were at Penguin—it was a very exciting time. I asked them so many questions; they were quite beleaguered by the time I went back to the United States, but it was fantastic. It was a defining experience for me.

The award dramatically increased my fascination with publishing. It also launched my career in practical terms, because as soon as I came back to the United States I was offered a wonderful job at Summit Books, a small, distinguished publishing house that was part of Simon & Schuster. In those days, because of the award I felt connected to British publishing. And so at Summit, for instance, I published Kingsley Amis: I did four books with him, including *Stanley and the Women*. It had been turned down all over the place, because it was thought to be misogynist, and then I bought it, so there was a very big fuss.

British publishing has changed so much since I was there. [But I know that] there are differences in taste. There are books we can imagine working well in the UK and not here, and vice versa, particularly in the case of literary fiction. The barrier falls if the prose reaches a certain level of lyricism, like Ian McEwan, but it has to be something written out of a profound gift.

SG *How would you say you learned the practice of editing?*

IS A lot of what happens in publishing is self-taught. But I learned a lot from my first boss Tom Stewart, editor-in-chief at Atheneum at the time. I typed his editorial letters and they were beautifully composed; they had a very big impact on how I thought about the editorial process. There was a powerful internal logic to his letters and a very nice tone. I think tone is extremely important in dealing with writers, and I try very hard to get that right. I also learned quite a bit at Summit Books from Jim Silberman. It was a great experience. Again, the size of the place worked to my advantage and I felt I could do a lot. I acquired books I cared desperately about. Summit Books came to an end through some sort of corporate upheaval...

SG *...of which there are many...*

IS Of which there are many...It was particularly sad because so many of the books we had acquired went on to do very well elsewhere. Many of them were absorbed into the Simon & Schuster system.

At that point I had two small children, so I decided to work freelance. I was cautioned not to do that, told I'd never get another job. I ended up working freelance for ten years. But contrary to all the warnings, when I decided I wanted to go back, there were options. I went briefly to Scribner, another imprint within Simon & Schuster. It was a bit of a shock, because the technology had changed so much. Email changed the pace. I'm not sure we even had computers at Summit Books.

SG *Was that about ten years ago?*

IS It was right after September 11, 2001. [After that] I decided I wanted colleagues again, and my children had grown up enough. I left Scribner after a short time, and spent a few weeks at [Henry] Holt. Then I was offered the chance to go to Random House with wonderful terms. I thought that if I didn't accept, I'd always be looking over my shoulder. At first I turned it down, because my conscience got the better of me. Then the offer came again, and I said: 'No, I'm going.' So I resigned my position at Holt and joined Random—and four days later the person who hired me there was fired, publicly—it was on the front page of *The New York Times* so I'm not being indiscreet. I felt like I'd been biblically punished for leaving Holt.

I spent a few very interesting and very turbulent years at Random House, but it didn't end well. The CEO was talking about the importance of doing 'books that weren't books'. I sought refuge at the Yale University Press, where I spent six years.

SG *It is fascinating to see that kind of career shift.*

IS Hardly anyone goes from trade publishing to university press. It's very unusual. For Yale, I worked out of my apartment in New York and went to New Haven once a week. And I became very interested in that world. I was a fellow of the Whitney Humanities Center and met the most fascinating thinkers. I thought it was a very civilised place after what I'd been through at Random House.

My mandate was to publish trade books within the Yale list. When I accepted the position, I thought it was a long shot. I wondered what I could offer that would bring serious authors there, because most trade authors don't think about being published by a university press. Also, university presses don't tend to pay as much, so there were some practical problems to surmount.

It turned out that what I *was* able to offer was an artisanal experience for the writers. I worked very, very closely with them. I never imposed my will on their manuscript but I think there's a real sense of connection that's felt by virtually all of my authors. One of the difficulties with publishing, in most houses, is that the imperative to acquire can make it difficult to serve the books you've acquired. It's a treadmill. But at Yale I was able to focus on the interior design of the book, the jacket design, the copy—every aspect of the book besides the text—in a way that the authors found very reassuring. What I heard again and again was that there was not nearly as much attention given to these details in trade houses as there had been in the past.

The first author I brought to Yale was Janet Malcolm. She is a very important writer and the fact that she would go to a university press after being published by Knopf sent a signal to other distinguished writers, and so I was able to form my list there very successfully. I published Alberto Manguel and Adrian Goldsworthy, a British classical historian. His books did very well. And I was able to bring trade writers to Yale through the 'Jewish Lives' program, a biography series endowed by [New York philanthropist] Leon Black. So we have Adam Phillips writing about Freud, Ron Rosenbaum writing about Bob Dylan, David Rieff writing about Robert Oppenheimer and Saul Friedlander writing about Kafka. It's a remarkable list.

SG *I thought that was a fascinating example of list-building as a creative act in itself. It seems to go even further than the average list, because of these pairings.*

IS So much thought is given to those pairings; it's quite a puzzle. We also have a series, 'Why *x* Matters', which helped me bring trade writers to Yale. I didn't officially manage the series but I was the main acquiring editor, and it was a fascinating parlour game to pair writers with ideas.

SG *When you are editing, what is your main concern and how is that resolved?*

IS One of the best acknowledgments I ever got was from an author who said I was a 'better-maker'.[3] I try very hard to encourage the best possible version of the book without imposing my will on the author. I don't insist, I suggest. I suggest very carefully, and the best authors take those suggestions, accept most of them, and transcend my suggestions. And those are very deeply satisfying relationships, because you know you've really had an impact on the book. But I never mistake it for my own work. The author's name is on the book and so I defer to the author in the end. Obviously, if a manuscript comes in and it's a disaster, that's another conversation.

I do a lot of querying, and a lot of talking with the author. Usually it's when we get away from the text and speak about the book more broadly that there's something very productive about the conversation.

SG *Are there examples that highlight the process of being a 'better-maker'?*

IS Well, it's coming up with the right title. It's figuring out how the jacket should look. It's that really painstaking work on the manuscript itself and it's pushing every aspect of the book in the direction of an ideal.

SG *Have you come across resistance to editing from writers? What kind of response do you give?*

IS I don't come up against a lot of resistance because I tend to sign writers with whom I feel an immediate kinship through their work, and most writers want a more objective view of their work: they want it to be as good as it can be.

SG *What about from other quarters? Are there conversations you have had, over the years, in which you have to defend the practice of editing?*

IS People at a great remove from publishing will tell me at a party that they've found a number of typos in some random book they're reading, and I'm not sure what to say about that.

Right now, I'm very privileged to be in a place where every manuscript is read about five times. This is a thrilling place, because it has maintained the very best standards of the period in which I entered publishing, at the same time as being very knowing and adaptive to the requirements of the twenty-first century. So it's very exciting to be here.

SG *I read that your first signing was a book about Blanche Knopf. Are the book selections entirely up to you, or is there some sort of brief?*

IS There's no definition. That was one of the things that was so attractive about this job. At Yale I couldn't do fiction. Here I do—you'll see from my list how wide-ranging it is. I think there's some internal consistency to the books I gravitate towards, and they relate to each other in very interesting ways. There's a conversation going on among my books, as wacky as that might sound.

SG *Could you describe a typical day?*

IS I have a pretty big editorial load, partly through books I inherited and partly through books I've acquired myself. And so there are entire days when I sit here and put my reading glasses on and edit. There are days when I barely get up, and other days are punctuated by lunch with agents and authors. An author might come in to go over proofs, that sort of thing.

There's not so much pressure to acquire here, because the pipeline is extraordinarily rich. But there's an internal desire to find the next interesting book and so I'm always reading and talking to agents to figure out what the next thing might be. There are very few meetings here at FSG—hardly any—and that's extraordinary. Instead, there is a very good improvised conversation about the books we are publishing. I'm in the office five days a week, which was an odd thing after being so freewheeling at Yale. But Jonathan Galassi, the publisher, wants everyone here so that we can figure out how to publish the books. The days vary. I'm never bored.

SG *Would you say there's any difference in how you approach fiction and non-fiction? Or are you reaching for the same toolkit?*

IS I think so. Both tend to turn on the coherence of the story, the narrative. I'm very attuned to matters of language on the page and I'm always one for concision, in both fiction and nonfiction. So there's never a sense that today I'm editing fiction, and then, today I'm editing nonfiction. For me it's really the same toolkit, as you say.

SG *We've talked about how unusual it is to move between trade and university publishers. Was there anything particular that struck you about that move? You mentioned that it felt more civilised.*

IS It was also highly procedural, and that took some getting used to. In a university press there are publications committees and acquisitions panels and all kinds of things like that, which were new to me. There were sometimes very good things that resulted from these procedures but university presses don't tend to be as editorially driven as trade presses. This house—FSG—is very, very editorially driven.

SG *The Amazon executive Russell Grandinetti said a few years ago, 'The only really necessary people in the publishing process now are the writer and reader'.[4] Do you agree or disagree, and why?*

IS That's just a very debased concept of the publishing process. It really deprives the writer of the constructive opportunities afforded by the editorial lens.

SG *Would you describe editing as a creative activity?*

IS It's a dynamic activity. When it's operating at its highest level it is creative; the editor's engagement with the text is creative in the way that a fine translator is creative. There's been books that I've half-written, although most books don't require that. But there isn't a constant sense of creativity because of the constraints, because you want to be sure that in the end it's the author's book.

I have a very distinct sense of what's editable and what isn't. Sometimes a manuscript comes in and needs a fair amount of work but if I feel like I can bring something to it; that's typically how it works. Then there are a very few manuscripts that require almost nothing, and a very few manuscripts that are truly uneditable.

SG *Is editing about judgment?*

IS Absolutely correct, yes. It's about making fine discriminations, advocating for the author but making sure not to overreach. I consult very closely with my authors on everything and I try very hard to get my authors their due as much as I possibly can, but there can be the sense of a pyrrhic victory if you push too far. Knowing how far to go, knowing when to stop is very important. And then, every mark on the page is a judgment; you don't want to be needlessly intrusive editorially and so sometimes I'll spend ten minutes figuring out whether to make a particular query. It's a very, very painstaking process, the work on the page.

SG *Do you call yourself an editor?*

IS I call myself a book editor.

SG *Is there particular imagery you use if you describe what you do? For example 'midwife'.*

IS I don't like that description very much. To explain what I do, I say that I read and I decide. I read in order to figure out what we might publish. I probably read more than most people, but I love to read and always have.

SG *Do you have any particular rituals or routines for getting in the mood?*

IS I listen to music when I do serious editing. Classical music, Bach or something like that. It seems to isolate me with a manuscript. But I take off the headphones as soon as somebody walks into my office, because I need to be available to what's going on out there.

SG *What do you like least about editing?*

IS I like least the feeling that I am not keeping up with the editorial load. Because of the very fastidious way I edit, it's hard to meet all deadlines. I just got in an 800-page manuscript, a translation of a Polish work by Anna Bikont about what happened in a village in Poland during the Second World War. It's really an important book, and a lot of publishers wouldn't do it, because it's so long. The great thing about this place is that if the book is important, they'll find a way to do it. I'm also editing three books for the fall list, and figuring out where the time comes from.

SG *We didn't spend too much time on your own personal background. I wonder, was there anything in your upbringing or education that explicitly connects to this work?*

IS Well, my father was a tremendous reader. Even as a small child, I remember memorising the names of the publishing houses on the spines of his books. I looked at them so often, the name on the spine became an indelible part of my memory of looking at his books. So there is that. I was a natural reader all my life—the child with the flashlight under the covers.

SG *It's as if the text is real, books are real—they are not separate from real life.*

IS That's right. They're interior. I read some things on a Kindle. But I find that if I love what I've read, I go and buy the book. The book is so much part of you—this idea of the 'end of the book' is preposterous for people like you and me. It may be a dwindling population; I don't know. My children both prefer physical books to electronic reading, and I think that's interesting.

Notes

1. Farrar, Straus and Company was founded in 1946 by Roger W. Straus and John C. Farrar. In 1964 Robert Giroux's name was added. See 'About FSG' http://us.macmillan.com/fsg/about, accessed 7 August 2014.
2. A bi-annual award open to UK and US publishing staff under 35, which supports a work experience exchange.
3. A phrase used by T.S. Eliot in *The Waste Land* in dedication to fellow poet and editor Ezra Pound (Eliot 1971).
4. See Streitfeld 2011.

Chapter 4

JEROME McGANN

*The John Stewart Bryan University Professor,
Department of English, University of Virginia
Interview: Friday, December 7, 2012
Charlottesville, Virginia*

The conversation offered in this chapter is reflexive to a high degree; a discussion about editing with an editing practitioner, who is also an internationally known theorist of editing.

The fields of bibliography and scholarly editing provide an important source of analysis about editing practice. However, debate about scholarly editions usually takes place in isolation from analysis of other kinds of editing. Often, it expresses itself in terms of paired opposites, so that typically, one approach aims to identify the author's original intentions and produce a work as close to that as possible, while the other puts more emphasis on the importance of selecting and interpreting the text.

McGann's body of work is an exception to that pattern. In a long career[1] he has become known for literary scholarship, such as the Byron edition discussed here (McGann 1980 to 1993); theoretical interventions (for example, 1991) and digital archives (2000). His influence extends across English studies, bibliography, book history and the digital humanities. His most recent book at the time of writing (2014) amplifies the theme of memory.

This trajectory provides an insight into the way theory in the field has evolved over time, partly as a result of his own interventions. In the earlier work, he describes 'final authorial intention' as deeply problematic (1983: 68) and argues for a 'socialized concept of authorship and textual authority' (1983: 8). But the practical experience of editing the Rossetti Archive brings about a shift from advocacy of 'un-editing' and Derrida's decentering as the 'rationale of hypertext', to an awareness that whole levels of meaning defy this kind of analysis. As expressed in the interview here, the result is a 'war on two fronts'—a familiar predicament for practitioners interested in theory.

McGann now uses the language of philology, albeit 'in a new key'. This reflects an interest in the development of institutions that will help sustain humanities teaching and research. Charting his own intellectual journey, he defines the early stance as belonging not with the French school, but with the Germanic influence of Jürgen Habermas. After a '50-year preoccupation with 'making it new', McGann now looks to the 'philological conscience', for which '[t]he past and the future are…obligations we keep forgetting and neglecting' (2014: 36).

SG *I am interested in talking with you, because your work gives a sense of looking at historical texts, and imagining what happened when they were produced for the first time. It shows an awareness of editing as a live practice, not just something carried out years later, for scholarly reasons.*

JM From my point of view, there is a sense in which even in scholarship, all editing is done for the first time.

Take the example of Byron. The edition that I produced for Oxford [University Press] at the beginning of the 1970s came after a hiatus of almost 75 years. The last time Byron had been edited in a serious, scholarly way was at the beginning of the twentieth century. There was no question that Byron needed to be re-edited in the later twentieth century. The great Ernest Hartley Coleridge edition was a classic, and very great, edition, but distinctively Victorian. And then there are all sorts of non- or sub-scholarly editions that are done in between for various kinds of educational purposes, and they all spin off the determinant work. And that is very typical. Certain kinds of edition are done, under certain kinds of circumstances.

Major editions transform the field. Take, for instance, the Walter Scott edition that's just been finished by David Hewitt and his crew. That has already begun to transform Scott studies. *That's* a particularly interesting edition because Scott, even more than Byron, fell out of attention for many years. In a sense there wasn't—as there was for Byron or Keats—a permanent edition that you would turn back to, and say, 'I'm going to move from *that* point'. There was just a whole series of reproductions of early editions. So Hewitt's is the first great scholarly edition since the earlier nineteenth century.

I got into scholarly editing by a complete set of happenstances…My MA thesis was on a theoretical issue of interpretation. My doctoral thesis was also theoretical…By chance, at that time I was interested in the problem of biographical scholarship and criticism. Given prevailing ideas about interpretive theory—I'm talking about the early to mid-sixties—the very idea of biographical criticism was professionally ridiculous. Criticism of all kinds was trying to get away from subjectivity, and especially away from biographical matters.

But if you were going to produce an edition of Byron, there was no evading biography. All Byron criticism and scholarship is biographical in one way or another. And so therefore, also historical. That was an interesting theoretical matter to me. I wanted to investigate the premises of a biographical approach, or an historical approach more broadly. That got me into manuscripts and primary data in a way that I had never done before. Still no ideas about editing at all.

Because Lord Byron's poetry was my first big editing job, I had to learn about scholarly editing. The reigning theory at that time was the Greg-Bowers theory of eclectic editing. Highly theoretical, very empirical. So I plunge into that, and I just read like mad. And I absorb the principles and I begin to test it out, try out a model. I think I approached it fairly intelligently even at that point—given the level of my ignorance. I chose what appeared to me one of the most difficult works to edit. I would try to edit it, and if successful, I would find out what more I needed to do by working on this difficult model. So I chose *The Giaour*, which is a real bear of a case. And I got into it in a big way, and after about two years I just ground to a halt. The Greg-Bowers approach immobilised me. I couldn't edit this complex thing according to the methodology. I was in a state, actually.

I went to my mentor, Cecil Lang, the great editor of epistolary materials. He said, 'Look, forget about theory for a while. You're theory-obsessed. Read the introductions to as many of the great editions that you can, from the classics to now. And just see what people *do*, and have done'. That advice changed my life in a great many ways. Not the least was immediate. A whole world of editorial methodology was suddenly thrown open to me that had been closed, because Bowers in particular had set out to revolutionise editorial theory and method.

But the move also began to reopen my traditional interest in interpretation and how editing itself was an interpretive methodology and set of procedures. I now see that every editorial work I have ever done has always been a theoretical action, a practical way of investigating editorial method, philological method, interpretive procedure. I just don't see that these things are separable, and when they are separated, both philological actions—interpretation/criticism and editing/information display—begin to lose their way.

SG *You have already anticipated many of my questions, such as 'What drew you to this type of work' and 'How did you learn'…*

JM [After Byron] I edited an anthology of Romantic poetry for Oxford. They asked me to do it and [at first] I said, 'No, this kind of anthology bores me, I don't see the point of *another* Romantic anthology'. Then I chanced upon Roger Lonsdale, the great…scholar. Specifically, his Oxford volume of eighteenth-century verse.

It was a revelation. I visited him and [asked] how he did it. And he said, 'When they asked me to do it, I told myself I had to read every single poem written in English in the eighteenth century'. He sat back in the chair. And he said, 'and I did, as far as I know'. Because, what he wanted to do was give a snapshot of what he took to be what they were reading. A snapshot of everything.

I came away stunned from that meeting, and I wrote to Oxford to say 'I will do your anthology'. I can't say I read every poem written in the Romantic period. But I did try to construct an anthology that gave a picture of what was being read in the Romantic period. Much of it is very bad poetry; much of it is not Romantic poetry. But I was aspiring to give a Romantic period snapshot like Roger Lonsdale's snapshot of the eighteenth century. Anyway, my anthology was less an anthology [than] an investigation of what people were reading. An editorial approach to reception history.

[After that] I edited Rossetti for analogous theoretical and methodological reasons. And I'm involved in a new digital editorial venture right now. It's called *The American World of James Fenimore Cooper* (McGann, in progress). I'm fascinated by the publishing world in America in the antebellum period. It is an amazing period of book and periodical production. Cooper and [Edgar Allan] Poe are key figures. I decided I'd take on Cooper. To this day I'm not sure why. I knew a lot more about Poe and still have a long-standing interest in him and his historical significance.

SG *Well, Poe has probably had a bit more attention.*

JM He has had a *lot* more attention. Although these blue volumes here [*points to shelves behind him*] are a scholarly edition of Cooper. These are eclectic editions with massive amounts of historical collation and scholarly commentary. Much of my life has been a critical engagement with eclectic editing and its limitations. I still regard all of this kind of scholarly work as fundamental interpretive activity, and I confess that I think a lot of theorists and interpreters remain deeply ignorant in these matters, especially when they celebrate what they do as materialist studies. Reading the work, it often feels like they've never really worked in a library, or been closely involved with documentary materials.

SG *I remember hearing a media ethnographer say, 'Theory is a practice too'.*

JM Yes, with all its attendant institutional mechanisms...

SG *Is it unusual for people to say to you, 'I'm interested in what you do as a practitioner?' That is to say, with the emphasis on your editing work as a practice, rather than your contribution to theory.*

JM For some editors, their work *is* a theoretical practice. I would say that, without question, Bowers was such an editor. Don McKenzie, especially with the *Congreve* edition which has just been published (2011)—that was a theoretical undertaking. Hans Walter Gabler's edition of *Ulysses* (1984)—definitely a theoretical edition. J.C.C. Mayes' edition of Coleridge (2001)—unbelievably great edition. [However] among many of the epigones[2] of these great editors—I think especially of Bowers, because he had such an influence—there's not a lot of reflexive thinking. They're well done, but you have to read them with an alert critical sense.

SG *Looking at what you do as a scholarly editor, how would you say it is the same or different from an editor working in trade publishing?*

JM I think a person who is editing now, say, an edition of *Mrs Dalloway*, what they are thinking about mostly is their immediate audience, which they will frame in a certain way. The work will be shaped by immediate circumstances and purposes. A scholarly editor, if she or he is any good, has as much on his or her mind about the past as the present. And therefore of the future, even the distant future. In a sense you might have your mind *more* on the past and the future [than the present]. Your sense of what the present needs entails a much broader sense of engagement with the past, because so much of the past is forgotten. We were talking earlier about how many times the editing takes place. What we call a production history, or a reception history—you can't really edit unless you get all of that under purview. And so that's why it takes 22 years to do something [for a scholarly editor], because you've got so much to do.

More and more, I have to say, this has grown upon me: that earlier, I was much more polemical and present-oriented than I am now. I have a book in press called *A New Republic of Letters*. I've grown quite obsessed by the problem of forgotten memory, how much memory is embedded in the materials that we inherit and that has yet been forgotten. And how you go about recovering it.

So, trying to work out a methodology for…an online edition of Cooper, I set a little exercise for myself. What's at stake is not just Cooper, you see— it's Cooper's world. Cooper is a kind of floating centre [which] an editor arbitrarily set for [that world]. We're talking about 1820 to 1850. It's this crucial period, right after the early revolution and what is called the second revolution of 1812. At that point, the United States begins to want a very clear sense of itself. No one at that time tried harder [than Cooper] to articulate such a sense, nor was anyone more successful. So he's a very important figure in American memory and American history.

I'm trying to find out how to do this. I'm still into a very methodological and theoretical moment of reflection with the edition. About three months ago, I set myself a test case. I took out the title page of one of his most famous books: an early book (1823) called *The Pioneers*. And I said, all right, what would be a complete annotation of this title page? That is to say, a recovery of the memory that's buried in it.

Now, if you go to scholarly editions of that page, there will be three or four notes—maybe a few more, maybe less; maybe nothing, actually. So I decided, 'I'm going to go in and see how far the annotation exercise takes me'. And I had to stop after a week; I had 22 pages. And I realised, this could go on indefinitely! But it was an extremely important exercise because it really did expose this matter of memory, and obscured memory, that is *in* the documents.

That's why editing is *so* crucial, because you have to go back to the documents. And the documents speak, if you know how to get them by the throat. You won't be able to hear everything that they have to say, but you'll begin to hear some of it, if you try. The dead can be drawn out. And we can teach ourselves to listen.

SG *I've been dipping into the archives at the New York Public Library, to discover material about editing. There is a huge collection about the Duycinck brothers.*

JM Oh that's fascinating; they were very important in exactly this period. I've been giving my library here at the University of Virginia to Special Collections.

They want to develop an archive around editing. It includes a lot of the stuff I was doing before being involved with digital tools. And then there are the computers I was involved with. The library here wants to use those materials as a lever, to develop a centre for the study of scholarly editing. It's a shame they didn't do that with Bowers [who] was here for many years…It is an important time in the history of scholarship because of the coming of this new technology. And now, it seems clear to me that the most interesting theoretical work being done in the world of cultural studies and scholarship is in editing, and editing theory and methodology; book history, bibliography; it's just exploded.

No one really knows how to use these machines yet. We were talking, a moment before, about theory and practice. The *only* way to get a grip on the capacity of these machines is to try to make them do things.

There's a great essay by a friend of mine, John Unsworth, now associate vice president at Brandeis for digital humanities. And his essay is called 'The Importance of Failure' (1997). It was an essay that he wrote when he was here. It's an idea that we deeply shared. It's [the idea that] what you do when you do anything, [is that] you fail. It came home to me, doing the Byron edition. Because once you get into [an editing project], you realise that [because of] various constraints, you can't do certain kinds of things. So what you are doing is already mistaken. That's very sobering, because you know you have to finish what you're doing and you want to do it in the best way that you can. And you do, knowing all the time that you're in a losing game.

The Rossetti edition was even more painful. I had the Byron edition behind me and I thought, OK, you learned your lesson about limits. Now, you're going to be *really* careful this time. And I was; I spent about a year and a half trying to be very careful about the logical structure of what I wanted to develop.

We started to implement it. And I was very pleased with what was happening. But after about three years…again, the limitations began to become very clear. And it almost all came crashing down. [With] the Byron edition, I was working within an institutional framework that is 500 or 600 years old, and that upholds you—you have to go *on* with an edition that is as much the press's as yours. You're going to finish it within the parameters that have already been set up. But the digital thing, you are inventing the parameters *yourself* as you're building it. So if it was coming apart…Well, there was a moment where I thought I had to stop and go back to the beginning and tear everything out…it was so painful.

We figured out a way to work around it, as they say in this business. And it works, it's a very good edition. But it's a failure in a fundamental sense because it (that would be 'I') didn't know what it (that would be 'I') wanted to do, and it (etc.) thought it did. And then I made what I thought I wanted to do, and then I thought, that's not what I wanted to do at all. But I wouldn't have known it until I made it, such as it is.

SG *In discussions about creative writing as a form of research, one argument is that in the very act of creating a text, you are discovering what you want to say.*

JM There's a writer who has come to mean a great deal to me—Laura Riding Jackson. She was a famous modernist writer; an American, although she spent a great deal of time in Europe. She began to write a kind of prose that interested me, because it became the kind of theoretical practice we're talking about. She wrote a book called *Progress of Stories*. They are stories that are about the writing of stories. They are not like narratologists who write about narrative structure. They demonstrate the telling of the story in the telling of the story. Dazzling. She has a masterpiece there called 'Reality as Port Huntlady'. All the stories in that book are about writing, and about learning what writing is, by writing.

SG *I wonder: is there an 'editing' way of thinking that is perhaps the same, no matter what you're editing? Even between, say, a scholarly editor and someone editing a magazine?*

JM There are certain fundamentals, aren't there? Accuracy, that is a *sine qua non*. A lot of people aren't any good at editing because they don't realise that they have an obligation to this basic requirement. I would say there are three criteria. Thoroughness, meticulousness/accuracy, and candour. Your cards have got to be on the table. So, no matter what you're doing, all those three things have to be adhered to. Then, there are other obligations, depending on the special objects you have in view, the audience you have in view.

SG *Perhaps the main difference with editing someone who is still alive, rather than a scholarly edition of someone long dead, is the human relations side of it?*

JM You also know, as a writer, the engagements you get into with your publisher. You write a book, you send in the typescript, and then you start to negotiate. There are house style rules, there are all kinds of lines that you will agree to follow, or there might be a line that you won't cross—'No, I can't do that'. That prevails, it seems to me, also in relation to scholarly editing. There are obligations that you have to the institution…

SG *To living people, in organisations that exist now?*

JM And also, to the dead! The [earlier] expurgation of Byron [was] acceding to obligations that [the publishers], the Murrays, felt they had to Byron. When Jock Murray came in, he had a different idea of what should be remembered about Byron—an idea that I share. But his father did *not*. One of the most fascinating things about Byron's editorial history is how long the Murrays basically controlled the view of Byron, by editorial control.

SG *We think of Byron being long ago, but there's a living link.*

JM Well, he was a celebrity. He and Goethe were probably the most famous writers of the nineteenth century, in Europe. Scott and Byron were certainly the most popular or successful writers. [They were also] cultural forces [that] transcend literature...Scott and Byron are feeding artists and cultural communicants for 100 years. How many operas are written off Byron poems or Scott novels? How many oratorios? It's *vast*. So there is an obligation, when you enter into an edition, to know where you stand in relation to it. You have to make a decision about it.

SG *This business about candour...it's right that one has to put things on the table. But when you have the living person right there in front of you, how you do that is perhaps different. The most successful editors seem to be the ones who translate that candour into a form that the author can hear, and allow.*

JM Very delicate!

SG *My impression so far is that it is not just the meaning of the words on the page that matters most when you're editing; it's always about the relationships. The other related, recurring motif is, thinking of the reader...*

JM Definitely. But I come back to something. I remarked earlier about the rights of a dead person, or the work that is in the past. There is a tendency, particularly by any contemporary scholar, critic or reader to read for your immediate purposes as you see them. I definitely regard my scholarly obligation as trying to persuade people that they want to try to read it, as Pope said, in the same spirit as the author. And that often doesn't mean that the author even *understood* the spirit in which he or she wrote it. It's back to memory again. Memories have their rights and the present *needs* them. That's really the scholar's perspective—how desperately the present needs the past.

SG *Yes, the importance of relationship applies just as much to people in the past. It is collaborative in that sense.*

JM You *do* collaborate. These documents that you work with, the remains of living beings and circumstances and relationships in the past, they have a kind of life and authority that you have to respect. Most people look at early editions, manuscripts, and documentary materials, and they actually don't *see* them.

There's a very great Renaissance scholar in Canada, Randall McCloud. Among scholars he's a kind of cult figure; a celebrated, strange and highly imaginative person, and an editorial theorist. He's never practiced editing in a traditional sense, but yes, he edits in a strange way. I've never known any scholar who is able to see a document with such acuity. It's like he lives with them, and suddenly they're able to talk to him in ways that nobody I know has been able to do.

He has a theory of what he calls 'unediting', because of his sense of the [damage done] by contemporaries when they approach things in the past. What he's trying to do is prevent this from happening, as much as possible; he sees the past as the locus of primary authority. It's a wonderful conception of the obligation that scholarly editors ought to keep in mind, all the time.

SG *I first drew up the working definition years ago. It occurs to me that another way of putting what I said there is that the editor is an 'embodied reader'.*

JM Yes, I definitely respond positively to that. The *most* embodied reader. There are other embodied readers—reviewers, for example—but no one is more an embodied reader than an editor, that's for sure.

SG *When I learned editing, working on a newspaper, that is how it was explained: 'You're standing in the shoes of the reader. You're looking at the story as if you were the reader. And you're anticipating all the different ways in which the reader might understand what is before you.'*

JM You can drop it down a level. My whole family are printers. My grandfather was a printer, my father was a printer, my brother was a printer. And printers...you hand in a book to the publisher. It falls into the hands of the people who have to design the book, the physical object. They *have* to read the book. The design of the book at that primary level is a reading of the book.

A famous example of this [is] the opening move in Don McKenzie's bibliography class at Oxford. Students sit at the seminar table and he passes around what a printer calls a 'dummy book'. That's a book that has entered the first stage of its reading, as it were. There's 'nothing' in it—no text, or print; that is to say, it's just a certain size, paper, whatever. He passes it around and says: 'I want you to look at it.' So, they all look at it. It comes back to him and then he says: 'Right, I want you to tell us, what was in that book.' And of course they go blank. But after about half an hour, they begin to talk about paper, about trim size, about all kinds of matters, and they realise that it can't be *this*, it might be *that*, and it becomes an arresting pedagogical exercise in this matter of reading.

As soon as you make a typescript, you are already reading. The writer is reading his or her book as it's being written. The writer is always really the first reader—the writer who's writing the book. But everybody in-between is always engaged in some kind of an act of reading the thing.

And then the scholar comes way at the end—this pedant, who tries to roll all that up. Why is it Caslon and not Bodoni? Or, why is it Bodoni? There's a splendid example in Whitman, the *Leaves of Grass*. It *should* have been set in Caslon, but it's not, it's Bodoni—why? Well, we do know that Whitman was a printer, and so he had some sense of making decisions that were deliberate, about these things. My sense is that he saw Bodoni as a much more modern typeface than Caslon. Which it *is*. But not *so* much more modern—he could have chosen some others that would have been much more dramatically modern. You could do a whole riff on this.

SG *When you say your family were printers, to me that makes a lot of sense; it would explain why you are aware of the meaning that comes through practice.*

JM When I was a boy, my father used to take us into the [print] shop. But I didn't *understand* anything. My brother and I would walk around and see what was happening, it was fascinating—I still have these memories in my head—where he would run linotype machines just for fun. But I didn't *know* anything. Even when I was in graduate school. It was only much later when I got into editing that all that stuff came roaring back at me.

SG *Almost 20 years ago, you wrote* The Textual Condition. *I was just looking it over before coming here, and a sentence jumped out where you talked about marrying the linguistic and bibliographical codes of meaning...*[3]

JM Which is what we were just talking about.

SG *Which is what we were just talking about. And about the inherently collaborative nature of editing. That jumped out because when you look at the history of editing, it seems to be in the collaborative media of newspapers and magazines where the modern idea of editor evolved. And book editing took its model directly from them.*

JM I was thinking, while you were talking, about nineteenth-century periodical publication. In America, that was the principal mode of publication. Cooper was unusual in virtually doing all of his publication in books. Poe has a number of books but he's principally a periodical writer. And he knows how to exploit the whole institution of periodical publication. He understands perfectly, for example, [that] under those circumstances, when he publishes a story or a poem it is going to be picked up, and it will metastasise—not least because of the copyright situation in America at that time. And he wants to *exploit* that. It doesn't matter to him, for example, that the poem or the story might be changed when it's reprinted. What he wants to do is get this stuff out to as wide an audience as possible. And so if it's mutated in some way, that's OK with him.

SG *Like digital mashups today…*

JM Exactly. So periodicals, just-in-time publishing of various kinds [are important]. There's a halfway house that involves…serial publication either weekly, biweekly, monthly, whatever it might be. Writing for deadlines, certainly. Dickens…was writing to deadlines, and sometimes he was still *writing* [when they came]. Dickens is such a fascinating example here, because not only is he writing to his deadlines for [serial publication] but his works…are getting reader feedback as they're still in process. He was a writer who could and did alter his stories because he could see what his readers were saying about those stories.

SG *That is what people announced as an innovation when digital publishing first arrived. Publishing a story in instalments as they go along, collecting feedback and building it into the story.*[4]

JM Yes, well, that was certainly happening [in the nineteenth century], especially in England. When you look at those serial issues, the publishers themselves write notes to their readers: 'We're changing the illustrations, they will now no longer be done by Mr Brown; Mr Seymour is going to be taking over from now on.' This sort of conversation [is] going on, [within] these objects that are coming out. And Dickens is by no means the only person involved in those conversations. The publisher will pull in comments that he's getting in the adjunct pages. Amazing.

SG *There is an account of Geoffrey Faber talking to students at Oxford (Faber 1934). He tells them that publishers spend a lot of time engaging with the text and changing it. He anticipates that they are going to be very shocked. He says, 'You might think, what business does a man of business have to go onto the author's own ground?' And he answers, 'But what if the author doesn't know his own ground?' He says, 'The art of authorship must take account of the conditions in which it is practised'.*

JM Yes! *No one* knows their own ground! You have an *idea* of what your ground is, what your purposes are, your intentions and so forth. But it's without question that you are mistaken, or that you have, as it were, edited your own ideas even though you may not even know that you have edited them. So it is an axiom that when you write one thing, you immediately don't write a bunch of other things.

In mathematics there's a remarkable book called *Laws of Form* by G. Spencer Brown (2011). It's an effort to develop a complete abstract language mathematically by as simple a means as possible. He begins by what he calls 'making a mark'. He says, 'As soon as you make a mark, you divide the field'. And so you make a distinction. And so, *there* is the mark, and there is everything that is *not* marked, that has now been marked by not being marked. To me this is one of the great thoughts about writing, that when a person starts to write something, you are immediately editing the material. And you are choosing *not* to put certain things in. That means they are there. They are there by the choice of not putting them there. They're there even if you yourself don't realize that they are.

Because what you're doing is, to go back to Aristotle—you are holding a mirror up to the world…but it only shows a certain part of the world. But having done that, it's implicitly saying, 'there are many other parts of the world that are there, and because I'm showing it to you in this way, if you look very carefully at what I'm showing you, you'll be able to start to see what I'm not showing you'. That, for me, is such an important rule to keep in mind in scholarly editing. All the things that Byron is saying by not saying something; or Scott, or Cooper, or whomever.

Problematic cases are especially helpful. For example, Byron writing a (love) letter to his sister as a 'poetical epistle'. Definitely a forbidden subject. He knows it, his sister knows it. Some of these poems he will publish, and so they are *really* coded. Others, he knows he can't publish. And so they pass on to us as historical documents. These poems present a very good example of a person consciously writing something and deliberately *not* writing something. And the 'not writing' is definitely part of what is being written. That's always occurring in writing.

SG *I want to ask, is there anyone who still defends a 'pure' idea of authorial intention?*

JM Not in the sense that it was polemicised, say, 50 years ago. As you know, I spent a fair amount of time hammering at that, but the idea of authorial intention is crucial. You cannot take that out as an important criterion. It is equally important to see that it can't be the criterion that shapes everything that you do.

SG *For the people who do think about it, it's become more nuanced. Although when students first come to a writing class, they may think that it is the only thing that counts.*

JM And, in a certain sense, so does anybody who is writing. At that point you are trying to carry out your intentions—as you must. It's true that in the last, so-called postmodern world, there are writers who pursue a writing that is trying to release expression that is not intended. And I find that quite fascinating…But it calls attention to the truth that intention is always in play anyway.

SG *Is there anything that you don't like about editing?*

JM Oh yes, I don't like a weakness in myself that I have worked at very hard, over many, many years, and it still bothers me…I'm painfully aware that I'm not a good proofreader. I'm much better than I was 30, 40 years ago. But it's not natural to me. And sometimes I am aware that [other] people have this skill, it's almost by nature. When they proofread, somehow they are able to see error, the material facts that are before them, much more easily than I can. I never proofread more than half an hour. It's just a rule, because as soon as I get tired, I really get bad. So, yes! That's something…

SG *I was going to ask if you had any particular rules or routines for your editing. It sounds like that's one of them.*

JM When I'm editing, I almost always multitask, as they say these days. And I know I do it almost theoretically. Because I want to be able to think about what I'm doing from as many different points of view as I can. So I will be constructing a bibliography; I'll be writing to, or visiting, archives; I'll be transcribing; I'll be doing a historical annotation. I try to do that all at the same time. I find it thickens everything that I do. If I'm just going to do the annotations now, I won't do it. That is definitely a style.

SG *Any other habits or practices?*

JM I like long-term projects. I didn't realise until many years after I began editing that I liked this aspect of the work, but I do. The Byron edition took 22 years…The Rossetti edition took 17 years. This Cooper edition—I know I will die before it's done.

SG *When you are editing, how do you know when you're finished?*

JM You never are; you know that.

SG *I know, but I'm asking everyone that question, because it's such an interesting one.*

JM The Byron edition is a good example. You're finished when the publisher is on your back, asking 'Where's Volume Four?' And there are all those deadlines that are effectively laid upon you. So, you're finished when you're finished. I was raised as a Catholic and I'm an unbelievably obedient person. Especially to authorities—at least on matters that don't involve, as the Pope likes to say, faith and morals. I'm obedient about my work.

The Rossetti edition is a good example of an edition that can't be finished. Its limitations are very apparent. And it's already obsolete. Nonetheless it's important historically, so I'm proud of it, even though I know only too well the constraints and limitations and weaknesses of it. One could theoretically just continue to add to it, because of the nature of digital environments.

SG *There is an argument that the digital environment means, one is never 'finished'.*

JM There's a terrible error, a theoretical error, in that thought. Okay, you can continue to add. But once you see the structural limits of what you're doing, then adding is brainless. What you really need is a whole new system.

SG *That's interesting. When new technology first came along, I remember print people saying that digital is more rigid than print. In print production you can rip up a page layout and redo it very quickly. People talk of information architecture, and it really is architecture—you cannot suddenly move the plumbing at the last minute. In that sense, digital media design is more rigid.*

JM I mentioned a while ago [our problems with] the Rossetti archive. I was in terror that we were going to have to stop. And it was because of an architectural limitation. I thought, 'Oh my god, I'm going to have to rip the whole bloody thing up and reconstruct the architecture'. The logical structure. Yes, that's true. That's one limitation.

But the limitation that I'm thinking of, is that I could go into the Rossetti archive now and update the bibliographies, I could update the commentaries. Every once and a while, another manuscript or drawing appears: I could be haunting the archives and see what's coming up for sale, paintings and drawings. I do add things from time to time. But my interest in the edition is such that I see that different kinds of editions are going to be needed. This edition was a theoretical intervention to try to figure out what you could do with these new kinds of tools. Now that I know the answer, or at any rate *an* answer, that's done. And it's done in the sense that it's also obsolete. So, I'm not going to go on with that. It's not meaningful for me.

SG *We have talked about writing a lot. When you're writing, do you experience a difference between editing yourself and editing someone else?*

JM I don't know if this answers your question, but I have a very particular way of writing. And it's been true my entire life, with the possible exception of the MA thesis and the PhD thesis. With books that I've written, I tend to think and take notes in random ways for a long time. So it could be six, seven years that I won't be writing anything. I'll just be reading and taking notes. Because I need to have a sense of what my own thought is. I don't really know my own thought.

I know friends of mine who say, the way they write a book is to start writing it. And in the act of writing they discover what it is that they want to say. It unfolds in the performance. For me, I'm not ready to write until I think I have a clear sense of what I want to do. Then, it's often the case that I can write with unbelievable speed. There are three or four books that I've written within five weeks. It's not as if I have everything in my head at that point. It's just, 'Now I *can* write'. Later, all sorts of changes take place, but I need that conception first, as a point to depart from. That's been true all my life. This book that I have in mind to do now, called *American Memory*, I know I'm not going to be able to do it for some years, if I live so long. I just don't know enough. The note-taking is really horrible. Because I don't even know how to organise the notes. I just have vast files of all kinds of stuff.

SG *Is writing more difficult than editing, or easier?*

JM The actual writing is a lot easier, and more pleasurable. The work-up to it is hard. Editing is a much more comforting thing. Because there are certain things that you *have* to do. That's very peaceful. I have to go to Harvard, I have to study those manuscripts, I have to construct a bibliography of them; I have to transcribe them; all these are obligations that I know I have to do, that's good.

SG *We've talked a bit about this, but—how did you learn the practice of editing?*

JM By doing; by doing…

SG *And if you had to sum up what you learned. Again, you've given some examples…*

JM Literate people study and read, and we believe we know what books are. I think probably the single most astonishing thing to me has been that I thought I knew what books were, and I got to know more and more about them, and the more I got to know about them, the more I realised I didn't know what they were. And that really came home with the editing of Rossetti, because at that point you have to tell an incredibly stupid machine how to simulate a book. It means that you have to be able to give the instructions to the machine about how to carry out the simulation. [Which] means that you have to know what you think a book is. That is when it came home with piercing clarity—that I did not know what books were. Because I couldn't tell the machine *exactly* how to simulate them.

SG *They say it's 'nonsense in, nonsense out'...*

JM Yes. A book is like a little moment in this [*waves to bookshelves*]. This is a glimpse of it. But the thing is vast. It's a history of writing that goes back to the dawn of time. And every book participates in that.

SG *Is it difficult to teach editing?*

JM It's difficult within a classroom situation. I find that the most rewarding educational scenes are apprentice-type scenes. So much of it is learning by doing. But the other really important thing about apprentice-type teaching is that you are learning all the time from the students. There is a terrific feedback that you get when you work cheek by jowl, close up with bright people who are interested in what they are doing. The classroom, it's such a hierarchical situation. No matter how hard you work at trying to alter that, the students are in a more or less passive relation and you are in a more or less authoritative position, and that's very destructive to all.

SG *What examples of resistance to editing have you encountered? Have you encountered resistance?*

JM Oh yes! Well, especially in our day. I mentioned that my early work was much involved with theoretical issues, and issues of interpretation. I've never not been interested in those things, and all my editorial work has always been heavily inflected by theoretical and methodological interests. Through the days of theory—the 70s and 80s and so forth—I found myself carrying on wars on two fronts. One was a battle with traditional editors who—well, Fredson did not regard me as a scholarly editor. He thought I was an interpreter, and that I didn't really understand what editing was.

And on the other hand, the theoreticians had no clue that what I was doing was theoretical. A lot of my friends saw me as going over to the dark side, involved in these dry-as-dust things. I now realise, being old enough to look back on those often painful days, that both conflicts were very good for my work; having to deal with those two separate parts of our world. But there were times when I was decidedly *not* a happy person. 'Despised and rejected of men' (!). But it was good, I now see.

SG *People can hold to a particular definition of theory, and think that anything else isn't theory. This came up in a recent Twitter exchange over whether the 'digital humanities' had their own body of theory, compared to 'new media'.*

JM Well, a lot of people who work in new media are completely ignorant of book history and the theory of textuality—what used to be called philology. It's very unfortunate. I know there are people who would say, 'We don't want to let our minds get infected by these models that come out of the past'. And I know I want to listen to that argument, though I don't agree with it. I think [those interested in] new media technologies and forms of communication need to study this ancient [form], the book—the greatest invention that those inventive creatures, Men and Women, have ever made, in my opinion. When you let your mind think into it, you see how amazing this machine is. If I said to [new media theorists], 'All text is marked text', I'm not sure [they] would understand what that meant. And how deeply problematic it is for anyone who wants to work with text.

SG *One last question. Is there an example where an absence of editing has made a difference? Because one way of evaluating editing is to evaluate its absence.*

JM I think Scott is a perfect example. Byron too. The reason why these two are such good examples is because they were so famous. When you go for 50 years without a serious editorial intervention in, say, Byron's work, then it's not without reason that they declined from attention through the twentieth century...until Leslie Marchand's edition of the letters and journals and my edition of the poetry, that's when he came back into view, and now he is restored to scholarly attention. It was the editions that did it.

Scott, it's even more scandalous. Because there has not been a scholarly edition until David Hewitt's now-completed edition of the Edinburgh edition. Scott is beginning to come back. We're talking about two authors of gigantic historical and cultural importance. That they should have fallen out of primary attention in the academic world is a scandal, I think.

Another way of putting it means that you're forgetting something that you really don't want to forget.

SG *So, forgetting and memory are about attention. And editing is about attention. So editing is about remembering.*

JM Yes. Calling attention to things that matter. Exactly.

Notes

1. See 'Vita', University of Virginia. <http://www2.iath.virginia.edu/jjm2f/vita.html>, accessed 7 August 2014.
2. 'Epigones' is defined as 'One of a succeeding generation. Chiefly in *pl.* the less distinguished successors of an illustrious generation' (OED 1989e).
3. McGann defines as 'bibliographical' the variations that exist, not in the word-for-word language of a text, but in the material, embodied *contexts* in which that language appears. An example is given of the first scholarly edition of Matthew Arnold's poetry, by H.S. Milford; in the table of contents, he 'includes a list of the separate tables of contents of all of Arnold's poems as they appeared in the different volumes (and magazines) up to 1867 [which] displays the dance of Arnold's poems as they appeared or disappeared or changed their positions in the various editions' (1991: 51).
4. For more detail, see Greenberg 2011.

Part 3: Legacy

Mary Hockaday at the BBC, John McIntyre at *The Baltimore Sun* and Philip Campbell at the scientific journal *Nature* are editors working in organisations with long roots in the past. The interviews in this section provide a chance to explore the meaning of 'standards' and 'judgment' in editing, in a period of rapid change.

Chapter 5

Mary Hockaday

Head of Multimedia Newsroom,
British Broadcasting Corporation (BBC)
Interview: Wednesday, July 4, 2012
Television Centre, London

At the time this interview took place,[1] Mary Hockaday was head of the Multimedia Newsroom, responsible for some 1,000 staff and the overall management of content for all news bulletins, along with the BBC News website. In this role, she oversaw the creation of a combined world newsroom, bringing together news teams from across the corporation[2] in a single location for the first time. New Broadcasting House, in central London, put out its first broadcast on July 9, 2012, just a few days after the meeting recorded here.

The BBC, funded by the UK licence fee-payer, is regulated by statutory rules about taste and decency and held accountable to an extensive set of editorial guidelines.[3] Within the organisation, all editors are responsible for maintaining the standards written into the corporate charter. In Hockaday's case, she was also a member of the News Board, which sets editorial policy and responds to complaints.

Hockaday joined the BBC in 1986 as a World Service production trainee. She held roles as a reporter, producer and editor, overseeing the World Service news and current affairs department before moving to wider news management.

The interview touched on a number of underlying questions that influence news editing, such as the difference between neutrality and objectivity.[4]

If resumed now, the conversation might extend into an exploration of cultures of practice, including the way editorial groups come to share assumptions about what 'everyone knows'.

Away from the constraints of news, Hockaday has explored the borderland territory of literature and journalism. After spending time in Prague during the early 1990s as a correspondent for World Service (the occasion for our first meeting) she wrote a book about Milena Jesenská (1995), a daring and charismatic Czechoslovak journalist in the early twentieth century, and for a few years an intimate friend of Franz Kafka.

Hockaday went to the city's archives—then only recently open to the public—to read Jesenská's work. The newspaper articles, which number in the hundreds, still convey the author's strong personal voice. Hockaday acknowledges that these texts 'cannot be taken as gospel truth' but notes with appreciation: 'At its best, her journalism is rich, perceptive and committed' (1992: xiii).

MH I should say something about the nature of my role. A lot of the specific outputs produced by the newsroom have their own editor. I am head of the newsroom, overarching that. So my role encompasses a broad range of activities; not necessarily the micro-editing of a particular piece of content. It is about…being another guarantor of the overall editorial direction and standards of those outlets.

SG *Do you think of yourself as an editor? If not, what do you call what you do?*

MH Yes I do think of myself as an editor, but it is [only] part of my identity. I also think of myself as a leader, a manager, a strategist, a problem-solver. Some of those [roles] are about being an editor, others sit alongside it. The part of my brain where I am focused on the content of what we are delivering and the service to audiences is the part that is about being an editor.

That includes looking beyond the obvious news agenda to dig out stories, to go where no one particularly wants us to go and illuminate what goes on in the world. To do original journalism. Many of our correspondents are brilliant at getting scoops, holding power to account, digging away at things. An editor's job can be to set them after something, or support them when they find something, and help them bring to air what can sometimes be a complex story. In other words, being an editor is both a reactive and a proactive process.

SG *Describe a typical day.*

MH It begins with the morning editorial meetings. First, in a very tight senior editorial group, then a slightly broader one, with the editors of individual outputs; we come together briefly but in a very focused way. We reflect on the previous day, how we think we did, and the big stories. [We ask], is our coverage meeting our standards of accuracy and impartiality, which is fundamental to everything I do as an editor, and is it providing context? Are we making sense and connecting with our audiences?

Then a look to what is coming in the day ahead; diary news events, the stuff we know will happen; stories that we discovered ourselves, or treatments or issues that we have chosen to focus on in a more proactive way.

Some days I will be close to the editorial content; on others, I will go off into a sequence of meetings about money, or people, or what we're going to be doing in five years' time, away from the emerging news of the day. But on most days, I will reconnect with the editorial. We have meetings at 3:15 pm, about how the day is going; [we ask], is it aligned with what we talked about in the morning? Of course on some days, you've torn it up and started again.

News is like a river, passing you fast. So the thing I try to carry in my mind all the time, and ask of the individual editors, is this: what is the story, what is the most important thing? Are we moving it on, are we being challenging, and are we being impartial? Are we reflecting a wide range of views, are we seeing it from every angle? Challenging received opinion about something. Making sure our tone is right, and attributing things. It's all about judgment.

We base a lot of what we do on reporting, and our own people being out there with the stories, and we look to them to report accurately and impartially, and to bring to bear their professional judgment. And so I think about ensuring that our coverage reflects the specialist knowledge and professional judgment of our expert, but doesn't stray into opinions. We don't have BBC opinions about stories.

Those are the things that are front of mind, if you're the kind of editor I am. We are serving a licence fee-paying public—that is an enormously wide range of people, we're not a niche operation. So all the time my concern is to be aware of that *breadth* of audience, and ask: are we telling the news in a way that will make sense, connect with people's interests and concerns? Have we done so with a *clarity* that all kinds of audiences can understand?

Similarly for our international audiences. It's not the whole world, it's a focused sub-set of people with an interest in international news, but none the less it is a very wide-ranging global audience where you're striving to achieve clarity and context.

SG *You've referred to the use of judgment. How would you illustrate that? Is it a quality that helps to distinguish what you do from, say, citizen journalism?*

MH I think citizen journalism, self-publishing, the incredible sense of openness and access that the internet brings, is a wonderful thing. But I don't think it kills the editor. I think it complements it. So, a couple of examples…

Take the day that Gaddafi was killed. We had to make judgments about the story, particularly the material: the video showing his capture and harassment, and ultimately his corpse. There were two aspects to that judgment. The first issue is, can we be sure what we are looking at? Is it what it purports to be? We have teams that are expert at verifying content and material. We didn't use it until we got through the processes of verification. The other sort of judgment was, what to show? We did not show everything. There was footage that was, in my judgment, too grisly to put in front of our audiences, and not necessary to put in front of them, for us to do our job.

That is a dramatic version of judgments that we make all the time. We're doing it within certain frameworks. First of all, we operate under the Ofcom code, which has things to say about taste, decency and the watershed. We operate under our own editorial guidelines. People sometimes think that's a rulebook but it's more a set of guidelines, based on long years of iterative practice and editorial thinking. Some things are very clear because of the law—for example libel or incitement to racial hatred—but others are based on working through our understanding of our audiences, and what the guidelines might be for a public service organisation, which might be different from a purely commercial organisation, or an operation with a different target audience.

I am also operating, all the time, as an editor in a public service organisation, funded in the UK by the licence fee-payer, with a strong ethos of public interest. And I'm operating based on years of experience. Years of making decisions, often very rapidly, sometimes with more debate, thought, conversation. That's the ethos that we all work within. It's not a science or a rulebook, but it is a very strong framework, and a ground on which to stand when making decisions.

There are other judgments that we make all the time. For example, what's the lead story, the most important thing that's happened today? It's a hard thing to define. Daily news is about the new, the dramatic, but there's also a sense of the important, and the interesting, and 'what are people going to be talking about'. And where the energy is. 'Importance' can be all sorts of things. It can be scale, or being unexpected, or drama, or impact on how many people's lives…A lot of the time it's just obvious. Other days, there are a couple of very good contenders, and at that point you're weighing up the audience; you might give a different lead to the audience of 5 Live, or Radio 4. You're mindful of a particular constituency.

We are also informed by colleagues in the BBC. As output editors we are generalists, but we work with correspondents and specialist editors who are experts, and it's often a partnership between what seems interesting and important to a generalist, informed by a specialist correspondent who may say, 'Well, this story may not look very interesting, but it is important'. Or, 'You may think that looks very dramatic, but actually, it's not as new as it appears'.

Ultimately, judgments are made knowing that there's an audience out there that will let us know when we get it badly wrong. It doesn't mean we are slaves to our audience or do exactly what our audiences want. It is about weighing up who the audiences are, but also applying our professional judgment and saying to them, 'You might not think you want to know about this, but in our judgment this is really important, and we think it is worth you knowing about, so that you can fulfil your duties as a citizen'.

SG *When people praise digital communications, they tend to stress how interactive it is. Did mechanisms did exist before that, for public accountability?*

MH Yes! And when I think about the digital space, I think it is great that people have a greater choice how they consume their news. People can choose to ignore our judgments about what we think are the most important ten things that happened in the world today. They can choose to consume their news through search on a particular story—that is the only thing they are interested in—or by what their friends happened to share with them. They can choose to compare several offers from several different news organisations. We know that our offer is not a tablet of stone, the only thing that people can consume when they sit down at 6 o'clock in the evening. But even where people have all that choice, we also know that many digital audiences users still come to a front page. People [also] come to us as a secondary source: they say, 'Well, people are saying *x* or *y*, but what does the BBC say?' We are a reference point.

We also now offer our own news in different ways. The home page is a curated thing, with a sense of the top story. Our Twitter feeds are more of a flow of moments and stories through the day, and people find us through other searchable links. But however people consume the news, the thing that is the same is the value given to accuracy and impartiality. It may no longer be a judgment of what the most important story is, but it is a judgment that a story is worth putting some effort into and putting out there, and our coverage of that story will be sound and can be a reference point for people, even if it's not the only way they touch that story.

SG *Can you think of an example where an absence of editing has made a difference?*

MH I can think of examples which I cannot cite by name. I can make a general point, pertinent to news. News is like a river; it never reaches a finite point. And in some ways, our output is like that. Of course we have programmes with a start and a finish, and for a brief moment there is a half hour that has to be filled, which can't be any longer than it is, and there is an attempt at that moment to sum up and capture the flow. But there is always another programme and another hour, and some of our channels are continuous, and the website is a completely continuous space.

So there is a constant challenge. As the river rushes past you, the first task is to report; to describe the river, what colour and how high and how fast, and all that. But the other thing that our audiences expect is not only what has happened, but also *why*, and why it *matters*; to fit a development into a bigger picture, and a bigger context; that day, that week, that month, that year...

Sometimes, we are so busy trying to report what's rushing past that we miss the moment to stand back and say, 'have we really explained to people why this matters?' And one can think of examples where we haven't necessarily done that. We usually get there in the end, but we don't always do it in as timely a fashion as we might. It's often on these big, long-running stories. I can think of our coverage of the Arab uprisings last year, the Eurozone crisis or the banking crisis—you get moments where everyone is pedalling very hard to capture what is happening as it rushes past. The best editing is when someone like myself remembers to stand back and say, 'What is the bigger picture, the sense-making we should be adding at this point?' It is not always possible to do it in the heat of the moment. News is news. But there are times when we want to do it and the moment is lost; sometimes we come back to it, but sometimes we don't, and that can be frustrating.

SG *You described judgment as being cumulative, based on experience. How did you learn editing? Is there anything that comes to mind that describes the process?*

MH What we require of everybody is that they recognise where a red light should go off and they think, 'I must go and check with a more senior editor or consult the BBC guidelines'. They should understand the general terrain.

For me, one of the joys of working at the BBC is that it's sort of Socratic. It's constant discussion, talking things through with other colleagues. As I have grown up through the organisation, I have been part of those conversations at a team level and department level, where people who have lived through it before me are sharing and discussing things, with all the accumulative wisdom and experience and judgment that they have. And so one soaks that up, and I hope others are now soaking it up from me and my other senior colleagues.

The other way you really learn is in the doing. And again, one grows up through producing a programme, through producing a longer programme, to producing the content of a network.

And one learns through the accountability processes, the relationship with the audiences. We get complaints, letters, emails from audiences. They are answered, we engage with them, and sometimes they have good points and one learns from that. We have forums and programmes where senior editors can be held to account. There are many mechanisms in the BBC where we are aware of audience view—the licence fee view—and reflect on it.

SG *Can you comment on some of the more detailed aspects of editing, about the 'how' rather than the 'what'? You mentioned earlier the importance of getting the tone right...*

MH That is not something I spend a lot of time on, in my current role. That is what the next layer below me is doing, and the layer below them. I might be involved in a conversation about which correspondent will cover something. Immediately in that choice, you are saying something about the tone, the direction of the story. Otherwise I might comment on the storytelling skill and the [multimedia] ingredients, such as illustrative sound. I will comment if I think something's been executed well and if the craft is good. But it would be the next layer below me that is thinking in a more proactive way about how they are going to do that story.

SG *These things can seem like details, but they have a way of affecting the whole story.*

MH You're right; all those decisions about the execution of something are done in the same world, with the same principles about quality, standards and service to the audience. What that translates into is, 'is it good quality, is it well written, are the pictures good, is the sound well recorded?' And then, clarity. Have we told the story? A lot of our output, we don't have much time. And even on the web, you don't have infinite space, people have only got so much time that they are prepared to put into something.

SG *Going back to judgment, there is a debate about the difference between neutrality and objectivity. Is that something you discuss?*

MH Oh yes, a lot. And again, one uses the word 'impartiality', but what do we really mean? A lot of people will play back impartiality as meaning, 'You all think as long as you have someone from one side and someone from the other—job done'. But actually, most things don't just have two sides. And so our sense of impartiality is about the *range* of views, and even within that, giving due weight to how the range of views are represented. Let's take climate change. We know there are a range of views about whether human beings have caused global warming or not. But we also know that the weight of scientific opinion is predominantly that there is a human factor in temperature rise, and there are a much smaller number of people who think that there isn't. In the overarching breadth of our coverage, we will include at some point the voice that says they don't believe that human behaviour contributes to climate change, but we will not give equal weight to that view in the broad spread of all our coverage. So it's a much more sophisticated thing.

We are absolutely making judgments. And it's why a lot of resource goes into specialist reporting correspondents. We have a business team and business editor. We have a political team and political editor, an arts editor, a science editor. All to ensure that we have people working on stories who are very well informed and experienced and therefore able to evaluate and reach judgments. And able to *evidence* the judgment reached, and make a clear distinction between an evidenced judgment and their own opinion.

It's something we talk about a lot, because we are obliged to do this within Ofcom in a way that newspapers aren't. And we know that this makes us not as noisy and shiny as some outlets. Opinion—strong opinion—and the drama that goes with that can be a very compelling thing. It's why we buy newspapers and we love Op-eds, and it's why people in the States watch Fox or whatever. We can't do that.

But what we do think about, and try and do, is engender our own sense of passion about being impartial, the energy about the journey to make the informed judgment, and a sense of the energy that comes from rigour and standards. And then the passion to communicate that to audiences in an engaging way.

Notes

1. At the time of publication, Hockaday had taken up a new position as Controller, BBC World Service English.
2. The newsroom creates output for BBC 1 television bulletins and the news channel; summaries and bulletins for Radios 2, 3, 4, and 6 Music; the news web pages; and the World News website, television channel and radio.
3. See, for example, 'Editorial standards', <http://www.bbc.co.uk/bbctrust/our_work/editorial_standards/>, accessed February 12, 2012; 'The BBC policy on discussion forum moderation.' <http://news.bbc.co.uk/1/hi/help/4180404.stm>, accessed 20 March 2009.
4. For further detail on this distinction, see Greenberg 2012.

Chapter 6

John McIntyre

Night content production manager, The Baltimore Sun
Interview: Friday, July 27, 2012
by email

John McIntyre has worked at *The Baltimore Sun* since 1986, with one year's interruption. And as a veteran, he has fun with the persona of the crusty newspaperman. The cover of a book of maxims, *The Old Editor Says* (2013b), features a white-haired McIntyre in braces and bow tie. The book is published by his students at Loyola University Maryland, where he has taught copy editing since 1995 (2013a).

McIntyre's prompt attention to my deadlines and the economy of his responses are all of a piece: the prose is spare but to the point, with plenty of telling detail. As on his blog, 'You Don't Say', the voice is wry, but this does not disguise an intense engagement with writers, readers and editors.

SG *What drew you to this type of work?*

JM First, economic necessity. I left the PhD program in English at Syracuse University, without completing the dissertation. Settling in Cincinnati with my first wife, who had landed a job there, I persuaded the editors of *The Cincinnati Enquirer* to give me a three-week tryout on the copy desk, on the strength of my English degrees and six summers' work at a weekly paper in

Kentucky during high school and college. They found my work satisfactory and offered me a permanent position on the copy desk, and I have been a working copy editor for the 32 years since.

Second, there was the discovery that editing was more satisfactory than scholarship. I learned that I could edit quickly and decisively, and had a knack for writing headlines. The daily deadlines provided a structure within which to work, and the companionship and collegiality of fellow editors, the exchange of information and badinage, was much more congenial than sitting in a library carrel trying to generate insights about texts.

SG *Do you think of yourself as an editor? If not, what do you call what you do?*

JM Yes, I am an editor. Sometimes a copy editor, but copy editing tends to spill over into primary [basic] editing, especially at publications where the primary editing is weak.

SG *How do you define editing? What imagery or metaphor would you use?*

JM Surgeon. I open up the patient, examine what is healthy and what is unhealthy, and excise diseased tissue. In a recent blog post, I offered a different metaphor, which also fits: craftsmanship, the satisfaction of seeing the publication launched, watertight, shipshape and Bristol fashion.

SG *What do you do? Describe a typical day.*

JM At home in the morning, after coffee, I usually write a post for my blog. I typically arrive at *The Sun*'s newsroom around 2 pm and catch up on messages and other details before the afternoon news meeting at 3 pm. After that, it is editing either daily news copy or advance copy, of which there is a mixture each day. Given our reduced staff, I do primary copy editing, slotting (that is, double-checking edited text), and proofreading. On some occasions, and this is deeply regrettable and dangerous, I perform all three functions for the same text.

SG *Think of a common activity: how long does it take to do?*

JM I edit quickly, which is a given under current circumstances, and sometimes too quickly. A routine article, say 600 words or so, I will read for 'media neutral'—that is, the same text to be used online and print—address questions of fact, correct grammar, usage and style, trim the print version to fit the available space, and write print headlines within 10 to 15 minutes. A front-page story of some length may take 20 minutes to half an hour. There are also a number of minor mechanical tasks to attend to, such as the front-page index, corrections and the like.

SG *Do you have any pertinent routines or practices? Mood-setting rituals?*

JM At home, I like to have music playing: Bach, Handel, Haydn, Mozart, Schubert. At work, I settle in and attend first to messages, both work and personal, and open the various websites I consult during the shift. Then I attend the afternoon news meeting, and then finally get down to editing.

I try to get up from the machine at frequent intervals and walk around the newsroom, focusing my eyes on distant objects rather than close ones, and getting some oxygen up to the brain. This is particularly helpful when I am stuck on a headline. I brew tea and coffee at work, and drink water.

SG *What is your main concern when editing and how is it resolved? Is there a particular example of editing that illustrates this concern?*

JM The principal concern is the factual accuracy of the texts, which is troublesome, because there is neither time nor staffing for extensive fact-checking. I have to have an eye for what looks as if it may be wrong. After accuracy, clarity comes next. I have to untangle awkward syntax and see to the conventions of grammar, usage and house style.

One example shows how the two emphases interconnect. A staff writer's article about the British bombardment of Fort McHenry during the War of 1812 was written in a way that could be understood as saying that the bombardment started at night and ended at dawn the next day. I knew that the bombardment lasted 25 hours and had to recast the sentence to reflect that.

Most of the prose I work with is not what could be called elegant, and a good deal is only marginally competent. What I have frequently been doing for the past three decades is to take inferior prose and render it merely mediocre, that being as far as it can be taken.

SG *How do you know when you are finished?*

JM When I have done all that I can reasonably do by deadline.

SG *Is writing or editing more difficult? How are they different?*

JM I enjoy writing, which is difficult in ways that are different from the difficulties of editing, and satisfying in ways that are different from the satisfactions of editing.

SG *Is editing your own work different from editing someone else's? How and why?*

JM More difficult. I miss more, editing my own work, I assume, because I know in my head what I want it to say, and thus fail to notice typos and other minor lapses. Because the blogging is more casual and immediate than other writing, I seldom hold on to a post long enough to go back on it with proper reflection. Also, I am not an accomplished typist and am prone to typos, which the readers of the blog are delighted to point out.

SG *What do you like most and least about editing?*

JM I like the sense of quiet superiority that rises from identifying other people's errors. I like the feel of tightening and clarifying sentences. I like the company of other editors. I like the structure that the daily deadline schedule gives to the work. I like the knowledge that my work is recognized by my masters, and that the published *Baltimore Sun* is better than it would have been without my presence.

What I like least is having to repeat the same damn corrections in text day after day for writers who pay no attention to what they are doing, or to do the work that the assigning editor should more properly have done.

SG *Is there a particular example where you feel your editing made a significant improvement to the text?*

JM On a Friday night at *The Baltimore Sun* several years ago, the main article for the front page of the Sunday business section moved late. The daily copy gets precedence, so it was even later when a copy editor picked up the article. It was a disaster. I'll enumerate.

The 'nut graph' (the focus graph) was delayed for a full third of the text, and then took the rest of the article in a completely unexpected direction. Sourcing was inadequate, and chronology was muddled. Finally, several passages were out-and-out libelous, the ripest and most egregious example of libel I have ever encountered directly.

Reporter and assigning editor were long gone, and there was a midnight deadline for the Sunday business section, which was printed as an advance. The copy editor and business slot editor came to me, and as chief of the copy desk I made this decision—excise the libel and publish the rest. It would make little or no sense to the readers, but they were accustomed to that in our business section.

Mind you, this story was not the work of a tyro, but was produced by a reporter with a quarter-century of experience at the paper, and edited by the business editor. The following Monday, I took the original text to the editor of the paper. The business copy editor and slot editor who raised the alarm got a commendation from the publisher. The reporter and business editor got an interview with the editor that I suspect is vivid in their memories to this day.

I can give another example, on my own editing. I regularly edit the reviews filed by *The Sun*'s music critic, which often had to be cut to fit. I edited by omitting surplus words and generally tightening sentences, rather than excising chunks of text. The critic regularly said to me afterward, 'You said what I meant to say better than I did myself'.

SG *Can you give an example of when editing has gone wrong, for whatever reason?*

JM When I worked at *The Cincinnati Enquirer*, the paper ran an article about a dinner at the Reagan White House at which monkey bread was served. A copy editor, not knowing what monkey bread is, turned to the dictionary and inserted a phrase identifying the dish as 'the fruit of the African baobab tree'. [In fact] what the Reagans [had] served was a Southern dish of sweet bread made from individual pieces of dough, dipped in butter and baked together in a pan.

This is the hazard of editing, to make a change of something half-understood that makes the text wrong. In my own case, I once changed a sentence in an article by one of *The Sun*'s Washington correspondents, based on something I assumed to be the case about arms negotiations, but which I did not check. I got a call from the reporter the next day demanding to know the source of my information, and I stammered in embarrassment. *The Sun* ran a correction, and I got a mild reprimand. The embarrassment was worse.

SG *Is editing valued in your organization?*

JM More than previously. When I started at *The Sun* in 1986, it was a common ambition among reporters to achieve the status of being immune to editing. Copy editors were openly scorned in the newsroom. *The Sun* had a managing editor for several years who habitually referred to copy editing as 'a necessary evil'. I myself was once called a liar—publicly, in the middle of the newsroom—by a reporter, and nothing came of it, because the reporter was one of the stars and copy editors, at that time, had no rights that a white man was obliged to respect.

Happily, most of the prima donna crowd is gone and the editing staff, though diminished, is allowed to edit.

I can also give a personal example of how editing is valued. I was laid off in 2009 along with 60 other newsroom employees. When the editor offered to bring me back on the staff as night editor, he said, 'If you accept, it will have an immediately positive effect throughout the entire newsroom, and it will make right something from a year ago'.

SG *Who has the last word: author or editor?*

JM Our intention is to be collaborative, and to discuss matters with reporters and assigning editors. The extent of discussion is determined by the importance of the issue (accuracy, clarity, organization, focus, etc.). But my hands are the last ones on the text, and as published it runs as I left it.

SG *Do you think of your reader? Why?*

JM All the time. Reporters tend to be drawn to their sources. They write for their sources. They write *like* their sources, falling into jargon. The greatest service that an editor can provide is to approach the text the way the reader would, to pay attention to one's own reactions as a reader, and to use them to identify difficulties or inadequacies in the text.

SG *How did you learn the practice of editing?*

JM Editing is a craft, and it is learned by apprenticeship. My university work in English literature gave me experience in analyzing texts, but it was by going through the [text], working alongside experienced editors and learning from them, that I became more effective.

SG *Do you see yourself as part of any particular tradition? Do you have a role model?*

JM I am in the journalistic rather than the literary tradition. My models are the editors I have worked with and learned from.

SG *How has your work changed over time?*

JM Through blogging about language, and through exchanges with lexicographers and linguists, I have examined many of the stylebook strictures and conventions of journalistic usage and found many of them bogus or time-wasting. The unfounded distinction between 'over' and 'more than' that many journalists embrace is an example. I am trying to focus on what is most essential for clarity for the reader, and less about fussiness over trivial details. Mind you, I understand that judgments within the craft about what is trivial and what is not vary considerably.

SG *How important is judgment?*

JM Judgment is all-important. Any editor makes thousands of judgments, most of them minor, in the course of a day, and any change an editor makes can be detrimental. Good judgment, Mark Twain said, comes from experience; experience comes from bad judgment. It is particularly important for editors to identify and learn from their mistaken judgments.

SG *What are the consequences of bad editing, in general?*

JM Some readers grow scornful and stop reading when they encounter errors of spelling or grammar or usage. To my mind, while such minor errors are annoying, it is far more urgent for editors to deal with focus and clarity. Lack of editing means that slack writing gets published; nothing is easier for a reader to do than to stop reading a text that is rambling, wordy, unclear or ill-focused.

SG *Should editing work receive more public recognition? How might that be achieved?*

JM Editing is inherently anonymous. It is a collaborative process in which it would be difficult, and largely meaningless, to recognise the contributions of the editors who have their hands on the text. To value it for awards, one would have to compare the original text with the edited text, and no one is willing to submit to that sort of embarrassment.

SG *Is it difficult to teach editing? What is the ideal form of training?*

JM I have taught editing at Loyola University Maryland since 1995, to [a total of] more than 500 students. Most of them arrived in class without the grounding in grammar and usage that used to be taught in elementary schools and high schools, forcing me to spend valuable time reviewing basics instead of more sophisticated aspects of the craft.

Beyond that, editing is an analytical endeavor, and most students have not been trained to read analytically. In writing courses, they have been taught to write intuitively, by ear. It is extremely challenging to get them to look at the structure and organization of articles, to identify focus, to challenge what the writer has given, to be productively skeptical.

Still further, the available textbooks focus on micro-editing (grammar, usage, house style, headline writing) instead of macro-editing (focus, structure, organization, tone). Happily, I have an extensive file of sub-par texts produced by professional journalists at *The Baltimore Sun*, from which I have been able to develop my own macro-editing unit.

SG *If publishers do not edit, who should do it?*

JM The current state of publishing puts more pressure on writers, many of whom are not up to it, and should not have to do without competent editing.

SG *What particular challenges and opportunities arise from digital publishing?*

JM Immediacy and involvement with the reader are each a plus, and the speed of publication can be a great advantage. That speed, of course, [also] allows first-draft, substandard work to go out. The greatest problem in digital publishing is the mistaken belief that editing can be safely gone without, or that an editor's casual swipe at a text amounts to adequate editing.

SG *Do you agree/disagree with the following statement by Amazon executive Russell Grandinetto: 'The only really necessary people in the publishing process now are the writer and reader.'*

JM Only a jackass ignorant of the functions of editing would speak this way. Or someone who sees paying settlements in libel suits merely a cost of doing business. Would Mr. Grandinetto prefer to have plagiarism and fabrication caught in-house by editors, or by the public?

Take a look at the facsimile edition of T.S. Eliot's *The Waste Land* and look at the comments by Ezra Pound, and the extensive passages of verse he simply crossed out. One of the greatest poems of the twentieth century was a product of editing, and aggressive editing at that. Eliot recognized the value of editing when he called Pound *il miglior fabbro* (Eliot 1971).

Chapter 7

Philip Campbell

Editor-in-chief, Nature
Interview: Thursday, July 26, 2012
Kings Cross, London

Philip Campbell, at the time of writing, heads the editorial operations of one of the world's oldest scientific journals. He joined *Nature* in 1979, following doctoral and postdoctoral research in upper atmospheric physics at the University of Leicester. After running publications for the Institute of Physics, he returned to the journal in 1995 as editor-in-chief. A Fellow of the Royal Astronomical Society and the Institute of Physics, Campbell advises public bodies on a range of issues relating to science and its impact on society.

The very high bar that *Nature* sets for publication makes it a good example of editing-as-selection. An account of the editing process at the journal also helps to illustrate the rhetorical role of editing in constructing arguments, and the difference this can make to the meaning of a text. Finally, it illuminates a long-standing debate within scientific publishing about how old and new publishing models can co-exist.

Nature was founded in 1869, a time of expansion and innovation in periodical publishing in the UK. The journal declares on its web pages: '*Nature*, above all, has been a survivor' (*Nature* 2014).

Its iconic status also makes it a target. Nobel Prize winner Randy Schekman, for example, made a splash late in 2013 when he criticized 'luxury journals'. He argued that existing open access alternatives such as Public Library of Science (PLoS) had 'not yet challenged the stranglehold *Cell*,

Nature and *Science* have on the biomedical literature' and the bias he felt they showed towards 'sexy science'. Instead, he was taking up the role of editor-in-chief of a new open access journal, *eLife*,[1] where decisions were made by 'experts who are practicing scientists' (Schekman 2013).

A previous staff editor at *Nature*, Philip Ball, describes the criticism as 'absurd' and observes that 'some authors felt in safer hands at *Nature*' than in the hands of academic peers who might have 'axes to grind' (Ball 2014).

In the interview here, Campbell gives his own robust defence, describing in detail the ways in which he sees editing bring value to the scientific process. The editor is a specialist not just in expression, but in critical thinking and the exercise of judgment.

The conversation starts with a discussion about the working definition of editing, and the role of selection.

SG *What kind of editing goes on at* Nature?

PC: Your definition talks about 'selection', and it is for this in particular that *Nature* makes its reputation.

I started at *Nature,* worked as a magazine editor elsewhere, and then came back. I [currently] have a team of 28 people here whose only job is to do what I used to do when I started. You spend your time in a lot of contact with academics; you find out what research is going on and you get sent, in the case of this journal, about 11,000 research papers every year, and you publish roughly 800 of them. The work involves an initial filter; our own editorial judgment about what not to publish. This is an extreme form of editing at the selection stage. Occasionally, we will come across work, approach the author and say 'you should send that to us, we'd love to publish it', but on the whole, the great majority [of papers] are unsolicited.

Next, for the 30% to 40% that we think might be suitable, we select two or three referees. Referees come back with suggestions and the editors themselves have constructive suggestions—[this is] developmental editing of the paper. By the time you've had something refereed, it's as likely as not that it will be published. Sometimes referees find fatal flaws, but we have a very high initial selectivity by our editors. We don't have an editorial board, we make our own decisions about what sort of science we want to publish. The referees give crucial technical advice, and as often than not, that is going to help us improve the paper rather than reject it.

That's basically what we do. It's something we probably take further than elsewhere; at *Nature* there is as much added value as you'll find anywhere in the academic editing processes.

Then it gets handed over to the sub-editors and they work on all the detail, which of course is not just text—it's all the stuff where publishers add value for electronic posting, adding in metadata. And then there's production.

So from my own experience, it is that upfront, upstream selection process before you hand it over to the subs that *Nature* depends on. Sub-editing is sub-editing; it's very valuable, it's absolutely essential, but for *Nature*, the value of the name—the entire brand—rests on our ability to do a good selection job and decide what to publish.

The other sort of editing that I know about from personal experience is on the journalism side of *Nature*. I have never been a news or features editor; I have some outstanding people just outside the door who do those jobs. I have, however, been the editorials editor.

The editorials are all internally written. It's an anonymous editorial so the voice is *Nature*, just like a *Times* leader. The editorials pages now have their editor, but for much of my time as editor I have run that page; if a colleague writes it I'll do the editing and see it through to the page. If I write the editorial, someone else will edit, it but I'm ultimately taking responsibility for the section.

Typically, we publish three editorials a week. Every week we'll look at what topics are out there and talk to our colleagues. Sometimes it's very straightforward; somebody comes out with a viewpoint that I think [should be included in] *Nature*.

SG*: You could say that the work you do on editorials is an example not just of selection, but also of putting things into context, because you're saying, 'this is why it matters'.*

PC: There are very varied types of content in our editorials, and one of my pleasures has been to make that as diverse as possible. Occasionally we run a think piece that doesn't do more than simply celebrate something—for example an anniversary. Sometimes we have a critique of behaviour by an institution or person. Sometimes we'll be very scientifically orientated and look at the way a research community can develop the integrity of the research—by which I mean, the robustness of the science that's coming out of labs.

Although *Nature* is very widely read, especially online, it is aimed at researchers. We're very, very conscious of that. We focused down a little, about three years ago [in 2009]. Before, if you'd asked me who we were aimed at, I would have included a wider range. But now we've focused on researchers; and there's a lot of other people who are very interested in the world of researchers. When you're thinking of who you are writing for, it's the researchers—not policymakers, not the general public, not industrialists—and that affects the way you edit something. When something comes in you immediately think, what's the researcher going to think about that when they open up the journal? Is it going to grab their attention?

SG: *In my own definition, I say that an editor is putting him or herself in the shoes of the reader.*

PC: Yes, I think that's exactly what we are doing when it comes to the news and features—that's absolutely the editors' job. Sometimes they will say, 'This isn't going to be of interest to everyone but it is of interest to one part of the readership', and that's fine. But it's completely audience-centric thinking.

When it comes to the research papers, awareness of the audience isn't so much of an issue because for *Nature's* readers, everybody knows how a scientific argument works, so in that sense you're taking the nature of the reader completely for granted.

SG: *Could we go back and look at the initial selection filter…*

PC: We publish about 8% of papers submitted to us and reject on receipt, without peer review, 60% to 70%. We have a time target; within a week, an editor will have looked at a paper and made the initial decision. That's our aim. What they're trying to do is to answer the question, 'how important is this piece of work?' In the end, we are trying to publish the most important science—that's what people look to *Nature* to do. If they see it in *Nature* they expect it to be really important. And so at that stage, we're not looking at the technical validity of the work, we're purely looking at its importance. Its scientific importance, not media importance; science for science's sake.

Just occasionally, we include a paper that may not be so impact-making scientifically, but [has importance for] the application of science to a policy question. For example, if you are in the middle of an epidemic of some sort, and you get an epidemiology model which shows where that's going to go, and it is of a very wide interest, we might publish that—even though, under normal circumstances, the model wouldn't be that innovative. But those are very rare exceptions.

SG: *Is it difficult to explain or describe the quality of 'judgment'?*

PC: It is true that it's something you know when you see it; the capacity to make a judgment. We select people for that capacity so I can tell you about the selection process. People who come into *Nature* must have experience doing research in labs. They will probably be postdoctoral. They will almost certainly have good papers behind them, published in good journals. They'll have their own confidence and track record. We take it for granted that if they've got through the door, they are good at their own research. But we are looking for additional skills and attitudes. So we ask for their general outlook on science, and give them a test.

One test is to take three scientific papers, read them for an hour, come back and answer questions. The papers are related to the applicant's own area of expertise but only in a general way. For example, if the applicant is a geneticist, the papers will be on biology but not genetics. They are expected not only to take in details, but also to form a judgment as to why it might be interesting, and how the arguments relate to the data.

We don't spell it out—we simply give it to them and say, 'Okay, you read this—imagine you are an editor and form your judgments'. And a good scientific-minded person will be able to ask questions, even if it's not an area of their own expertise. For example, they can say: 'They're making that statement but they only have two data points [on which] to judge it; that's a weakness.' That sort of critical thinking, that ability to defend their judgments, to articulate why the paper is of interest—all of that is what they're expected to do.

The candidates have been through the manuscript test and answered very well; and then, you get to their interests—what's going to get them out of bed. Because they're going to be faced with this pile of manuscripts every day, for the rest of their time with us. They've got to develop relationships with the authors out there, and the referees. So they've got to be reasonably personable, hold good conversations, and resolve conflicting opinions from referees—which happens all the time.

SG: *Do you have a view about the new open access publishing models that are coming up, such as 'publish first, edit later'?*

PC: We trained some of the people who set up the first PLoS journals. They were my colleagues; some of them left *Nature* to do that. They were extremely good. *PLoS Biology* and *PLoS Medicine* I believe have rejection rates similar to ours. The job of *PLoS ONE* is to publish anything that's valid, provided that it's technically okay; my guess would be that it is publishing about 80% of what it's sent. It has been extremely successful at doing what it does. I think that particular organisation, above all, deserves credit. There were others as well but I would say the Public Library of Science was the most radical, and the most determined; the publisher who did the most to break the mould.

The thing you should note, in terms of editorial, is that the processes used in *PLoS Biology* are pretty much identical to the processes used by us. There has never been a suggestion that it holds to different quality standards. It's true that *Nature* is seen as the most prestigious journal, and you'd expect me to be competitive in terms of what we achieve, but their journals are nevertheless very selective. And in terms of the processes, it's exactly the same mindset. In that sense, we're all part of a community.

In my head, the issue of open access is distinct from the issue of editorial selection. The question is often asked: is open access bad for editorial quality? And the answer is no, it isn't—not in itself, as long as the business model actually works. In principle it is not in opposition to good editorial. If [the publication depends on] an author fee, the highly selective journals would need very high author fees for each paper. But there are all sorts of ways in which some publishers can get round that problem, and some funding agencies haven't yet decided what or even whether they are going to pay.

SG: *Are there any examples of decisions that stick in the mind—'I'm really glad we made that decision', or 'I really wish we hadn't done that'?*

PC: We never discuss specific cases without getting permission. But I can talk in general about the sort of decision I'm proud about. It relates to the times when we go against the recommendations of the referee [and] publish over their heads. Because sometimes referees have their own reasons for rejection.

If any referee says, 'This paper is wrong because…' then we won't publish it, absolutely. But [sometimes] three referees say, 'Well, it's all right but it's not really interesting, we don't think it's what *Nature* should be publishing, but technically speaking it's fine'. We will on occasion disagree with them because we have our own view. There are loads of other cases where referees disagree and we have to work our way through that.

There will be times when we reject a paper but say, 'Look, if you can go away and do all sorts of work, come back, we'll reconsider it'. Sometimes, a much easier problem, we'll say, 'Two referees have said this is fine but one has asked for a very specific thing. You need to go and do that because we agree with them'. That's the standard interplay between the various views of editorial and referees.

SG: *Are there any examples of a 'before' and 'after', where everyone agrees— including the author—that the 'after' is much, much better and they're grateful?*

PC: Here's an example, which I can give you because this was said in public at a conference. We published a paper about the first full mouse genome; in those days it was a big thing to celebrate. And there was a party in Boston near the labs that did most of the driving of the project. The leader of the project stood up, saying 'thank you' to different people. And he said thank you to *Nature* because 'you really made us work hard. Your referee's comments helped us make the paper much, much better'. We all knew we were going to publish the paper. It was a very good piece of work, an important piece of work, and we could have just put it through and I'm sure it would have been okay. But the referees came back with page after page of constructive suggestions as to how to make it better, and we all wanted to [make it better], so we did.

SG: *Let's turn to the shaping function—the sub-editors adding metadata, checking. What examples can you think of, that illustrate what they do?*

PC: Research papers are standard formats and do not involve much shaping. But the journal also includes something called a 'review'; with this format, the commissioning process is absolutely crucial to the success of the article. You're finding the right author but if you're good, you're also thinking, 'Why am I commissioning this piece? Why are we doing this particular piece on this topic, right now?' That involves a lot of judgment. That's an editing function right at the outset. And then you really do help shape the article with the author, because [they vary in how good they are] at presenting ideas in a coherent way. At that point, the editors need to take a look at the thing and reshape it.

SG: *In an interview you once said that some people criticise* Nature*'s use of professional editors on the grounds that they are supposedly second-rate or failed scientists. Are there examples you can think of, where people have criticised the very practice of editing?*

PC: Well, yes, you will hear people say that. They say, 'These people are not active scientists, therefore, they don't understand, right?' And my answer is, 'Bollocks to that one'. Because what you get with professional editors are people who are talking to active scientists all the time; they were active scientists themselves so they know exactly what it's about, they know what the rules are.

Of course, when it comes to a very specific debate between what one referee is asking for, and what an author is saying, if the author doesn't have faith in the editor's ability to resolve that and make a good decision, then one easy answer is to say, 'Well don't come to *Nature*'. But I think I can honestly say that our track record speaks for itself. And actually, people who get to know the editors do have respect for them.

I have a litmus test for that. People come here occasionally to work on secondment, and those people are academics who are active. They work exactly as any other member of staff; they're integral to the team, they see everything, they hear everything, they contribute, they bring their expertise, which is immensely valuable. I talk to them near the beginning of their time, and at the end. And I'll say to them, 'You're an academic, you've come in— have you been surprised by anything? Are you happy? Did you feel that this is all okay?' They've got nothing to lose by saying, 'I've got concerns'. And I've yet to hear it; no one has ever said that. They've always said, 'Actually I think it really works. I think it's good'. Of course, there are wrinkles, but in terms of the essential robustness of what we're doing, I stand by what we do. And where we have specific concerns about robustness, we always review our policies to strengthen our processes.

I do understand that academics out there have a real concern about non-active academic editors. All we can do is do our best, and communicate what we're doing and how we're doing it, when it comes to those difficult decisions. But there is another thing to say. We're on the road a lot of time; these editors spend six weeks every year visiting labs, talking to people. Because of the way we do the job, we will often be *more* aware of what's going on, we will often have a *better* sense of alertness to what the community is doing and will be systematically more dedicated to the process of decision-making on behalf of the author than many [scientifically active] academic editors.

I say *many*, because there are some absolutely stellar academic editors. And I think that if you look at the most inspiring editors, they tend to be the academic editors. But they are very few and far between. I can think of an astronomer who edited the *Astrophysical Journal*, and a physicist in 1905 who published several of Einstein's seminal works, and I can think of a climate researcher who edited a multi-disciplinary journal. These are all active scientists, either revered or greatly respected because of their knowledge and dedication. But they are the exception that proves the rule, because of the way they applied themselves.

SG: *What is it that the editor does that improves the outcome?*

PC: In the selection process, they're making sure that the advice they get is the best advice that can be got. The added value of the editor is making the science as good as it can possibly be, in order to justify the paper's conclusion. If it's a *Nature* paper, it should be an important conclusion, so a lot hangs on it. We have the most critically minded audience, because academics are very critically minded.

When it comes to anything else, the editor acts on behalf of the reader. You've said it yourself and we all know what the editing process involves and that's how they do it. They form their judgment at the commissioning. But the best editor's thinking, how can I make an impact with this, in the way it deserves?

SG*: In a way, what you're saying is that editors are specialists—but what they are specialist at is editing, and that's a distinct set of skills and knowledge.*

PC: Yes, but the important thing to add is that the editors are [not outsiders, they are] *also* in the scientific community. That six weeks out in the community is something I set a great store by. If they were just sitting at their desks, after a bit they would definitely get stale, and they would lose the sense of how the field is moving, who the good people are, why they're respected by other people. It is only by getting out and having conversations that you get tacit knowledge about people.

SG*: Another complaint I've heard is that a journal title acts as a brand and readers become complacent. They think, 'Oh well, it's in that publication, so it must be good', and there's therefore a lack of independent judgment.*

PC: Yes, and I've written editorials that completely support that [concern]. It's not just the *Nature* brand at play, it is the trust that people have to put in a research paper. In some disciplines like biology, the experiments are very difficult to replicate, so people have to put a huge amount of trust in it. But the truth of the matter is that we're not going into the labs to replicate this work before we publish it. So like the reader, we can only base it on what we see—and I think that's true to a dangerous extent. There are some papers which are considered important because they are in *Nature* which will turn out to be wrong, because people make mistakes in laboratories, or even [commit] fraud—very, very rarely but that happens. If the *Nature* brand is put on something and makes everybody think, therefore, it's a safe piece of work—then, they're not being scientific. In my view, there is too much of that sort of trust within the research community.

The second concern is that when people judge individual researchers they [may] look at them and say, 'Oh well, he's had a paper in *Nature*, he must be good'. And that too is a worrying substitute for a proper conversation and a proper look at that person's papers, even if they haven't been in *Nature*. It's certainly true that many researchers will tell you some of their best work did not appear in any of the top journals; it appeared in other journals.

SG*: Would you say that editing is creative?*

PC: Yes, absolutely, if you're any good at it. All the editing I have been talking about is creative, because right at the outset, you're not just taking something you're given. In many cases you've helped to decide that it sł ··

be given; you've commissioned it. That's certainly true of the editorials. Then when you're looking at a piece of text, if you're a good editor, you're thinking about the problem, asking—are there other aspects [worth exploring]; you're using your imagination and knowledge to make it a better piece. That's a creative process.

SG*: Thinking about your own experience, how did you learn editing? Was it all on the job? Were you watching, listening to others?*

PC: I would see other people do different types of editing, and see how other people edited my copy, how people talked about the copy in conversation; how they talked about the criteria they brought to bear. It was being part of an organisation that thought about readers and what they wanted. But I was never trained in any formal way as an editor.

SG*: Not many people are. Do you feel that editing receives sufficient recognition? Someone once suggested giving editors a byline so people can follow them.*

PC: I haven't given that much thought. There is no reason why one shouldn't put in a byline. I think transparency is a perfectly good thing. In bigger publications [with more staff it could be good in principle] to know that a particular piece was edited by certain person.

SG: If publishers do not carry out the editing, for whatever reason—who should do it?

PC: I find it hard to answer to that one…I think it's interesting why it's hard to answer. I do believe very, very strongly that an editor acts on behalf of the reader. If a writer writes direct to a reader, [for example in a blog], you may get self-indulgence, and assumptions that the reader understands, and therefore you won't connect as well as you would otherwise. The best bloggers are either talking to [a very specialised audience], or just very good at articulating their ideas. So, will there always be a need for editors? I think the answer is yes actually. I really do believe that.

Note

1. The business model of *eLife* is discussed in this book in more detail in the interview with Peter Binfield.

Part 4: Devolution

This section follows acts of editing as they move to new positions in the circuit of communication. In this process of devolution, publishers sometimes push responsibility for editing down the chain towards agents, freelance editors and the authors themselves (Greenberg, 2010). And so the interviews move to novelist Louise Doughty, literary agent Carole Blake, and freelance book editor Constance Hale.

Chapter 8

LOUISE DOUGHTY

Novelist, journalist, teacher
Interview: Wednesday, April 2, 2014
by telephone, London

Louise Doughty is a London-based journalist, critic and novelist. At the time of writing, the most recent of her seven novels was *Apple Tree Yard* (2014). An earlier work, *Whatever You Love,* was shortlisted for the Costa Novel Award and longlisted for the Orange Prize for Fiction, and she has won awards for radio drama and short stories. Doughty was a judge for the Man Booker Prize in 2008 and has chaired other panels including the Orange Award for New Writers, the John Llewellyn Rhys Prize and the Somerset Maugham Award. She gives lectures and classes on the practice of creative writing, for example at the Faber Academy and the Arvon Foundation.[1]

In this interview, Doughty's account of how and why she puts her work through a developmental process of her own devising—*before* submitting it for publication—provides an example of editing taking place across the communications circuit. Her experience also confirms the gap in public awareness about this process; for example, in the questions fielded (or not fielded) at literary festivals.

SG *Do you think of yourself as an editor?*

LD I am a novelist, but I do think of myself as an editor as well. What I say to all my writing students is, don't think of yourself as just a writer; think of yourself as a re-writer. Unless you have the capacity to edit your own work, you're finished. I'm very hard on the students about that and I would go so far as to say it's not possible to be a writer unless you are also an editor of your own work, because nobody gets it right the first time. It's an absolutely essential skill. New writers often don't understand how important it is, and I think the more experienced you become as a novelist, the more you realise just how vital it is. So, yes, I would call myself an editor. I don't think I'd be able to be a novelist unless I was one.

SG *A recent book (Sullivan 2013) argues that the current obsession with re-writing is very culture-specific, and traceable to the modernists. Do you think that is true, or have writers always had to edit?*

LD It may have become a more formalised process. It's certainly a more self-conscious process. But if you look at the manuscripts of any number of classic authors, they are covered with scribblings and crossings out. All writers, even if they don't re-write their manuscripts endlessly, make notes and then edit as they put words down on the page; or they edit in their heads.

That's something else that people often don't take on board: there's an awful lot of editing that goes on in your head before you even type a single word. You write a sentence, and while you are writing it you are already editing the sentence that follows. Because you're already anticipating; you're thinking of several options, rejecting a couple, going for one, rephrasing it in your head...and it's happening as your fingers type the previous sentence. So I think editing is a completely instinctive process. I don't think a writer has ever existed who hasn't edited on some level.

SG *do you call it editing, or do you have another word that you like to use?*

LD I call it editing or re-writing, but I use the two words as interchangeable.

SG *Looking at your actual practice, can you describe a typical day?*

LD If it's a writing day, I leave the house with my laptop and disappear to a café. I will be there anything between two and six hours, depending on my available time, writing and editing as I go along. I'm constantly reading through what I've just written and editing it.

SG *What do you like the most about editing?*

LD I love editing because the definition of editing is that you've already written the first draft, and the bit that I find most difficult is the first draft. I love the idea that I've got a body of work and I can kick it around the room and lick it into shape. The fact that I've got to that stage is wonderful, because to me it's the most enjoyable part. It's where I actually get to feel like a writer, as opposed to a machine trying to churn out words [for] the first draft on the page.

SG *What do you like least about editing?*

LD The fact that I would always like more time for it. In an ideal world, if time and money were no object, if I didn't have to earn an income from the books…at the end of the editing process I would stick the book in a drawer for a whole year and then come back to it and edit it all over again.

SG *What is your main concern when editing, and how is that resolved?*

LD My main concern is that by that stage, I am so close to a book that I can't see the wood for the trees. At the end of each novel I start to feel fed up, I'm emotionally exhausted by it. Once that starts to happen, it's easy to lose faith in your own sense of judgment. The novelist has already done the marathon, and is being asked to go around the block a couple more times. My main concern is; is my judgment still sound or have I reached a point where I just can't tell anymore?

For example, my fourth novel *Fires in the Dark* is my longest novel, and my most ambitious in some ways. I think it has some of my best writing, but it also has some significant flaws. It is an uneven book and that is probably to do with the fact that I was very, very tired when I got to the end of it.

SG *At the micro-editing level, what matters to you most about style?*

LD Clarity. If I can write beautiful prose that is a thing of beauty on its own, that's great; but clarity comes first and foremost for me.

SG *For people who are editing someone else's work, developmental editing is a major concern. For example, is the story structure working? Do you think of those issues as editing questions or authoring questions?*

LD I think they are editing questions for the author as well. All aspects of writing are a part of the editing process for the writer, and I think you should be getting all aspects right before it goes to the [publisher's] editor.

SG *Can you describe the developmental side of editing, from an author's point of view?*

LD Restructuring is a huge part of the editing I do, but only later in the process. I don't think you can do the structural edit until you've got a first draft. Obviously it's in the back of your mind with each chapter, and there might be days where I spend my time structuring, and don't write anything

[new], but I will only do that when I've got a large body of material under my belt. I won't be thinking about structure every single day, because I will be concentrating on a particular scene.

SG *Do you involve other people in the editing process?*

LD At the end of every book, before it goes anywhere near my publisher's editor, I show it to—ideally—six or seven people who are completely separate from each other, and get their feedback. That's absolutely essential because you need a broad range of opinion. The people who do that for me are not professional editors. They're what you might call ordinary readers; friends, or people who've helped me with the research. Often what I get from them is an instinctive response. It's not the kind of detailed feedback I get from a professional editor, but it's still invaluable. If all six of them have the instinctive response that the beginning is too slow, for example, then I know I've got a problem and I try and fix that problem before it goes to my publisher.

SG *Do you think of your reader? Literally, or in an abstract way?*

LD I *do* think of my reader. I think all writers need to do that. Not in the first draft, when I'm concentrating on getting the words out of me and onto the page. It's only when I'm re-writing that I think of the words going off the page and into a reader's head. At that stage you have to think of a reader, because you have to start thinking of how the work is going to be received.

SG *How do you know when you are finished?*

LD I know I'm finished when my publisher starts screaming for it. I know I'm finished when I get told I have to deliver because they have a schedule to keep. Left to my own devices, I would re-write endlessly. That's why I sell my books in advance. I sell them on proposal because I need the deadline and I find the deadlines healthy. I don't think you ever know that you're finished on a creative level. There is that Paul Valery quote; a poem is never finished, it is only abandoned (Litz 1969). It's exactly the same with any form of writing. You could go on endlessly making it better. There's no such thing as a perfect work. So for me, finishing is all about publishing schedules rather than feeling that a work is completely done.

SG *You said earlier you worry that by a certain point, your sense of judgment might not be reliable. How do you explain the role of judgment?*

LD Quite often, you know something's not quite right and it's a question of listening to the voices in your head. What you don't always know is *how* to put it right. But you get a gut feeling for when a sentence isn't working. Sometimes it's obvious; the sentence is too long or needs to be rearranged. But sometimes it's more nebulous than that. You just have to go with your gut feeling.

SG *Is editing creative?*

LD Yes, of course. In fact, in many ways I think it's more creative than the first draft, because in the draft you're getting through the mechanics of a story. When you are editing, that's when you give the work some sort of poetic shape, some sort of internal dynamic. I think in many ways it's arguably the most creative bit of the whole process.

SG *For you, how is writing different from editing? Do you tell yourself at each stage, 'Now I'm writing, now I'm editing'?*

LD I'm always editing as I write, but there is a bit at the end which is pure editing, when a complete first draft is finished. It's the bit where the real art comes in, and I think that's why it's the most enjoyable.

SG *Have you come across examples of resistance to editing, or criticism of it? Have you been in a position where you had to suggest changes to other people and they didn't want to accept it?*

LD I come across it a lot in my students. I would identify it as the single major issue that any new writer has to address; the ability to edit their own work. That's what creative writing courses are for. The course I'm teaching at the moment is for people who have already finished a first draft before they come. So in that sense it's an editing course, not a writing course, and the biggest issue is persuading writers to edit their own work. You can feel people's resistance to it all the time. You sense it in the room; you make a suggestion about their work and they stiffen in their seat.

The people I identify as the ones who might have a career as a professional writer are the ones who are prepared to edit; the ones who listen, take feedback on board, go away and see what they can do with it. It's not about following the exact suggestion that's been made, it's about finding another way to make the work better. Those are the ones who've got futures. The people who are not prepared to address re-writing their own work are the ones who are frankly going to go nowhere.

SG *How would you describe the effect of bad editing, or just absent editing?*

LD Sometimes you can tell when someone has written down the thoughts in their head, unmediated, on the page. Quite often, the absence of editing can be seen in the sentence word order. Or they've written a piece of work that's rambling, where the main character goes off on a digression and comes back into present tense, and there's no indication of that in the text. And the person who's written it knows full well what's going on, but the reader is not going to have any idea. Or they'll start writing a scene in which a character's in the kitchen, say, but then the character is talking or thinking and there's no indication where that character is now, or what day of the week it is: they haven't placed the character at all. And because *they* know where the character is, they forget that the reader doesn't know. Spotting that is all about going back over the work and looking at it as a reader, and not as the person who wrote in the first place. That's what teaching editing is all about. It's teaching them that skill.

SG *How did you yourself learn to edit, and how do you teach it? Is it difficult?*

LD As a novelist you learn on the job, and you learn by giving your work to other people and getting feedback. It's exactly the same with teaching. You give people feedback and you tell them what you think is wrong, and then they have to go away and work out whether they believe you or not. The only way to learn it is by doing it. Writing is a practice, not just an art, and the only way to do it is to roll up your sleeves and get on with it.

SG *Thinking more generally about editing, is it something that has sufficient public recognition or value?*

LD No I don't think it does. I'm not sure whether it's reasonable to expect the general reader to recognise the value of editing. But for anybody within the industry, yes, they [should] do that a lot more. For people who want to write themselves, editing needs to have a lot more value and a lot more recognition, because the major problem with people on writing courses is that they don't recognise its importance. There's no real way of understanding just how much editing is involved until you've done a fair amount of writing.

SG *Have you come across attitudes that devalue editing? For example, people who say, 'Nowadays everyone can just press a button and their work is distributed, so why bother with all the middlemen?'*

LD I think the people who say that tend to be people who think that they are being unreasonably excluded from literary success. It may be that a small proportion of those people are unfairly excluded. There is work that's rejected because it's not fashionable; because the agent or publisher can't make money out of it; because it's too difficult; and some of that undoubtedly should be published. But any agent or publisher will tell you that the vast majority of unsolicited work that is rejected is simply not good enough to be published—it is not good on a technical level, it needs editing and it needs a lot of work—and that's the end of it.

SG *How do you respond to the Amazon comment that 'the only really necessary people in the publishing process now are the writer and reader'?*

LD I would say that you have to look at the proportionate numbers of writers and readers. There are too many producers and not enough consumers. If everybody can publish everything they want with no editing, no gatekeepers, and no filter, then how are readers supposed to find what they want to read? No reader, however passionate and however engaged with the book world, has enough time to read every self-published novel and work out which are the good ones. That is why we have filters, otherwise known as publishers and agents and editors. The vast majority of readers want guidance, and I don't think it's elitist to say that. It's to do with the practicalities of time. That is why they're paying a publisher for the published book, because somebody else has done that job for them. Somebody else has edited it, filtered it and said, 'This is what we think is good'. I think it's very naïve, the idea that there can only be readers and writers.

SG *If publishers do not edit, who will do it, or who should do it?*

LD I think it's the writers themselves. They have got to be a lot more ruthless, and that's why I give my work to other people to read before it goes near the publisher. Editors don't have enough hours in the day to edit as thoroughly as they would like, [so] the onus is on writers to get it right before it goes near the industry. That is part of the writer's job. I don't think any writer should be handing over something half-baked and relying on the editor to make it right.

SG *Could you talk us through your background?*

LD I've been publishing novels for nearly 20 years now; my first book came out in January 1995. I write what is loosely referred to as literary fiction. During the eighties I studied for a BA in English literature at Leeds, and then an MA in creative writing at the University of East Anglia, with Malcolm Bradbury and Angela Carter. I've done a huge amount of journalism for almost every national newspaper, and broadcasting. I also do radio drama and short stories. But I always wanted to earn a living as a novelist, and I would be very happy if all I had to do was write novels. That's at the heart of what I do and that's the most important part of my career.

SG *Do you see yourself as part of a particular tradition? Do you have a role model?*

LD There are writers I admire, such as Margaret Atwood, Alice Munro, Hilary Mantel, Helen Dunmore or Rose Tremain. But I wouldn't really call them role models because I think every writer's different. All writers are individuals and each of their novels are individual from each other. I wouldn't put it any more strongly than that.

SG *Is it unusual to be asked about editing?*

LD I don't think I've ever been asked about the editing process before, in a serious interview. Students have asked me how I go about it, and I've talked about it when I give readings. But in a way it's surprising, as a novelist, how little you get asked about editing. People normally ask about the other end of the process. They want to know about your inspiration; where you get ideas, where a novel originated. Whereas, of course, that is often just the seed. In some ways the original idea is the smallest part of the process and the editing, at the other end, is far more important.

SG *Can you speculate about why there is so little interest, considering its importance?*

LD I think that the general reading public isn't really interested in the mechanics of how a book is made. The public tends to think that an idea comes fully formed, unmediated. One thing that always astonishes people outside the industry is when I tell them I'm supposed to deliver in June for a publication date the following June. They think you deliver a book and it comes out a few weeks later. People have no idea at all that there is a whole process that goes into making a physical book, part of which is editing the text. So I think a lot of it is just down to a general misunderstanding of how much work goes into producing a book.

SG *Does the experience of discussing editing with me, in a formal setting, prompt any new thoughts for you about the process?*

LD I think it's good to be reminded about just how important it is. Particularly as I'm in the middle of a new novel myself at the moment. Hearing myself answer the question, I'm reminded that yes, it is a really important part of the process and it's something I have to leave time for; I can't take it down to the wire too much. Perhaps all writers are guilty of taking it for granted until they reach that point and tell themselves, 'Oh yes, that's right; I always need a lot of editing'. It is only when you think seriously about a subject that you realise just how important it is.

SG *Is it different discussing editing in this context rather than, say, with a student or at a literary festival?*

LD I'm not sure really. With students one is always trying to convince them of the importance of editing, because that is something they resist. So obviously it's different answering questions for you, because the whole reason you're doing this project is that you understand the importance of editing in the first place.

The difference is also there at literary festivals. They will ask about how you come up with an idea, about how you construct a plot or how you do your research, but the actual tweaking of the words on the page is not something they really understand and they don't understand just how long the process takes.

SG *When you look at the transcript of this interview, is there anything particularly funny, silly, or interesting about editing a text about editing?*

LD Yes, it was fun editing an interview about editing. It reminded me that editing exists on two levels: objective judgment *vis à vis* correction of facts, and subjective judgment, which is not [about] what is wrong so much as how I would do it if it was me. On [that] level, I would have kept the interview shorter and tighter, and asked more about the influence of [new media] on the public's perception of 'editing' themselves. To what extent [do] people rush to present an unedited version of themselves in a public arena, and how does that affect our perception of what a text should be? But at that level, you are talking about a personal response that will vary with each individual.

Note

1. In addition to the novels, plays and journalism, Doughty has published a book of writing advice, based on a regular newspaper column (2007). Biographical details are sourced from the author's own website, <http://www.louisedoughty.com>.

Chapter 9

CAROLE BLAKE

Co-founder and head of book division,
Blake Friedmann Literary Agency
Interview: Thursday, August 30, 2012
Camden, London

Carole Blake, a pioneering literary agent with an international profile, received the Pandora Award in 2013 for a 'significant and sustained contribution to the publishing industry' over 50 years. She is a former chairman of the Society of Bookmen, former president of the Association of Authors' Agents and former president (now lifelong patron) of The Book Trade Charity. Her book, *From Pitch to Publication* (1999), is now in its 19th UK printing.

The Blake Friedmann Literary Agency was founded in 1982 and currently represents some 200 writers. The company's stated aim is 'to represent writers' careers, rather than individual books or projects, and to sell those writers into as many markets, languages and media platforms as possible' (Blake Friedmann 2014).

As the interview ended, Blake commented: 'It's very interesting talking about something that is a piece of what I do, but which I very rarely separate out, and think about in that way.'

SG *To start, a little bit about yourself…*

CB I grew up in a very working class family. I left school at 16 and was convinced that I wanted to be a librarian, because that was the only job I knew about which involved books. Until, thank God, a history teacher said to me, 'You'd die of boredom if you became a librarian—why don't you go into publishing?' It hadn't occurred to me that there was a business that produced books. So I got a job as a secretary at a packaging company that made art books. They did the editorial work, the production work and they made co-editions with publishers from around the world, sharing the illustrations and text but translating it.

It was completely fascinating. I was there for eight years. Then the man I worked for became managing director of Michael Joseph: I moved with him and became rights manager there. Later, I was headhunted to go to WH Allen. That was an unmitigated disaster, because I hadn't researched properly what they published—a lot of nonsensical showbiz bios and such. But they had a book that came in the month I joined, André Brink's first novel, and I fell upon it like a drowning girl and sold it to about 18 languages at my first Frankfurt [Book Fair]. Then I realised it was just about the only readable book they published.

After a year, I was headhunted by the man I had worked for at Michael Joseph and became a marketing director of Sphere, a paperback company that Thompson started. I was phenomenally bad as a marketing director. I was running the contracts department, the rights department and the publicity department and the man I worked for was very volatile: we used to argue all the time.

One Friday afternoon we were having an argument, and he fired me while I was in the middle of resigning. So, I said, 'If you're firing me, I will withdraw my resignation and I will sue for wrongful dismissal'. And he said, 'You'd never do that to me'. So I put everything in order, left and sued him. They had to settle out of court because he hadn't told Thompson that he'd fired me, and he couldn't fire me because I was on the board. I was employed by Thompson, not by Sphere, and the first they heard of it was my lawyer's letter. It was all deeply satisfying, and they paid me off.

I started my agency on [the back of] that. Authors I'd sold rights for, at the various publishing houses, were ringing up and saying, 'If you're going to become an agent...' It hadn't occurred to me [to be an agent but] I realised that, without trying, I had a client list. So I started in a room in my [home]. But I've enjoyed every day since, I have to say. Every day is different and I've been doing it for a long time.

It was a very low-key start, which would be extraordinarily difficult to do these days. Money comes in very slowly in publishing, and it used to be said that it takes at least three years to make money as an agent. Now, I think it's much longer than that, because it's much harder to sell books.

I've got to the stage where I can pick my clients. I have only taken on one new client in about the past five or six years, because the clients I've kept are published everywhere. We sell rights individually; we don't sell world rights in all languages to one publisher. Peter James, for instance, is now published in 38 or 39 languages. Every time a manuscript comes in, you rub your hands and think, 'Wow 39 deals to do', which is very pleasing. And every book he publishes goes straight to number one in hardback, straight to number one in paperback here. That happens with Sheila O'Flanagan too.

So, I'm in the nice position of being able to choose authors whose words I admire and [whose work I] think I can sell, but also [authors] who I like. I said in a radio programme once that I would only ever take on somebody that I would invite home for dinner. The other agent being interviewed was horrified at that thought, and said so on radio.

SG *Dinner might be a bar too high for some, but I have a rule about expecting basic decency from people I work with.*

CB Yes, I'm absolutely with you on that, and I can cheerfully say that the 19 clients I represent now are all dear friends. I've even been on holiday with one of them—which might be a step far too far for anyone else. So it's a close relationship. I've represented Barbara Erskine for about 34 years—a longer relationship than I've had with both of my husbands put together.

It's completely about trust. It doesn't completely obviate the difficulties but it allows you to handle the difficulties in a smoother way, I feel.

Here is an example. I took on Lawrence Norfolk when he was 24 years old, on the basis of a one-page synopsis that he left on our London Book Fair stand. It took years to write the book, an incredibly complex, intellectual read. Brilliant. Sold everywhere. The first royalty cheque from Germany bought him a house in London. I'm not talking about the advance, I'm talking about the earned royalties, and it was a bestseller in many countries.

He wrote another two books after that, each becoming more complex. And then he got stuck on his fourth novel. I kept reading drafts, and it got more and more difficult to understand. [He wanted] editors to see it, so I sent it out on multiple submission. Masses of [eager] publishers were following him, and his editor had left the last publishing house, so it was an open situation. People fell upon this manuscript with cries of joy, wanting to love it. [But after reading it] everybody turned it down, sorrowfully.

I asked him to come in, and he sat where you're sitting, and I said to him, 'You have to put this book to one side. You have to give it up, it's killing you and I can't sell it'. He was incredibly tense, and he said 'Are you firing me?' And I said, 'Absolutely not: I'm telling you to leave this book alone because you can't make it work'. It was the worst meeting of my career, ever. I didn't sleep the night before, I didn't sleep the night afterwards. He walked out and I thought, 'I'll probably never see him again'.

Three weeks went by. He rang up and said, 'Can I come in and see you?' I thought, 'Well, he's a very honourable gent, he's probably going to fire me face to face'. And he came in and said, 'Thank you for saving for me from that book. Can I tell you the story of the one I'm going to write now?' I said, 'Please do'. In 20 minutes, he outlined the complex plot of that new novel. I said, 'Right; I've just got one instruction for you', and he said 'What's that?' I said: 'Go home and write the bloody thing.' And he's put that in the acknowledgments, in slightly sweeter words.[1]

When I got a few sample chapters, I sent it out on multiple submission, had a big auction, and sold it for a lot of money.

Agenting, and editing, are both about not being afraid to make suggestions and take *decisions*, although the final decision is always the author's. For example, 'At what point do I get this character into the house? At what point do we see the love story developing? Do you think I should echo this point earlier, so that we know what's happening?'

SG *So, developmental editing.*

CB And structural, rather than pencil on the page. In commercial publishing they tend to talk about 'structural editing' and 'copy editing', with the function of copy editing seen as much less important and usually done out-of-house, as opposed to in-house. Whereas many in-house editors do the structural editing, if they do any at all. That is a great bone of contention, of course, because publishers don't want to pay editors to sit in a room with the door closed and a keyboard or pencil in the hand. They want their editors to be book buyers.

SG *This is something I'd like to explore. I'm always hearing, 'Oh, publishers don't do editing anymore', but I have seen it in some places.*

CB Some do. [One example is] Liz Fenwick—the only new author I have taken on for years—and her novel *The Cornish House*. I did a bit of editing on it, sent it out, got quite a few rejections. Then I got a call from Kate Mills at Orion, who I'd never sold a book to before. She said, 'I really love this book but it's making me furious'. And I said, 'That's a very odd statement; what do you mean?' She said, 'I can absolutely see ways it can be better'. I said, 'Then buy it, and do the work with the author'. And she said, 'Well, I need to know from you—will she accept editorial work, and will she work on it?' I said, 'She would feel that was the best privilege a writer could have'. And it's true: Liz has a very professional attitude and Kate did some wonderful work on it, and Liz is very open about saying how grateful she is for that.

It's made it a much better book. But [before that], a lot of people [had] rejected it. They did it with rave letters, saying, 'It's absolutely wonderful but it needs work', and you think, what is your job title? Your job title is 'editor' but actually, your function is just 'book buyer'.

When editors buy books, they do edit them every so often, but they often turn books down because they need editing, and because they know their house doesn't want them to spend time editing. Or because they're nervous about putting something up to an acquisition board that they know needs work. It's much less risky to say 'no' than it is to say 'yes'. That's not entirely on the subject of editing; it's on the subject of book-buying.

SG *Well, it is about editing because the question is, where does editing happen? I wrote an article a couple of years ago called, 'If the editor disappears, does editing disappear?' And the answer was 'no, it doesn't'…*

CB It just moves somewhere else in the chain.

SG *It just moves somewhere else in the chain, and that was why I wanted these interviews to include the places it moved to. So, there's yourself…*

CB There are literary consultancies. And there are some very good schemes. The Romantic Novelists' Association runs a new writing scheme and lots of writers have been helped tremendously by going through that. I believe the Crime Writers' Association is doing something similar at the moment.

SG *I teach on a creative writing programme and basically what we teach is, how to edit your own work.*

CB Yes, and some authors can produce that distance—and some can't. One of my authors is brilliant at [editing her own work], and the books are wonderful as a result. Her name is Elizabeth Chadwick and she writes very upmarket historical fiction. I've represented her for at least 25 years. I took her first manuscript out of the slush pile, when the agency was much smaller and I used to open the post myself, and I remember taking the three chapters and synopsis out of the envelope and being completely mesmerised. I read it at my desk and rang her straight away. She was very surprised because she'd only posted it the day before. I had a very quick auction and sold the book very well.

Little, Brown have been re-issuing some of the earlier books, which they didn't publish [themselves]. Elizabeth said to me, 'I'm quite happy that they want to re-publish me but I don't want [those books to appear] as they were. I need to go through and edit them again'. She wasn't being paid any more to do that, but she did an absolutely rigorous edit herself, and tightened the books. It was mostly taking out adjectives, taking out scenes that didn't need to be there. That's a discipline that not many authors have. The ego gets in the way, too.

I used to represent a thriller writer called John Trenhaile. He ended up with a hardback editor and a paperback editor in the UK, plus a hardback editor and a paperback editor in the US—this was in the days when publishers didn't necessarily do both formats—and me. And somebody said to him, 'You're mad; how can you get five sets of editorial notes?' And he said, 'I'm very lucky to get five sets of editorial notes because sometimes there will be one thing that only one person notices'.

SG *There's a big debate within creative writing about how students learn to provide their peers with good quality feedback in a workshop. The problem is that less experienced people tend to go to extremes: they say, 'Oh it's wonderful' or 'it's terrible' and they don't...*

CB ...Don't say why.

SG *They tend not to make distinctions and say, 'I like this, but I don't like that'.*

CB I have this theory about group activities. Everybody thinks they can deal with things on the surface but nobody believes that it's their particular responsibility to deal with deeper problems. They think, 'I can mention these few things but somebody else will do something about the rest'. Whereas, when you are an editor or an agent and you are trying to make a business out of that piece of writing, you have to answer to the person who wrote it, and you have to be pretty articulate about why you're making suggestions.

Someone was over for dinner last night and saw all my books, and said, 'Oh you must read very fast' and I said, 'No, it's just the opposite'. When you're reading to edit, and you're going to speak to the person who wrote it the next morning, you have to read very carefully, and reading becomes slower. It's not a choice, it's a necessity, because you have to be able to remember everything well enough to debate it with the person who wrote it.

SG *Let me come back to your own practice. Do you think of yourself as an editor? If not, what do you call what you do?*

CB I suppose yes, but I don't present myself as an editor. I know that if I'm reading a new manuscript, I never read it without engaging the critical faculties. I think an agent's job is to engage editorially with the first manuscript by an author, because you've got to get it into as saleable a shape as you can. But that actually means editing it so that all the possibilities can be seen, rather

than locking it down so that no one else can get it into it. I'm not very articulate on that point…

SG *No, that's a great way of putting it.*

CB The old joke is, you put six editors in a room and you'll get seven opinions. So I always say to an author, if I say I think this needs doing, don't be
surprised if an editor who buys it tells you just the opposite. Because it is
down to opinion and we all bring our own emotional baggage to every piece
of work that we read.

Once you've got the author on the road to publication, it ought to be
possible for the agent to step back and do less work on future manuscripts because it is more the responsibility of the editor that's going to publish it. And
part of my job should be to create a tight relationship between the author and
the editor. I want to be a conduit, not a barrier.

SG *How do you define editing? Is there a particular metaphor or imagery that
you use?*

CB For me [the meaning of editing] is to make sure the author is telling the
reader what the author *thinks* they're telling the reader, and to make that
book as saleable as possible. Saleable in terms of me being able to sell to a
publisher's editor; the editor being able to sell to their acquisitions board
and sales department; and the sales department being able to sell it to the
bookseller. And only *then* does the bookseller get to sell it to somebody
who is going to put their hand in their pocket, and become the eventual
reader.

SG *Is it possible to unpack that just a bit? Obviously 'making it saleable' varies
from book to book, but what are some of the components?*

CB Well, if you're selling commercial fiction, [it has] to be clear who the
central character is, because you're telling the reader whose eyes they're going
to experience the story through. You need to have various crises that the
character goes through and there must be ways in which the characters are
thwarted. It must end with a resolution, which doesn't necessarily mean everybody's happy but it's got to be emotionally satisfying for the reader.

SG *The narrative arc?*

CB Yes. And obviously the rules are slightly more elastic for literary fiction,
if there are rules at all, but I don't analyse it because I have been doing it for
such a long time. I'm always trying to present as satisfying an experience as
possible for the eventual reader. Always bearing in mind that the book has

to be re-sold, and re-sold, and re-sold, at every layer within the publishing company and the bookselling chain.

SG *Could you describe a typical day?*

CB Every day is so different. If I don't have meetings in the office, I often work at home. I'm always at my keyboard by seven a.m. My computer is linked to the office; I can get into every system as though I was here. This means, joy oh joy, you need never stop work. Over the period of a week, I send emails in every hour out of 24, I imagine. Very often, I'm corresponding with an author late into the night or very early in the morning, because they don't work office hours. I have one author who lives in America. We do business with Australian publishers. So we have to do things out of hours, making phone calls in what's laughingly known as your spare time, of which there is none. Some days are completely meeting-filled. Some days I can still be sitting in my pyjamas at home, 13 hours after I [first] started typing emails.

And then there are the book fairs, which throw the schedule into chaos. Frankfurt doesn't take place until October, but the influx of visiting overseas publishers and agents and scouts start next week [September 2012] and we won't look up from Frankfurt until the end of November. And then it's nearly Christmas, and then you blink and you're making dates for the London Book Fair.

At [a book] fair I never get to anything except meetings. We have five people there who sit at our little tables...and we swap partners as the publishers go round. An appointment every 30 minutes; parties and dinners in the evening; get up the next day; do it all again. The day it finishes, you realise you've got flu and then you have to type all your meeting notes.

SG *When you are editing, what is your main concern and how is that resolved?*

CB My main concern is always; get this book to be as good as it can be. As good as the author can make it. When I do editorial notes, I always say to the author: 'These are my ideas but you don't have to follow them. It's your book, it's your name that's going to be on the book.' Sometimes the advice is purely practical: for example somebody's having an 11-month pregnancy. Sometimes it's more subtle: the pace has slacked, you need to tighten up; or, you can drop the first two chapters and start on chapter three. That's something that often happens with inexperienced authors. The writer may need to know all the stuff that's in the first two chapters but I don't need to know it. There is that old saying, 'wear your research lightly'. I want [the author] to know, for instance, what every character has for breakfast, and which way they'd vote, so that they are whole people. But I don't need to know it.

SG *And how do you know when you're finished?*

CB You don't. I mean, you really don't because, like so many aspects of being an agent, you can go on working on something forever. One thing I like about selling foreign rights, for instance, is that you can always do a bit more work; you can always find another language you haven't sold that author to. With editing, in a way the problem is the opposite; you have to know when to stop but you can't be sure. There is no right and wrong. It's not a science, it's a business married to an art form. If there was an absolute right or wrong you could teach it, and the authors could learn it for themselves.

SG *How would you say writing your own work is different from editing someone else's, even if they might involve a lot of the same things?*

CB I can be slightly flippant, because I am six years overdue with my next book [about the publishing business]. A very famous writer said, 'Writing's easy: you just take your heart out and lay it on the table'. I enjoy editing; I don't think I enjoy writing.

Actually, that's not even true. I do enjoy writing, but [not] the pain of trying to find the time to do this bloody book. That's how I think of it in my head, as one word: 'mybloodybook.' It's the guilt of thinking, 'If I'm writing my book, I'm ignoring some of my clients. There's going to be a phone call from [my publisher] saying, 'Are you delivering it in January?' You know what? For the fifth year running I'm going to have to say no. I enjoy writing, I like writing about the business, but there just isn't enough time, and so the guilt factor is huge.

When you're editing, I find that if I've got a very clear idea of what the problems are and how to solve them, it's absolutely joyous doing the notes; particularly if I [have a sense of] how the author is going to take them. If I'm puzzled because I know that something's wrong, but I'm not sure what's wrong and I don't know how to fix it, [then editing is] quite stressful.

SG *So, you like problem-solving.*

CB I like things cut and dried, and you can't always do that. But the pleasure of working on a smaller client list, and the pleasure of working with those clients who are, in every case, very close friends, is that I do know them very well, so I can sometimes say the toughest things. There was a time with one of my biggest authors...she delivered a book, and the editor and I read the manuscript at the same time. The editor loved it and I loved it, but I said, 'It can be better'.

The author cried every day [that weekend] and we had long, long conversations. I said, 'Of course it's publishable as it is'. And she's got a big following, it would have been a bestseller. But would the next one have been a bestseller if she had disappointed some of her readers? Hats off to her: she said, 'Okay, I'll do the work; I'll say to [the editor], "Hold off: I need another month or so"'. And she did it, and the book was better for it. That doesn't happen very often. It was quite stressful having to say to the author, 'I know your editor likes it but you know what: you can make it better'. Gulp-making, that is.

SG *In a way, you have answered another question here: What do you like most about editing, and what do you like the least?*

CB What I like the least is the mirror image of what I like the most: if I get to a point where I know there's a problem, but I don't know what the problem is. Sometimes you think, 'This book isn't working', but you can't put your finger on why. I'm sure any editor would say the same thing.

SG *At the detailed level of style rather than structure, is there anything that you feel is very important?*

CB It differs, depending on the kind of book. Usually I find that most authors have a style that they don't choose: it comes naturally, and it would be wrong to try to force them into doing something else. I've seen authors try to make themselves write in a different style and it very seldom works, because it's awkward.

SG *How do you think you learned to edit?*

CB I was never taught it. When I first worked as an agent, I didn't edit. There wasn't so much need for it, because it was easier to sell books then, and editors edited. But Julian Friedmann, my business partner and at that time my husband, did a lot of editing himself, and I think I picked it up from him, and from other colleagues. And when you're an agent, you send a manuscript to a publisher and later you see the edited version. You're always seeing the manuscript progress through professional editors. It's a slow, long process. Having taught yourself in that way, you start instinctively to edit as you're reading.

SG *Would you say editing is creative?*

CB I think so, but you have to put your own ego to one side and remember that it is always the author's book. Their name goes on the spine, they're the ones who are going to be criticised. The critics will think it's their fault if they don't like something. So I always make a point of saying to authors, 'Here are my notes, do what you like with them'. If an author said to me, 'I'm going to ignore everything', I would have to question whether I'm the right agent to be representing that author, but it doesn't happen.

SG *How much is editing about judgment?*

CB I have no idea. I don't know how you'd measure that. If I'm reading a manuscript and deciding whether to take the author on, what I have to judge is, first: do I love the writing, do I think the writing is good enough to sell? And secondly, can I picture who I would sell this to? Because I make my living by selling books, not just loving them.

SG *In terms of helping to shape the work, is part of what you're doing about bringing out the meaning? Or does that sound a bit airy fairy?*

CB No, because the editing process begins at the synopsis stage, before the author has written something. Sometimes authors will say, 'I've got three ideas, I'm not quite sure which to do next'. That's a form of editing: telling them, *that* one will follow the one you've just done better. Very often we'll talk about an idea, and a plot, and a character, before the author's written it.

SG *What are the consequences of bad editing?*

CB Bad reviews, lower sales, lack of translation deals—it hits you in the purse. Very often, the book that's badly edited may be a best seller if the author [has a following]. But it's the book after that which may suffer. And these days, with every sale through the tills tracked by Nielsen [BookData UK], booksellers will often buy 'down' to what they sold before. When I was bright-eyed and bushy-tailed, booksellers would say, 'We can make this book a bestseller'. Now they go to the computer [and say] 'Oh, we took 50, returned 30 and sold 20—we'd better buy 10'. Bookselling has become much less creative than it used to be.

SG *Do you think editing should receive more public recognition, and if so, how would that be shown?*

CB No I don't, because I don't think the public wants to notice the business of publishing. The author has to be the central person in the whole business. If the publishing business inserts itself into the imagination of the reader, that would make for a less satisfying read. I don't think readers want to think about the process of writing, or the process of editing. Most people who aren't in this business know very little about it and I think they are content to believe that a book springs fully formed. They might know that the author had great trouble writing it, because the author gives interviews and talks about that, but it would be unreasonable for an author to know that the editor was being interviewed as well, for instance.

SG *In some media, editors get bylines of their own, and there's been talk of readers 'following' an editor as well as an author.*

CB Well, writers follow editors around; I don't know that readers do.

SG *If publishers do not edit, who will do it, or should do it?*

CB Obviously agents do, but there are many authors who find it impossible to get an agent. Companies like The Literary Consultancy do some work. Some publishers run creative writing courses.

I have a general worry about people who can be hired by an author. They will take the author's money, they will do an editing job in isolation but they don't have to be responsible for turning that book into a saleable project. When I edit, I'm doing that for free and I only get paid when the author gets paid, so there is a very clear motivation and responsibility. I'm not necessarily trying to turn the work into a Pulitzer Prize-winning novel, I'm trying to get it published: I'm trying to get the author paid, and paid well.

It's easy to part wannabe authors from their money, because everybody thinks they've got the talent, it's just that they just need to polish it a bit. There's so many people who want to take money off authors these days, so I do have a slight suspicion about their role. [A literary agency's in-house course can] cost more than £2,000. When they started, I asked, 'When people have gone through your course, presumably you always represent them?' They said 'No', and I said, 'Well, there's a disconnect there, if you have taught somebody that you think is teachable and they have passed through your course, and you won't represent them'. And I asked, 'If you did represent somebody who came through your course, and then sold their book, presumably you'd give them their money back?' I didn't get an answer to that one. I admire them on so many levels, but I just think there's got to be some level of responsibility.

[Even between publishers], there are different ways of editing. For example, I took on a woman called Kobie Kruger, the wife of a man who runs a game park in South Africa. I happen to be passionate about wildlife and I've been on safari many times. She'd been published in South Africa by Penguin, [but] she hadn't been published here. Her publisher recommended her to me and said, 'Will you take her on? I know you like wildlife and this is a wonderful memoir'.

I read her two volumes and thought, there's *one* book in this. These two books need to be knitted together; they need to be tightened and shaped, and you need to bring the personal story more to the fore. It was a huge amount of work. I was literally editing line by line and putting these two books together. The author was marvellous about it. The book became a bestseller here, and I sold it to about 11 other languages. It was an incredibly laborious task, but I could see that there was a single sparkling narrative to be got out of [the two volumes]. If the author hadn't been willing to do a lot of work, it would have been impossible.

SG *What particular challenges and opportunities arise from digital publishing?*

CB Getting the author paid properly is the biggest challenge at the moment. I can't tell you how many hundreds of hours we have all spent here talking to publishers, talking to contracts departments, about the royalty rate for ebooks. It drives me nuts.

One of Peter James's novels was chosen by Sony for a price promotion. They said to Macmillan, 'We want to sell it at 20p'. Macmillan said, 'You can sell it at what you like, but you have to pay us the regular cost'. Okay, fine, Sony were going to absorb the loss, Peter got the regular royalty, Macmillan got the regular price. The minute that Amazon saw that, they price-matched, and they were still doing it months later. I said to Macmillan, 'I want to make sure you are not taking the hit'. No, everybody else [is taking the hit]; Amazon were losing so much money on every sale.

Stepping back and taking the wider view, I'm very unhappy about it, because books are being devalued. People don't think they need to pay a real price for books anymore, no matter what format they're buying in. When Retail Price Maintenance went, all those years ago, that was it: you can't put the genie back in the box. These days, people feel that they're being taken advantage of, if they pay the retail price for a book.

SG *That ties in with a last question, a quote from Amazon Executive Russell Grandinetti. He said the only really necessary people in the publishing process now are the writer and the reader. Do you agree or disagree?*

CB I would say, they need to be the only *visible* ones, but without all the people behind the scenes, you wouldn't have a cover design; you wouldn't have a properly edited text; you wouldn't have the book in bookshops. That's not Amazon's concern because they don't care. I think that's disingenuous, but he would like to believe it.

Note

1. The identity of the author is only given in this case, exceptionally, because he has already put the episode in the public domain: see Jeffries 2012.

Chapter 10

CONSTANCE HALE

Freelance book editor, teacher, journalist, author
Interview: Friday, October 19, 2012
Brooklyn, New York

Constance Hale is an articulate advocate for the editing arts, and a founding member of the editors' collective The Prose Doctors. In a long career as reporter, writer and editor, she combines an editorial practice with postgraduate teaching at Harvard and the University of California at Berkeley.

The interview, held in a noisy café in Brooklyn's Dumbo[1] neighborhood, was snatched during a book tour taking Hale away from her home in Oakland, California. She was in New York to promote her latest title, *Vex, Hex, Smash, Smooch* (2012). This follows *Sin and Syntax* (2013; first published in 1999) and a *Wired* stylebook (1999).

Hale's experience provides insights into the teaching of editing culture and skills, and the devolution of those skills away from traditional publishing houses. She occupies a particular spot in the 'circuit of communication': as she puts it, 'I'm usually hired as a developmental editor for a book that has been more or less accepted for publication, and I know what the publisher wants from the book'.

SG *Would you call editing creative?*

CH Absolutely. I go through a process of needing to 'see the book'. That's the only way I can put it. I hold the book in my head and I get to a point where I have a vision of the book. And then I edit from that vision. Coming up with the vision is a creative act. It's an act of imagination.

By the time a writer comes to me, he or she is a little lost. The writer had a vision of the story when starting out, but in the process of writing loses that vision, or gets lost in the material. So the editor has to come with a fresh vision that is sufficiently close to the writer's original vision, but also infused with the editor's imagination as well.

SG *I'd like to bring out in these interviews what editors actually do...*

CH Would you like me to describe my process when editing a book? I have an absolutely clear, practised method.

The first thing I do is to meet the writer informally and get to know him or her as a person, before I have read the manuscript. So the interaction is not tainted by any judgment on my part, or anxiety on the writer's part. And I say to the writer, 'I want our first conversation to be just you and me, getting to know each other'. I ask the writer what it is that he or she is trying to achieve— the most important thing—and what's the greatest frustration, and if there is anything that he or she wants me to look at, in particular.

Then I read the manuscript. I'm a compulsive editor, so I try to sit on my hands and take it in; [I won't] start editing before I've read the whole thing. Maybe I'll take a *few* notes, but the first read is about seeing what I have in my hands (and, by the way, I read only hard copy at this stage).

That first read I want to be absolutely open, naïve, uncontaminated, and I'm reading it as a reader. I tell writers I am a proxy for the reader. Often an editor at the publishing house has hired me, so I do know what the publishing house thinks. But if there's been a peer review process, I don't read the peer reviews until after I've read the manuscript myself, the first time.

By the time I start the second read, I've got my own ideas about the major weaknesses and strengths. So the second read is to continue to identify those, and work them out, as well as to consider the concerns of editors and reviewers. The second read, I'm really drilling down. I do a lot of line editing; I move things around. I start tabulating notes. I mark up the copy a lot and prepare a memo as I go along.

And then I schedule a chat with the author. If there's another editor involved, I involve that editor in the chat as well. By this time I have articulated my vision. This conversation is about me saying: 'Here's what I see, here are the problems I have identified, and here's what I want to do. Here's my road map.' It's very important that I have a road map, so the writer feels that someone is coming in with positive suggestions.

Before I lay out my road map, I write up and share a paragraph summarising what I think the book is about—these are the themes, this is what I think we have in front of us. And I ask, 'Did I get it right, did I miss something?' I'm trying to be a mirror, I'm trying to reflect back to the writer 'this is what I see', in the most sensitive and articulate way I can. The writer is usually relieved to hear that someone 'gets' what she or he is trying to do.

Then I have a stock set of questions that we usually talk through. First I ask about readership: who is your audience—primary, secondary, tertiary. We have a conversation about that; the reader and the author's relationship to the reader. I often find that the author's stance as a narrator, and the author's voice and point of view, shift around a lot. I point this out and ask, "Who are you talking to? Let's be really specific about it'. A lot of people think they are writing for a general audience—they *want* that, because they want their book to be a bestseller. But unconsciously, they are writing for their peers. And so I explain about tone and language, and a lot of things that flow out of understanding who your audience is, and speaking to your audience.

Usually, in this conversation, we also talk about the title and subtitle, because frequently there is some adjustment that needs to be made. We often have a 'metaphor' conversation: I ask, 'what's the central metaphor of this book; is there a way to express the title metaphorically?' Sometimes the writer has a metaphor but it's a flawed one, so we work on finding one that is fresher or more exact.

Then I look closely at the table of contents, the overall structure of the book. I may say, 'Gee, did you think of dividing this book into three parts? It might be helpful'. Or perhaps the way the ideas are expressed in the table of contents is not crystal clear. Again, we need a central metaphor—or at least a clear organizing principle.

The last big question I often ask is, 'What kind of a book is this? Is it going to be picked up and read from cover to cover? Or is this a workbook-type thing? How practical do you want this book to be? How literary?' That's going to guide how we organise it.

I take notes throughout the meeting. After that conversation, I send the manuscript to the author with the memo, using the author's answers to help me address certain questions. So the memo is the real road map. It's not a judgment about the manuscript, it's not a criticism of everything that's wrong, but rather the expression of this vision of the next draft.

And then usually there's a rewrite, and sometimes I do another round of edits after that.

SG *Do you only ever work on non-fiction?*

CH I almost never work on fiction. I do a bit with writers whom I've worked with a lot, who trust me. I don't consider myself a fiction editor. There are people who have much more experience doing that. But I'll work on memoir, I'll work on any nonfiction. The subjects that I've worked on, in more than two dozen books, have been all over the place. I've done a lot of business books, leadership books, organisational behaviour, academic history books. I've edited books by journalists and books by psychologists. On a shorter magazine length, I've edited memoir, travel and first-person essays. And journalism! I've been an editor at two different newspapers and three different magazines.

SG *Can editing be taught? How should it be taught?*

CH I once asked Orville Schell [then dean of the Berkeley Graduate School of Journalism] about the school's editing classes, and he said, 'Editing can't be taught'. And I said—'Hunh! Why do you say that?' He almost treated it as though it was a magical, intrinsic talent, and the only way you could learn how to edit was to be mentored, to sit at the knees of an editor.

I disagree with that. Having taught editing quite a bit myself, I know there are a lot of things you can teach about editing, things that *should* be taught about editing. Unfortunately, most editors are *not* taught; they learn through a messy process of trial and error, and there are many not-very-good editors out there as a result.

To teach editing, you can spend time talking about how to be better listeners to writers, and about how important the writer-editor relationship is. You can have exercises—not role-playing, exactly, but ways to test a person's comfort level with the very particular kind of communication that has to happen with editing. You are basically telling people all the time that they are going to have to do a shitload more work, and you are trying to make them excited about doing it. It's an almost impossible thing that you're trying to balance: stern marching orders, along with unbridled enthusiasm, such that the writer feels jazzed about going back and doing a whole lot more work. It's an iffy proposition, but there are ways to do it effectively.

So that's one thing to convey to novices: the delicacy of the editor-writer relationship and how important it is to deliver the bad news in such a way that the writer is excited about going back and doing another draft.

On the skills level, a lot of editing skills can be taught, whether they be copy editing skills, or line editing skills, or various ways to structure a big work.

What makes a difference between a really good editor and a not-so-good editor is the ability to see the potential of the piece and to articulate it for the writer who is doing his or her best but is often lost in the material. The editor can show the writer the path; the editor can understand the material in a way that the writer doesn't, and articulate that for the writer.

Instead, so many editors just tell the writer what is wrong. But editing should not be a process of passing judgment. It's a process of seeing what is latent in a manuscript and helping the writer make it more explicit. It is a skill that involves a lot of emotional intelligence, but many things can be explained to a new editor.

SG *I have heard journalism school faculty say they offered editing courses in the past, but they were taught in a very narrow way—basically, how to mark up copy—and they thought it was a waste of time.*

CH I think it is, too. Journalism schools in the US are very focused on reporting and writing. That is what you go to journalism school to learn. And there might be one editing course, which is often a copyediting course. I don't know why journalism schools seem to have this prejudice against teaching editing in a more comprehensive way. Because what ends up happening is that you have a whole bunch of untrained editors. Often a good reporter is promoted to editor—but reporting and editing are completely different skills. Someone can be a great reporter and a terrible editor. Although, being a good reporter helps you to be a good editor. Because you spot holes, and you know how to fill the holes if you're in a pinch.

I teach at UC Berkeley Extension. Most of the editing courses that I'm aware of are at these continuing education schools, where you can get a certificate in editing and publishing, after taking courses in 'beginning copyediting', 'intermediate copyediting' and 'advanced substantive editing'. There might also be a preparatory grammar course, for people who aren't ready for the introduction-level course. Altogether, it is a three-semester programme and you come out of it ready for an entry-level editing job. You have practical editing skills. You just don't necessarily have the journalistic skills.

So that's the problem. The journalism schools teach reporting, and they don't teach editing. And then these other schools teach editing, and don't necessarily teach journalism (which raises awareness about the meaning of a 'fact', the essence of a 'story' or legal and ethical concerns). An awful lot of editors have never been trained as journalists, and this can be a weakness.

SG *Does new media publishing make editing more important?*

CH I wish editing were made more important in new media, but I don't think it is. There is so much unedited work out there now!

I have a website, and I wish I had an editor. The trouble with blogs, for example, is that you add from the top. The weird thing about the blog as a form is that the reader views it upside down. The reader meets the most recent post first. So how do you reverse-engineer that? Someone like me needs an editor because I can't see how to make it make sense.

Webmasters use the archive metaphor, but after a while a website starts to feel like a messy repository. I'm not really talking about navigation, I'm talking about synthesising the ideas in the right order. You need someone with an editorial mind to come in and look at the whole thing and work out a way of organising the material so that the reader can comprehend it.

Even though I'm more of a book editor than a magazine editor, the magazine is my metaphor. And so I try to look at my home page as a magazine table of contents. I want to have a lot of rich content, but I do want a structure. I'm at a point, though, where I want to hire an editor to come in and help me make sense of it all.

SG *Perhaps one can treat blogs like serial narratives?*

CH With people like Dickens, Henry James, you had a readership that saw the magazine every month, reading things in order. Now, people are getting things much more randomly...That subverts the whole idea of narrative. It's so different from a book where I *know* how a reader is going to hit the manuscript. I value the idea of a table of contents, a cumulative approach to information.

When you have no way of knowing whether people are going to get the information in the order that it's delivered, literary [narrative] is subverted. Structure is an essential part of storytelling, rhetoric, argument. But structure is by definition subverted on the web.

On the other hand, works don't have to be narrative. The book I just published is not a narrative book. But it has a very clear structure, an organizing principle. Readers need signposts. I consciously carved up the text in different ways, creating resting points. You can pick up the book at any point, and there will be a discrete morsel on almost every page. It makes the material more accessible. I know that the subject matter makes people feel anxious, so I don't want people to feel that it's an overwhelming book they have to sit down and read, cover to cover.

Depending on the subject, you're either trying to construct a really artful narrative, or you're trying to *de*construct something and make it approachable, by giving people bite-sized chunks that they can digest in all sorts of random ways.

SG *You have said, 'the magazine is my metaphor'. Could you expand?*

CH Firstly, I'm a visual person, so I love magazines because of the graphics. The colour, the layout of the page, the table of contents that leads you to articles you can read, one at a time. I like the artfulness of the layout; it's more interesting to me than a book. Even in books, I spend a lot of time on page design. I'm fortunate that my publishers have given me really good designers. I think typography is even more important to me than photos or graphics per se. I love what you can do with type and colour. And a magazine article or short story is my favourite length. The newspaper's not my metaphor. Some people think in metaphors like 'above the fold', but not me.

SG *From an editing point of view, what is the difference between magazines, books and newspapers?*

CH The newspaper grants the least individual voice to the writer, but that is because the prerogative is to get information to a mass reader as efficiently as possible. There often isn't *time* to spend on the craft, because of the urgency of the deadline. Magazines are in-between. They give a little more focus on voice and little more range to the writer. But the readership, the 'demographic', can be tightly defined by the publisher.

With books, the writer gets the most leeway. It's really the writer's book, sink or swim. There's relatively little editing in books today. I know these stories about Maxwell Perkins[2] and others, but my experience is that editors touch the manuscript little or not at all. That can be wonderful, but it can be dangerous. I don't think people buy a book because of the publisher. There is a taste factor, perhaps, or some prestige attached to the publisher, but a book is identified more closely with the writer.

On the web, there are some brands like *Salon* or *Atlantic* that are based on the magazine model, but blogs are generally writer-driven. And then you have all the excesses and indulgences—all the flaws—of non-edited copy.

Although I say the magazine is my metaphor, I don't actually prefer writing for magazines. I have felt manhandled at many magazines. I often felt that I couldn't figure out what editors wanted. Sometimes they say they're going for something and then they contradict themselves. I have encountered the worst editing in magazines, in general. It's the way they are structured. There may be this brilliant person at the top who is setting the course of the magazine, and everyone else is trying to figure out what that person wants. Junior editors are often not very good.

Some magazines allow a kind of gang-edit that is, at least for me, quite unpleasant. There's an assigning editor; but once the manuscript comes in there is an editorial meeting where six editors sit around and talk about an article, and the editor-in-chief has the ability to weigh in. There's very little autonomy and trust given to the individual editor. The best work comes out of that relationship between editor and writer. But I think magazines often subvert it. In newspapers, editors are generally given more autonomy. There may be a top editor but they're not rewriting leads, asking lower-level editors to change the whole thing. On magazines, there's a lot of messing with your head that goes on.

I wrote a front-of-book piece for a major national magazine, 400 words; I had to rewrite it four times. You can't go that wrong in 400 words. You can't improve it that much in 400 words. That's just bad editing. It's not trusting the reporter to get the best story. One of those rewrites happened because the time hook changed, since the process took so long. Such editing is inexcusable, to me.

The kind of editing that I cherish is incredibly intense, incredibly special, a true creative collaboration. As a writer you dream of an editor who understands you, like a intellectual soulmate; the editor has powers that you don't have and brings them to bear, so that the manuscript gets better. And that editor is a champion for you with other editors. That is what most writers want.

And that's what I want to be, as an editor. As a freelance editor. I only want to work with other editors who grant me autonomy to deliver. There's a contract; they trust me to work with the writer, I get the writer to trust me; the writer and I collaborate, and then together we deliver something to the publisher.

I used to own a restaurant with the chef, and our definition of a good waiter was: 'Your glass is always full; the waiter is never there.' This kind of elegant attention…your needs are met, you're always happy, you don't ever need to *ask* for the waiter, and the waiter doesn't put himself in your face, that's analogous to my definition of a good editor. Somehow the writer feels his or her piece came out exactly right, it is what he or she intended to write, and the editor's fingerprints aren't there. The writer feels that the piece is entirely true, and there's no evidence of the editor. The editor may have been there quite actively, but doesn't manhandle the copy or leave traces. It takes an incredibly good ear, and that's what you *can't* teach about editing.

My editor at W. W. Norton didn't touch the manuscript—she's not a line editor—but she engaged with it. She pointed out sentences she especially liked, and we had long discussions. She also gave me tough love, and I went back and rewrote the manuscript. And then she fought like hell for a good cover design, page design, and a very careful copy edit. I call her a lioness of an editor, and that's a good metaphor, too.

SG *When you work for a publisher, what are the circumstances in which the in-house editors hire you?*

CH I have an unusual deal with Harvard Business Press. They hire me when they want to publish a book that may reach an audience beyond the [business] school or the C-suite [the top executives], but whose author may not be used to writing for a wider audience. Or just needs more help than an in-house editor can give. They know I will deliver a book that they can publish. To pay me, they take money out of the author's advance. (Many of their authors are professors or consultants who can afford it.)

Otherwise, I am not hired by editors; I'm hired by writers. That's increasingly what's happening. The cost has shifted onto the writer. If you don't pay, you may end up getting a book between covers that hasn't been edited much. I hire line editors for all my books. Line editors normally just look at sentences, not for punctuation and spelling but for content, phrasing and music. The line editor helping me most recently ended up doing a little more developmental editing than she intended, identifying things to cut, since I fall in love with my own material a bit too much.

In speaking to potential clients, I try to define the different types of editing—line editing, copy editing, developmental editing. I like to give writers a vocabulary so that they can better articulate what it is that they want. They might say 'editing' when they just want someone to proofread. Or they might think they need just line editing, when the work needs an overhaul.

Then there's ghostwriting. Some people call themselves editors and they're really ghostwriters. I have to have a conversation about that with a lot of my authors. I say, 'I don't ghost, I edit. If you want a ghostwriter, go ahead but it's not me. Because, when I write something, my name gets on it'. That's just my personal policy. For some people it's part of a continuum, but I don't consider that editing.

SG *Is that because it's a euphemism?*

CH Many academics have a lot of pride; they don't want to say they hired a ghostwriter. They want to say that they wrote their books. They don't mind saying they had an editor—of course they had an editor! Plus, they're used to delegating to graduate students, they're used to having other people *do* stuff, so they are OK with hiring an editor. But they don't want to say they haven't written their book, so they don't want a 'ghostwriter'. But they might, either secretly or quite openly, want the 'editor' to ghostwrite.

SG *Do you identify yourself as 'editor'? If not, what do you call what you do?*

CH I think of myself primarily as a writer. My business card says 'Constance Hale. Scribe'.

Usually, if I'm writing a short bio, I call myself a journalist, just because that's the most all-inclusive label for what I do—both editing, and writing. And I'm trained in journalism. That's an important thing for me to signal. You're getting that set of skills in my work. It distinguishes me from many editors. My background in journalism gives me an ability to question facts, and I am trained in finding stuff out fast. It's easy for me to interview people. And I have a journalist's sense of story. Sometimes I can step in, as an editor, in a way that maybe other editors cannot. As a job title, 'journalist' encodes a lot of things that I think are very important, and which I think many editors don't offer.

SG *What metaphors do you use? You mentioned 'waiter and glass', and 'lioness'.*

CH The other common metaphor I use is 'collaborator'. To me the ideal relationship between a writer and editor is one of intense collaboration, where the editor is OK with the writer getting the credit. It's the editor's job to step out of the way. To coax things out of the writer and sometimes to articulate what the writer is not able to articulate. But to understand that it's the writer's story. So there's a selflessness about editing that's important. I guess 'midwife' is another good metaphor. You're helping the delivery but it's really *not* your baby. I am working with one writer who was born in India and we say that I am her 'didi'—her older sister or cousin.

The magazine editor has two functions: One is curation. The editor-in-chief is a curator. What makes Adam Moss [of *New York* magazine] a brilliant editor is his powers as curator. The individual story editor is quite different. Some people are real geniuses as editors-in-chief, but not great at a one-on-one level with writers. I never wanted to be editor-in-chief, because what I really love is working with a writer on a story. The most inspiring editor I've ever worked with might be Kevin Kelly at *Wired*; he had a way of seeing possibilities in a story that the writer might have been blind to. I long to work with editors at *The New Yorker*, because of the gentle way they are said to work with writers.

SG *When you are editing, how do you know when you have finished?*

CH I run out of time. Or the author runs out of money. Often, I am working within a contract and I use up the budget.

SG *Can you give any examples of conflict over editing, or pushback?*

CH I have had clashes with writers where I don't get what I want. I make my case but ultimately it's not my book.

I can give you an example. One author had worked at a high level in the federal government. It was a smart book, but where he [described] bad experiences, he refused to name names. Where he had good experiences, he did name names. I said, 'There are reasons why we journalists don't like anonymous sources'. I pushed him and I pushed him, but he just didn't want to be negative, he didn't want to settle scores. That was honorable, but it undermined his credibility in a subtle way. In some cases I was able to get him to identify some people more clearly (senior White House official, for example). But overall, I lost the argument. And indeed, when the book came out, more than one reviewer said the book would have been stronger if it had named people. It was a flaw in the book, but it was his book.

Apart from that, I can think of very few times when I have had a clash. Not that I don't push—hard. When there's something that bothers me about a piece, I try to talk to the writer about the craft in such a way that I persuade the writer to come my way. But I think that's because I approach it as a craft. I mark up hard copy a lot and I always say to the writer, these are all just suggestions. If you find another way to deal with this sentence, change it in a different way. Most good writers will see if something's better, and they want it to be better. I don't say, 'this is a bad sentence'. I usually point them in a direction. I have no ego about them not taking my edit.

One area of conflict is jargon. I try to rid the text of jargon. Whether it's a doctor or lawyer or, especially, a business professor or CEO, I get a lot of pushback. They defend it. And it's hard because a lot of times, the ideas are encoded in the jargon. They say, 'This is how we talk'. I have to invest a lot of energy in talking to my writers about language because, again, I'm working with them to understand the notion of audience. Who are you talking to—your peers or a lay audience?

A lot of times people say they're talking to a lay audience but then they use language that is for their peers. I say: 'You have a different reader now.' Sometimes we have jokes about it. One writer drove me crazy me with the phrase 'cross-domain synergies'. We ended up with 'four-way wins'. To me, all these conversations about language and metaphor are creatively exciting.

SG *Do people misunderstand the role of editing?*

CH The biggest misunderstanding is that oftentimes, people say they want to hire me as an editor, but what they really want is a proofreader. To me that is an interesting misconception about the publishing process. The more naïve people are about publishing, the more they think that editing is just fixing mechanical mistakes. They don't realise why I charge the money I do [*laughs*], because it's a high-level, intense, hard project, and I have a high level of skill.

To give you an illustration of this: at The Prose Doctors, we posted on our website an essay about the cost of editing, because most people who come to us have absolutely no idea how expensive high-level editing is. We're cheaper than a therapist, cheaper than a doctor, cheaper than a lawyer. But people have a low regard—they'll pay a massage therapist an hourly rate, but they don't see editing as worth that kind of money.

SG *Is that because it is invisible?*

CH I think that goes to a larger question. I study about language and writing and have become aware of the extent to which people feel they own language. We don't think of language as an art or a separate skill, we think of it as something that is part of our humanity. We all think we ought to be able to write naturally. Most people don't slave over revisions the way seasoned professionals do. Even though there is a tremendous amount of anxiety out there about grammar, people don't think they should pay for copyediting. And this is more true now than ever. We want free content, and that means there isn't money for editing. In the background, there's this sense of writing not having the same value as painting, or other arts.

So I consider my books works of evangelism. I'm an evangelist for good writing and craft. What I try to do in my books is to show how 'natural' expression is inferior. And that it takes a tremendous amount of work, discipline, talent and experience to take the natural, and craft it into something beautiful, something deeper, more meaningful, more impressive—in the sense of making an impression on the reader.

My books try to help us tap into this natural affinity for language, this desire to communicate. I try to give people a path to becoming more skilled at it. And incidentally, making them more appreciative of the people who do take the time and do all that work.

I was giving a reading recently in San Francisco and a colleague of mine, a writer, said: 'Do we have a word for what it is you do? Just as we teach art appreciation, should we teach language appreciation?'

He had a good point. We look at art and music a certain way, we study them to understand how they work, but often studying literature is not the same. We don't study the actual craft. A good model is the literary critic James Wood, who encourages his Harvard students to practice 'close reading'. To me, that's the missing link—we ought to be learning how very skilled great writers are.

We can all draw, but none of us equate ourselves with Rembrandt. We can all speak and tell stories, but…somehow we don't have the same sense of how difficult it is to be Hemingway, to get from A to Z when it comes to language. So that is a subtext of my books. We all do these things, but only literary artists or craftsmen put themselves through all this. It is a practice.

Notes

1. 'Dumbo' is an acronym for 'Down Under the Manhattan Bridge Overpass'.
2. See Berg 1978.

Part 5: Digital

This section continues the journey into digital experimentation. Peter Binfield left *PLoS ONE* to set up *PeerJ*, Phoebe Ayers is a member of the Wikimedia Foundation, and Evan Ratliff is a co-founder of the media and software company Atavist.

Chapter 11

Peter Binfield

Co-founder and publisher, PeerJ,
San Francisco and London
Interview: Wednesday, August 1, 2012
via Skype and email

Scholarly publishing has been a key site of change in publishing. This does not come without conflict. In the UK, for example, there has been a mixed reaction to new rules requiring all research to be published on an open access basis. As is often the case, it comes down to money. One argument in favour of open access is that the public already funds research through taxation, and should not be expected to pay twice. However, if the reader does not pay, the gap must be filled from another source.

At the time of writing, some models (commonly described as 'gold') propose to charge the author a fee, but an individual writer cannot always count on an institution to cover the cost. The 'green' model makes conventionally published texts available without restriction, typically after an embargo of not more than 12 months. However, professional associations that depend on reader subscriptions are worried that this may not be long enough.

In all these debates, attitudes towards editing can occupy a central place. Not all costs can be stripped away by the new digital platforms, and editorial mediation is one of them. The question arises: who will carry out acts of editing on academic texts, and how will that be funded?

The interview here with Peter Binfield throws light on these questions. Binfield trained as a physicist and worked in academic publishing for 21 years, most recently with Public Library of Science (PLoS). His latest publishing venture *PeerJ* went live in February 2013, six months after this discussion was recorded. The project was co-founded with geneticist Jason Hoyt, with startup costs provided by Silicon Valley's O'Reilly Media.

At the start, Binfield was concerned that the book's working definition did not apply to his own more entrepreneurial role, commenting: 'In some ways, what I do isn't editing, but I facilitate others to do editing.' In response, the explanation was offered that the interviews follow acts of editing to new places. In this case, Binfield's experience encompasses the publish-first-then-filter model—a type of editing that takes place after publishing, not before. It is also helpful to ask what happens when professional editing is *not* there, as a definition can arise as much from its absence as well as presence.

The conversation touches on the longstanding question of how writing skills can influence meaning. Binfield acknowledges that an absence of such skills during the process of making a text public can have an impact not just on the work's reading pleasure, but also on its scientific quality.[1]

SG *There is a debate about the meaning of 'gold' vs 'green' open access, and whether the author should pay to be published. Where do you stand on those distinctions?*

PB My understanding of the 'gold' model is that it describes the publication of an article on an open access basis but as a primary act—the publication of record for that article. And that's different to 'green' open access, which is about taking a previously published article—or the almost-final version—and making it open access by putting it in a repository. In my opinion, green OA is not 'publishing': it's simply a way to take a published article that's been through a process and open up access to it.

That is the distinction—primary or secondary—rather than whether the publication is paid for by an author fee. There are plenty of gold open access journals that have no fee at all for the author or the reader. *eLife* is the most recent example of that, on a large scale: it's free for authors and that's very much a gold open access journal.

SG *Am I right in understanding that your current model is: the author pays, but only once, not per article?*

PB We're a gold open access publisher, but with a membership model. Academics become a member of *PeerJ* and that membership gives them the right to publish with us for free. There are different tiers. So if you are a basic member, which currently costs a one-off fee of $99, you're allowed to publish one article with us per year for free, for life. Then there's a $199 tier, which allows you to publish two articles, and a $299 tier which is the real 'unlimited'—you can publish as much as you want every year, for life. The catch is that every author has to be a member, so if you have a paper with five authors, it's five times the individual membership fee.

SG *Should the author have to pay at all? Thinking of my own experience, I went from being a journalist who was paid for my work, to being an academic, expected to do everything for free. Now it's going one step further. Obviously, publishers are looking for different models and have to get money from somewhere...*

PB And that's the problem, isn't it? There are genuine costs in the system that need to be covered, so somebody has to pay, somewhere along the line. The question then becomes, *who?* In the old model, the reader paid via a subscription. In the case of *eLife*, they have found wealthy funders—the Wellcome Trust, the Max Planck Society and the Howard Hughes Medical Institute. Other models require the author to pay per article. In this model [*PeerJ*], it's the author paying to become a member, in order to publish.

The other question is, *what* are they paying for? Are they paying for an incredibly expensive, wasteful process or are they paying the minimum possible to get the job done, professionally and correctly? If you start going down that route, how can you make it more efficient, how can you shave more of those costs out of the system to make it cheaper? And also, you need revenue to pay costs, but the question arises—can you perhaps find a different way to get that revenue, rather than charging the authors?

We have this very low-cost service for authors. We hope to drive that cost down even lower to zero, so our long-term goal is to make this free—free to publish for an author, and free to read—and recoup the costs some other way, still to be determined. But right now, this model covers the costs and we're going to explore ways to bring that cost down and find other ways to replace the revenue.

SG: *Keeping you afloat, so you can experiment and find what works?*

PB: That's one way of thinking of it. We think this model will work at the moment [and] the market will accept it. But if you look at the geo-political landscape of the open access world, where it might be going in the next five to ten years, there's going to be downward pressure on price or cost, and there's going to be new ways to make revenue out of open access content— ways that aren't even invented yet. So, we've got a model that we think works right now, and while this industry's in transition. But this isn't necessarily our final business model that exists forever.

SG: *You say you are covering your costs, providing a stripped down service—can you explain what service you're providing? What costs do you need to recoup?*

PB: This is where what I do differs from a more traditional editor. If you imagine an editor at *Nature* or *Science*—one of the elite, highly selective journals—those people are often closely involved with the content. They are genuinely editing content, they're working with the authors, they're working with the text; they're crafting a thematic issue out of different articles, and so on. They're doing what you might traditionally think of as real editing work. But out of around 28,000 academic journals in the world, probably no more than a few hundred are doing this.

Then you've got this big group of journals run by the community, for the community. They're run by academics and there's an academic editorial board and they worry about peer review, putting the thematic issue together, and so on. They have a publisher who will publish those journals, but typically, the publisher is almost just a service organisation. The academics deliver the final approved articles to the publisher, and the publisher does the production and makes a journal out of it. I would say that is probably representative of the majority of journals in the world.

And then, *PeerJ* and *PLoS ONE* are a third version. It's easiest to describe how *PLoS ONE* works because I spent three or four years there, and *PeerJ* hasn't started yet. There is a very large academic editorial board that handles the peer review of papers, but in addition the publisher—the editor in this story—is heavily involved in overseeing the process, facilitating the whole process and making sure that it's conducted professionally, making sure the standards are adhered to: the ethical standards, peer review standards and plagiarism standards.

In this model, the publisher is doing much more than the publisher at one of the journals in the middle of the market. At *PLoS ONE* I was involved with advising editors on plagiarism and data manipulation, and on the ethical standards of animal experimentation in particular countries. I was making sure that the journal is professionally and adequately managed and produced. Rather than just taking whatever the professional academics have submitted to the publisher.

So you get much more involved that those journals, but not as much as an editor in *Nature*, or *Science*, or even [specialised open access journals like] *PLoS Medicine*. In the *PeerJ* or *PLoS ONE* set-up, I never read the articles and I'm not hands-on with the content. I don't make any decision on the content at all, whether it should be accepted or not. That's all done by the academics. I provide the structure, the process that needs to be followed, and all of the checks and balances—more than an average journal would.

SG: *Do you think of yourself as an editor, and if not, what do you call what you do?*

PB: I don't think of myself as an editor—my title is publisher, and it was the same at *PLoS ONE*. My role has elements of editing, but it also has elements of managing the business, and managing the process, workflow and standards. So I'm more comfortable calling myself a publisher than an editor. I can't do the kind of editing that the professional old-school editors do—that's not my skillset.

According to your working definition, what I do is 'process'. [*He works through the list.*] 'Selection' is done by the external academics: they select author content, decide what will or won't be published; they're the gatekeepers. 'Shaping'…I wouldn't shape individual articles, but I shape the overall direction of the journal, the standards, how it works. Shaping of an individual article is done by the academics, by the peer review and revision process. 'Context' [or linking]—there is the functionality of the website, how you navigate around it and the taxonomy that's used. The 'relationships'—that's interesting. Right now I'm building the editorial board of this new journal and I'm forming relationships with the editors, and that's important, so they understand my vision. And then, they'll form relationships with the authors and the reviewers going down the line. The publishing process is still a human interaction, isn't it?

SG: *My working definition talks about the editor's concern for the reader, the person at the end of the whole process. How does the reader fit into your model? For example, are readers expected to do their own selecting?*

PB: Yes, you're right—if that is part of editing, then we're pushing that out to the reader. In this model, the only selection that is made by us is whether or not the article deserves to join the scientific literature. It's peer-reviewed and it goes through revisions and corrections, but the only decision made by the publisher is—is this scientifically sound? There is no determination whatsoever made about whether it is good or bad, or relevant. The reader is expected to read the article, and make their own determination.

Then we provide various tools to try and aggregate that information *vis à vis* article-level metrics. The reader reads the article and makes some determination of whether it's good or bad, and we can track how they read the article; we can track the number of readers—that tells you something. If an article has a lot of readers, then it's an interesting article in some way. We can track citations and tweets and Facebook likes, and we have comments on the articles. And so it's a digital crumb trail of the activity around an article that's conducted by the reader that you can mine, as it were, to try and discern whether or not the readership thought it was good or bad. And then you can give that information back to the readership and help them navigate better with it. So there is a circular act of selection, putting things in context.

SG: *Is it possible that the* PeerJ *system will work well for groups of people who share a base level of specialist knowledge, but not so well with a much broader base of readers?*

PB: We're only just collecting the data and nobody's analysed it properly yet. This kind of thing works best on open access content because it's openly available. People can re-tweet it, and 'like' it, and comment on it, and so on. That is typically harder to do in a subscription model, and still only [a fraction of the literature] is open access. So there's still not a big enough corpus to work on, to do these studies properly. Potentially it will improve as the ratio improves.

SG: *What steps are taken to prevent people from gaming the system? For example, people who write bad reviews about their opponents, or buy more 'likes'.*

PB: Yes, that's a common question, whenever we present. And yes, people will try to game it, of course. But the current system is gamed too: it is counting citations within a scholarly journal to another scholarly journal. And the way of measuring those citations, the impact factor, is gamed. And so the counter-argument is: yes, people will game it, but more data is better than less data, or no data. The more data sources we provide, the harder it is to game. Because, effectively, they have to game all of these different data sources consistently. If you just game the Facebook likes and not the tweets, someone is going to notice; there'll be algorithms that can spot unusual behaviour. So, you'd have to game everything consistently in this new world: if there's ten metrics, one would have to game ten different things.

The other argument is that this is a self-regulating, self-policing community of professional academics, and there are consequences to behaving badly. Perhaps if you're a fiction author on Amazon there is no real consequence if you get caught gaming; you've still got readers. But if you're an academic and you get caught, it's unprofessional behaviour and you are ostracised, thrown out of your department.

I think that in the future, if someone is caught gaming their tweets it will be seen as being as bad as plagiarism or data manipulation. It may be harder to catch and spot, but as an academic you don't want to have your reputation ruined because you tried to game a number of Facebook likes. So I think it will be self-policing.

It all comes down to whether or not people value these metrics. If they start gaming them, that's potentially a good thing because it shows that they value the metrics enough to want to game them. So these have become a valuable metrics. Once they start gaming them, we know this movement has been successful.

SG: *I'm wondering, again, whether there is a difference between communities. Are the metrics more valuable in fields where there's more agreement about what everyone 'knows', compared to others? Does it depend on the community?*

PB: It depends on the community, and the reader. One of the arguments put forward against the way academic publishing is currently done—selection *before* publication—is that the decision whether or not something deserves to be published is the opinion of two reviewers and an editor, and it's only their opinion, from their perspective. They're interested in a specific thing, whatever that is, and have made a decision as to whether or not this entire article is read by a group of people. Does it see the light of day at all?

In reality there is a very large spectrum of readers who read articles for different reasons. So, some people might read them from a scholar's point of view, and for that the articles have to be scholarly and advance the field. But as a research funder, for instance, you might be reading that article to see whether it influenced public policy—did it change policy in a country on how to treat AIDS, for instance? If you're the author you might be interested in a wider public reading your article, because you've got a book out that you want to show off. If you're a librarian, again you're reading it from a different perspective. There's a vast spectrum of readers that may or may not find it interesting, so give them a big spectrum of metrics.

Some readers simply sort all their search results by usage, because they're only interested in seeing the most-read articles. Some people sort by number of citations: they want to see the ones most people have cited within that field. Others are going to sort it by the comments, because they're interested in that debate. It allows a lot more potential for people to find their own value in a work than the previous system of two people making a binary yes/ no publication decision.

SG: *When we talked about the 'shaping' function, you said that you shape the overall direction of the publication. Is it right to say that this assumes that some kind of centralised decision-making is necessary?*

PB: Yes and this includes professional standards. Some are obvious, such as 'no plagiarism' or 'no data manipulation'. But there are others. For example, all the authors on a paper should meet a definition of authorship, and if someone is mentioned in the acknowledgments, they should have agreed to be so acknowledged. Otherwise it shouldn't be published. The industry tries to police these things.

A good example is clinical trials. Ten to 12 years ago, a group of the leading medical journals got together and said, 'We aren't going to publish any more clinical trial articles unless they follow a specific protocol and provide documentation'. That is what I mean by shaping the standards. And then there are journal-specific standards. One interesting rule we had at *PLoS*, for instance, was that we wouldn't publish any paper that had funding from the tobacco industry. That was a specific criteria that other journals may or may not follow. But that is a form of shaping again, isn't it?

SG *Yes, and I would say that building an editorial board is also part of shaping, as it is part of maintaining standards*

PB It is, although it's hard. *PLoS ONE* has an editorial board of three and a half thousand people covering all scientific fields; it's very hard to shape that board and select people into it who meet a specific requirement. I'm doing the same thing [here], building an editorial board for the new company. Right now, I have 450 people across all of biology and the medical sciences. In that scenario, what you tend to do is not so much 'shape' the board, but set standards for membership. A board member has to be a seasoned academic, a principal investigator or above; someone who has published 35 papers or more; a real academic that's capable of making the right academic decisions. In addition, there's the training. You need to explain to them the vision of the journal, train them, and correct it when they make a wrong judgment call. So there's that level of shaping as well.

SG *When you say training, what does that entail?*

PB The training is interesting. Everyone involved has been selected because of their track record. They've all reviewed papers, they all think they know what publishing is about. But with *PLoS ONE* and now with *PeerJ*, the criteria being applied are very unusual. If they have worked on selective journals, they may come into the process with the notion that they need to make a judgment call, based on the impact of the paper. So we must make sure they understand the vision of the new type of journal, and how it works. The criteria is simple—is it scientific or not? You have explain it to them, and hope they listen. Then there is an element of checking as they go forward, going back to them if it looks like they've made the wrong kind of decision.

The training is hard with a board that big, especially with academics who are very busy. They're not going to sit and do a training course, and they're probably not going to read your emails either. At some level you're simply hoping that they 'get it' at some level, and do their job professionally because they're community members of good standing. At the end of the day, there's an audit trail of everything that happens in the system; there's an appeal process if an author feels unfairly judged, and so on.

SG: I remember editing something years ago about the regulation of psychotherapy. The author argued that one shouldn't try to prevent harm by imposing strict limits to entry—what you need is a good appeals process so that if anything goes wrong, people have somewhere to go. He said that control of outputs prevents more harm than controlling inputs, in that case entry qualifications. Would you say that your approach is similar?

PB: Yes, that does sound quite parallel to what we're talking about. What we're doing, of course, is taking away a lot of the control traditionally held by the editor, the traditional gatekeeper in this process, and giving it back to the community.

One of the questions in your list was about the metaphor I would use to describe what I do. One of the examples was 'midwife'. This fits quite well: I don't write the papers, I don't edit the papers, but I deliver them to the world in a healthy state and then the world deals with them as they wish. And so I think midwife is not a bad metaphor here. I think the publishing industry hasn't really respected the needs of the academic community that it's serving, or respected its knowledge and skills. What we do, and we're quite clear about it, is to be a service to the academic community. We're not telling them what to do; they don't have to come and beg us to select their paper. We're just trying to set up a very professional service-oriented environment, where we give them what they need to publish articles for their community.

SG: You've talked about three types of publishing; you seem to be saying that it's only the bit in the middle that is not serving its community. Would you say there is some value to traditional, intensive editing—the 'luxury' kind?

PB: Definitely, there is. Open access is about to disrupt this entire industry quite soon, but the group it's going to disrupt is the large one in the middle. The highly selective brand journals at the top—*Nature, Science, PNAS*—these kind of journals add genuine value in the process, they really do, and the editors there do a good job and people still value that, to the extent that they'll still pay money for it, and submit work to those journals. But people don't value what happens in the middle and it becomes almost parasitic on the system. That's the bit that's open to disruption.

That said, you need to be careful that the business model isn't conflated with the publishing process as such. The question is, does editing have to be attached to a specific business model? In this case, a subscription model and a restrictive copyright licence. And it doesn't: you can still have that kind of highly selective editing, where you select the best of the best, and you craft it and edit, and work with the authors. You can still do that and it doesn't have to be in a restrictive copyright licence subscription journal.

That is what *eLife* is trying to do, of course. It's trying to do the same thing as *Nature* with the same level of editing, but without the business model attached to it. That's also what *PLoS Medicine* and *PLoS Biology* have done. Those journals are run by professional, good editors but without the subscription business model wrapped around it.

The problem is financial. The traditional open access model doesn't work in a highly selective environment, because if you're rejecting 99% of your submissions and only publishing 1%, the fees you charge authors for that 1% can never cover the work. The *eLife* solution is to find a very rich benefactor to fund everything for eternity.

SG *You've referred to the fact that the editorial process costs money, and has to be funded somehow. You've just said that being selective about content limits the funding you can get from your own model, and not everyone can emulate eLife because there aren't enough institutional funders to go around. So the question remains—where are people going to get the money for selective editing?*

PB Perhaps you do still get it from the reader, but it doesn't have to be via the traditional subscription model, with a copyright licence on top of it. You can get it from the reader using an open access model. I don't pretend to have a solution, but I think that you're absolutely right—the finances are harder to figure out in that model.

SG *A similar debate has been taking place for many years about journalism. Everyone's looking for a business model that will pay for good reporting; the problem is that it's very expensive to spend time on discovering new things, and that's been difficult to fund.*

PB Some people are trying writing consortia. Journalists are forming groups to pool their efforts and sell it. You can see parallels here. For instance, *Nature* and *Science* reject about 99% of the work submitted to them. One reason there's so much inefficiency in this model is because those 99% of articles go on to be submitted somewhere else, and are then rejected again, and submitted somewhere else. So an article might be submitted to five, six, seven journals, and re-reviewed at every single one until it gets accepted. This is very wasteful in the system. But in principle, that work should not have to go back through the same process at another journal. These highly selective journals could pool their knowledge, so that if *Nature* rejects a paper, *Science* might accept it without having to re-review because it meets their criteria differently. That would save cost, and make the system more efficient.

SG *From the author's point of view, it might be helpful to get five or six sets of reviewers' comments.*

PB I guess there is the occasional masochistic author that would appreciate that, yes.

SG *What drew you to publishing in the first place?*

PB I have an academic background. I did a PhD but decided that was more than enough. At the same time, I loved science and the environment and the academics themselves. So publishing was a great job to go into. I went from a physics PhD to work at the Institute of Physics Publishing. I was still dealing with academics, with science, with physics that I loved, and had the ability to influence that in a bigger way than I could have done individually. As an individual academic there's only so much you can add to the world. It's where you sit on the fulcrum, isn't it? You can't move much when you're just one person researching your own thing, but if you're publishing the work of thousands of people, read by millions of people, there's a much bigger opportunity to make a difference in the world.

This is a theme throughout my career. It's got to the point where, at *PLoS ONE* at least, I was making a significant difference. I was running the largest journal in the world by a factor of five; publishing 3% of the literature, according to PubMed statistics, roughly doubling in size every year, disrupting the entire industry. And, at the same time, accelerating science, improving people's ability to get science out there quickly and effectively. What I was doing there, and hopefully will continue doing, was making a much bigger difference in the world than anything I could have done as an academic, and a not very good academic. So that is what interested me.

As my career has gone on, I've dealt with bigger and bigger programs, more and more journals, more and more content. I arrived at Sage Publications and ran their US journal programme. It had 220 journals: more content, more articles than *PLoS ONE* later on, but in a very traditional, unchanging model. And then five years ago or so, I saw the promise of open access, which was just starting to pick up steam. I could see that this was a better way to get content out there faster, better. And *PLoS ONE* was the most interesting kid on the block, working to do that stuff.

It probably looked a bit odd to some people that I jumped up from running 220 journals to [just] one, but history has proved me right—that one journal turns out to be the most interesting thing in the industry right now, making a lot of positive change. This starts to get a bit teary and sappy, but if you can get good content out there faster—if a peer-reviewed article is published in one month instead of one year and suddenly people can read it and use that content—you're potentially going to save lives.

SG *If a publisher doesn't provide hands-on editing and it is left to the author, do you think authors have the right skills? If not, how could they acquire them?*

PB It does depend which aspect of editing you're talking about. For instance, a lot of authors don't know the ethical standards that we enforce—for example, making personal information known by mistake—and don't give it a high value. The academic may know what these standards are, at some level, but then they go and write a paper that mentions a person's name or shows a photo of them. So from that point of view, they don't have the skills.

[As for the writing itself], in theory the writing should be very information-heavy. The ultimate academic paper is just a picture of the experiment, a table full of data and the conclusion. Everything else that gets put in is only there to help a human being understand the paper. They're telling the story of their research, but it should just be the facts. But because there's humans involved—there's a human writing it, there's a human reading it—you end up with a lot of semantics loaded into it.

Do academics have the skills there? They probably have the skills to write a paper that contains the facts, but [when] they're asked to write a paper that tells a story, transmitting information to another human, all sorts of interesting things happen: they overplay the results; they try and make things sound sexier than they are…Because for them, the results are great; they think everyone in the world should read about it in *The New York Times*. Or they don't report the negative results, or they downplay them. So again, they're not very good at that either.

The process that I operate doesn't help them there. It doesn't pick up on those kinds of things. The peer reviewers should notice that the contributor is overstating their results, or omitted to mention all the negative results; they should ask for revisions. But those people are also academics who also make the same mistakes when writing their own papers.

I don't know if this is answering your question. We're relying on the academic community to educate themselves about the standards needed to produce a good paper, rather than ourselves trying to fix that for them.

SG *You mentioned getting 'push-back' from authors. I wonder, could you possibly expand on that? For example, if you enforce standards about giving away confidential patient information, how do authors respond when faced with that kind of editorial constraint? And how do you respond to their response?*

PB Usually the push-back arises from misunderstanding the standards we are imposing, or not being aware of them. So they might argue that they don't *need* to provide *x*. We then get into a debate. Often they can be persuaded of our opinion, but on some occasions they become so frustrated, they withdraw their submission.

SG *Do you agree or disagree with the statement by Amazon executive Russell Grandinetto, that 'the only really necessary people in the publishing process now are the writer and reader'?*

PB I think the answer is, 'it depends'. The simple act of publishing no longer needs anyone other than author or reader. But if you want to maintain standards, professional levels of consistency, then a professional publisher is needed.

Note

1. At a conference on research integrity, the executive editor of the Nature Publishing Group said that editors had noted a 'certain level of sloppiness' creeping into research papers, particularly the biomedical sciences; many items needing correction were 'avoidable errors...and I think that is a very troubling trend' (Gibney 2013).

Chapter 12

Phoebe Ayers

Member, Wikimedia Foundation board of trustees, reference librarian at the University of California at Davis Interview: Thursday, September 20, 2012 via Skype

Phoebe Ayers, a professional librarian, began editing Wikipedia in 2003 when still a student. She is co-author of a user's manual (Ayers et al. 2008), with chapters ranging from 'The Life Cycle of an Article' to 'Becoming a Wikipedian'. At the time of writing, she is a member of the Wikimedia Foundation's board of trustees, elected by the community of users.

A recurring theme of this book is an exploration of how editing, like other practices, tacitly or explicitly develops a culture that helps to sustain it over time. The importance of social practice to Wikipedia is acknowledged by co-founder Jimmy Wales, who says about the guidelines: 'This is as much "a social technique for getting people to work together" as it is an editorial policy' (Waldman 2004).

What is perhaps unusual about Wikipedia is the way it acts as the focus of contradictory expectations. It is open to all, but most edits are carried out by a fraction of the millions of registered users. After years of concerted effort, the proportion of women editors remains small.[1] It has a structure to overcome disputes, but decisions remain contentious.[2] The hierarchy itself—in which some editors are elected to have different levels of access and privileges—is under constant fire and, as in all other social groups, individuals sometimes abuse their privileges.[3] The project's pivotal policy, the 'neutral point of view', comes under fire from many directions. This includes constructivists who challenge what they see as a positivist frame, and sceptics who worry about the danger of false balance.[4] Effective use of the neutral point of view depends on the identification of good sources. In the interview, Ayers underlines the difficulty of doing this well.

The main challenge, in such circumstances, is to tease out the details that throw light on both the unique and generic aspects of editing for Wikipedia.

SG *Within the Wikimedia Foundation, you go to the annual conferences, you know the concerns that people have. What issues are discussed relating to editing practice? Is there anything particular you think needs 'fixing' or not?*

PA That's a big question. I was thinking about this. The foundation is a non-profit organisation that does the administrative work. It's important to realise that everyone who contributes to Wikipedia considers themselves to be an editor. That's what we call ourselves; we call ourselves Wikipedia editors. We don't call ourselves Wikipedia authors. And so the entire spectrum of things that we do, from writing a draft of the article to copyediting it, formatting, merging in changes, deciding whether it should be deleted—that whole spectrum comes under the heading of 'editing'. And so when we talk about how Wikipedia editors should do their work or how the projects work, we're talking about everything. About how people interact with each other, how articles are written and produced. Some of those activities are related to traditional editing—making an article coherent, or proofreading—and some of them are more curation-based. For example, deciding whether two entries should be merged together or split apart, or whether something should be deleted or kept. Some of it is more to do with fact-checking or research.

When we think about any of these things, we tend to focus on getting more people involved. How do you get people to become Wikipedia editors; how do you train them; how to create a good environment for them. The second thing we can talk about is, processes for doing things. How do we make the process better, more efficient, easier, less contentious. How do we make it easier to create Wikipedia in a new language; how do we make the editing platform code better.

Working on Wikipedia, you have to put your ego aside. We have this principle of 'no ownership'. Nobody 'owns' an article. Nobody is solely responsible for a piece of text. Of course people put more work into some articles than others—they may put in hours and hours, trying to make a particular article good—but that doesn't make it theirs, right? We all share in the burden of making it good, in some respects.

As a consequence, nobody is in charge of the process. Nobody reports up to an editorial board. And I think that's the real extraordinary thing about Wikipedia. People still have a hard time, even after a decade now, understanding how it works in practice. As a community over the years, we've created stylistic guidelines, a big style manual, trying to work towards the ideal encyclopaedia article. We've also created a body of practice about how you do things; how you interact with each other, how you contribute to an article. As editors, we all judge each other according to those standards, the body of practice that's been set up.

SG *You say there's no ownership, but Wikipedia editors are following an agreed process that is enforced in the culture, using a body of guidelines and best practice. So there is some structure.*

PA A lack of ownership does not imply a lack of process. That's the key bit about the collaborative part. We've developed processes and the guidelines as a community, and so those decisions are made by the people who show up and act in accordance with those guidelines. What I mean by ownership is that if I work on an article about volcanoes, that article does not become mine, to dictate what stays in and stays out. I can work on it, make it as good as I can, but it does not in any particular sense belong to me as an editor. And no one is particularly responsible for the enforcement. There's no editorial body, no group of people who are in charge of that process.

SG *When you talk about putting egos aside, that can't be easy. Are there any particular examples where that's been a problem?*

PA The reason I'm stressing it is that it has developed over the years. Nobody came down from on high, but over the years it has developed as a guideline. You don't own the things you write in the sense that you don't dictate the final article. And there is no final article. Things are constantly changing and shifting. It's a difficult concept to get your head around. It leads to conflict all the time, especially with new people coming in. They may submit an article, and then wonder why it's been changed dramatically, or even deleted, for example if it doesn't fit the scope of Wikipedia. Often those decisions are not clear-cut, and so that leads to a lot of potential conflict and confusion.

You asked me what issues the foundation is worried about. That's one of them. Getting new people inducted into Wikipedia culture is difficult because it is super-complex, a little bit counterintuitive. And it's difficult because you've got hundreds of people working under the umbrella of these practices. How they interpret these practices may not always be identical.

Getting used to that rhythm and figuring out the guidelines, learning how to work within them, how to make your case—in short, learning what Wikipedia thinks an encyclopaedia article should look like—all of that takes some work and some time. And as you know, writing and editing are not easy. And so while Wikipedia is entirely open, it's not always very transparent. It's not always easy to figure out what's going on. And it's not always easy for people to think about writing for an encyclopaedia, and Wikipedia specifically. It's a specific genre and very different from most other things. So yes, there is the potential for a lot of conflict there.

SG *Sue Gardner [then Executive Director of the Wikimedia Foundation] launched a debate a couple of years ago about women not feeling welcome in Wikipedia. It generated a significant volume of comment. Is that still a concern?*

PA It is still a concern, very much so. And it's a concern because of all those issues I just mentioned. It's difficult to get people to start editing and once they start, they may encounter a hostile or confusing environment.

A couple of years ago I wrote a book about Wikipedia. A sort of how-to manual about how it works. The reason we wanted to tackle that was because the guidelines on the site are so incredibly complex. There's thousands and thousands of pages, which is too much for anyone.

The concern is that compared to the population at large, and the population of Wikipedia editors, the percentage of those editors we identify as female is quite low. It's somewhere between nine and 13 percent. It's part of a broader concern about making the editor population diverse in terms of age, profession, gender, geographical location—getting people from around the world, not just Northern Europe and the US. It is a debate that has run over many years. And the reason for that, is we're very focused on being a global and inclusive project. As an encyclopaedia it's meant to be about everything that matters. And that doesn't mean some of the things that matter.

SG *I can imagine all sorts of reasons why diversity is a good thing. But can I check, is the benefit conceived as having an impact on the range of content, or is it thought that there would be a different kind of process, a different type of editorial judgment?*[5]

PA Well, both, because those things are so tightly linked on Wikipedia. The idea is that there would be different content, potentially. This is the hypothesis; nobody knows, because the decision-making about that content is an integral part of Wikipedia.

There was a debate in the news recently about Kate Middleton's dress. The Wikipedia article about the dress had been nominated for deletion. And the argument was, who cares? Lots of people got up in arms—millions of people cared about this dress. It was a big deal! Whether or not you cared personally about this dress, it was objectively a big deal, in the news and the fashion world. That argument, back and forth, is an example of the kinds of editorial decisions that get made about content and these decisions, in turn, shape what Wikipedia looks like. And so yes, the argument is that with a more diverse population, there would be more people in Wikipedia who cared about fashion. They would say this article mattered. And in fact they did show up; the article is still on Wikipedia.

Those are the kinds of decisions we make every day as Wikipedia editors. That's why we identify ourselves as editors. It's not about who's going to write an article in the first place, but what happens to it.

SG *Earlier, you described some activities as 'classic editing' and others as 'curating'. In my own working definition, I include those other activities as part of editing. Did that make sense to you?*

PA It does make sense to me, but here's the difference. You talked about the role of the author versus the role of the editor. I don't think there's a role for the author on Wikipedia. I think we're all editors.

SG *I understand. The question is more to do with the way editing is defined. What is called 'classic' editing can be understood as shaping or micro-editing, and what's now often called curating involves selection, which can be understood as a form of macro-editing.*

PA Yes, sure. Those decisions on Wikipedia are rarely made by a single person. The deletion process, people weigh in with comments, and you see if there's a consensus one way or another. If there's no consensus, the article is typically kept. There's quite a bit of gatekeeping done, but not on the level of making decisions about importance or content value. The gatekeeping that is done without a prior collective consensus is typically when the article is spam, or so far out of scope that the decision is obvious. If someone contests it later, decisions can be reversed.

SG *There have been concerns about political manipulation, for example when a conspiracy theory is expressed in a Wikipedia article as fact—the theory itself, not the fact of its existence—and then it takes a while for the community to realise it's up there. There are other cases where the subject is valid but there is intense controversy over the way it is covered.*

PA Yes, it is tough, there's been plenty of cases, you see it in the news all the time. Let's say there's a politician whose staff edits an article, tries to make them look great; or tries to take out something that doesn't make them look great. That happens to varying degrees. It's not supposed to. We have big guidelines about it. It's not always caught.

The cases where there's a real debate—there's a point where they can be included without controversy, depending on the way they are covered in the rest of the world. If something causes a stink in the world news, we will often say as Wikipedians, 'All right: this happened in the world, it's notable enough to be reported in the article with citations. We're not going to pass judgment whether this is true'. It's like the foundational principle of neutrality (Wikipedia 2014). The idea is that you report what happens in the world but you give people's minority views their due. You cite everything. You don't yourself pass judgment but you report the consensus that other people have come to, in other forums. So, people think the world is round, there's a small minority that thinks it's flat, there's a citation, and you get on with the article.

This is more difficult when you've got a public figure who is maybe known for only one scandal, or when the scandal overwhelms the rest of their career. Nobody likes their Wikipedia article to report on that. It's tricky, right? It doesn't always get done correctly, but I think our goal is to report what happened and to give it its due. And the same with conspiracy theories. Some of them are notable in their own right—for example, that the moon landings were faked. There's an entire article about that whole thing, because that's something that people believe out there in the world.

SG *One case that caused upset in the UK concerned a journalist who created sock puppet identities. Over a long period of time he edited other people's entries under a false name, to portray them as negatively as possible. Eventually he was exposed but in the meantime, people's reputations were seriously harmed.*

PA Yes, and the best way we have developed to deal with that is to focus on sources and not to make Wikipedia the primary source on anything. So if you say 'Politician *x* has been accused of embezzling', well—accused by whom, and where? And in what circumstances, and can you give me a reference to a newspaper article to that effect? Without all of that, it shouldn't be in the article.

As individuals, Wikipedia editors don't necessarily know about the subject—we're not experts, we're not writing from our personal knowledge. We're bringing together the knowledge that exists out in the world. That's true whether it's someone in the news or whether it's a scientific article, or what have you. There are plenty of experts on Wikipedia, people with PhDs and practitioners and people who really know their fields. But it's a not a prerequisite and it's sometimes actively unhelpful.

SG *The issue of sources is an interesting one. In a recent case, the author Philip Roth spotted something in a Wikipedia entry about the source of inspiration for a character. He told Wikipedia the detail was wrong, but then had trouble getting it corrected. What struck me in that case was the tone of the correspondence, which probably added to his sense of injury. Perhaps someone with more experience might have said to him, 'What you say is important, so let's find a way to resolve the problem', for example, by putting it on the record so that it could be referenced.*[6]

PA I think that's exactly what happened in the end, and the article did change. I'm not going to try and justify anybody's tone. I didn't look at the exchanges myself, but I'm sure we could have been more polite and done it better. But I have mixed feelings about this case, because essentially Roth was saying, 'The critics are wrong, and you should take my word for it'. If you think of yourself in the position of a Wikipedia editor, this is tricky, right? The place to debate those things is not in pages of Wikipedia but in literary forums. If he wants to rebut his critics, then doing it in the encyclopaedia article is unfair to everybody. The article relies on the public record.

Part of the reason Wikipedia editors are a bit wary of people saying, 'I'm so-and-so, correct my article' is that I could write in and say, 'I'm Philip Roth', and there's no way to know if that is true. And not only is there no way to know, but there's no way to know someone's intentions. That's where the heavy emphasis on sources comes in. Wikipedia relies greatly on the mechanisms in the world that exist of editing and publishing and everything. So yes, I wish that Roth's concerns had been handled better, we make those mistakes and fail a lot. But on the other hand…

SG *You began editing on Wikipedia in 2003, so you're coming up to your tenth anniversary.*

PA Yes, and the project's tenth anniversary came up a couple of years earlier—it started in 2001 and I joined fairly early on. Which is interesting, because I've seen the evolution of the site over time.

SG *What drew you to the project?*

PA I began as an editor, as people do. I stumbled on the site, thought it was really cool, and started making edits. And I've always been interested in it from a research perspective, too, as an information scientist. A couple years in, I went to our first international conference and was introduced to people around the world. It was the first time many of us had ever met face to face. That was pretty extraordinary.

As a result of that experience I got more involved in the organisational side of things. I started organising conferences, and became involved in various projects. The foundation itself was quite small when I joined as a volunteer; just a handful of paid employees, taking care of the computer servers. The foundation is still small but has grown over the last couple of years, both in terms of what we're trying to do and staff numbers.

Somewhere along the way, I wrote the 'how-to' manual with a couple of other people. I was elected to a seat on the board of trustees for the foundation in 2010. That's the governing board: it doesn't control Wikipedia but it thinks strategically, and looks to the long-term for the foundation and the projects themselves. There are currently 11 projects in total—Wikipedia, Wikisource, and so on. I served a two-year term on the board; I just finished this summer in 2012. And here we are.

SG *Does Wikipedia fund you in any way, or is that still voluntary?*

PA I've never been paid for any of this—I've always been a volunteer. I am a librarian, it's still my day job. My professional background and interests overlap a great deal with Wikipedia. I'm interested in how people get knowledge about the world; how they interpret that knowledge; the politics of getting access, copyright, open access; scientific communication; I think all of that is pertinent to Wikipedia, which is this grand collaborative experiment.

SG *I ask everyone in these interviews: what imagery would you use to describe what you do on Wikipedia?*

PA We sometimes half-jokingly refer to the administrators as 'janitors', and there's some truth to that. There's a constant clean-up to be done; that will never end. I sometimes feel I'm doing my part in that, in the great...[*laughs*] I'm not sure what is the right metaphor.

SG *I like that—'janitor'. I sometimes use 'housekeeping'. Can you describe a typical day as a Wikipedia editor?*

PA It has varied over the years. I skip around a lot. I tend to focus more on types of things to do, than I do on subject matter, although I specialise a bit in science articles and biographies.

I do a lot of things that sound—and probably are—quite boring. People post references to a journal article and sometimes they need to be formatted, checked, verified—I do a lot of that. I add references, I do a lot of fact-checking. That's my librarian background coming through.

You'll see those tags saying that an article needs a citation—those are meant as flags, both for the reader, but also for the Wikipedia editing populace. It's part of our workflow, our management of the article system. There are categories that list the articles that are unreferenced. You can go through them, pick them out, add references, and take the tag off. I may see an article labelled as needing work and I clean it up. The grammar's bad, the formatting is bad, I'll fix the grammar, I'll fix the formatting.

There are big tasks where you might rewrite an article, or write something up from scratch. Sometimes I'll do that but I don't do a whole lot of straight-up writing. I tend to work on things that have already been started, and try to improve them. Sometimes I'll tackle small things that need to be done across a group—for example, all the articles about glaciers need to have their references improved—and you'll just go through, boom boom boom. There is a multilingual component to the work—a process to link articles so the Spanish articles link to the English ones, and vice versa, so that you can see there are equivalences in both languages. That's a specialised thing that I've been working on lately.

There's always more to do! We're talking about 25 million articles across all 280 language projects, four million in English alone; almost all of them are mediocre.

I don't think there's such a thing as the 'typical' Wikipedia editor, because people find their niche. There are people who focus on writing articles about trains, or history. And then there are others who specialise in a particular type of administrative work. They only work on deletions, or welcoming new editors. And then there are people like me who skip around and do a lot of cleaning up work. I think most people do it as a hobby. They're working in their free time, or multitasking. I know a few people who spend eight hours a day on Wikipedia, for one reason or another, but they are not typical.

SG *Do you have any rituals or habits when you're going into Wikipedia editing mode? For example, do you always do it in the morning, or evening? Have a cup of coffee before you start, or play a certain track...*

PA [*laughs*] I do a couple of different things. I edit at three different times. Sometimes I'll take a half-hour out of my working day, when I feel I need to do something else. I find it very relaxing. I do a lot of editing in the evenings, just after dinner. There's a lot of tasks that are minor, so you can multitask and watch a movie and do some Wikipedia editing. I almost never sit down to watch TV without doing some editing while I'm at it. I always have a list in the back of my mind that I can tackle if I have half an hour in the airport with internet access. I know other people who spend an hour religiously working on Wikipedia at night. It just depends.

SG *I understand the idea that editing can be relaxing. There's a satisfaction that comes from making something better, smoothing it out. Obviously, not everyone feels that way.*

PA And I'm not trying to do it eight hours a day, either, right? Oh! Sunday mornings! I love to edit on Sunday mornings [*laughs*]. If I'm at home, it's great. It feels like such a luxury, to take a couple of hours. Part of that is related to what I do with Wikimedia. My organisational responsibilities are much more like work. Actually editing Wikipedia itself is totally fun.

SG *What is it about that couple of hours on a Sunday that feels like a luxury?*

PA It's a good question. I think there's a bunch of layers to the answer. It's partly the satisfaction of putting something into a project, losing yourself in the rhythm. I find the activity fun, and I think most Wikipedia editors do, or they wouldn't do it. There's something about making something better, as you say, and maybe working on something that's interesting, something that you care about...getting absorbed in it, interacting with other people.

There's a lot of people who make a few edits and then go away again. That's the vast majority of Wikipedia editors. Or they work on it occasionally, or on a particular topic. But there are people who stick around for years and years, like me, and make tons of edits, and I think for us we find something joyful and compelling: it's hard to stop.

SG *What is your main concern when you are editing, and how is that concern resolved? Is there an example you can give?*

PA I have an overriding concern, which is that there's so much that needs to be done! If I could somehow convey that to the world, I would. Concretely, I often worry about finding good sources for articles. That's very difficult. I'm probably as much of a professional as you can be for that particular task, being a skilled Wikipedia editor and a skilled librarian, and I still find it incredibly difficult.

SG *I understand that in Wikipedia, the term 'editing' is used to cover everything. But if we make a distinction between originating something and revising it, would you say there's a difference? And if so, how would you pin it down?*

PA Within the world of Wikipedia, writing an article requires that you have some sense of sources and you think about the subject holistically. You sketch it out. You have to make decisions about whether there should be an article on this topic and if so, how to frame the subject. Many of those decisions can be made later but you do have to think about those questions as an article author.

Aside from Wikipedia, I do quite a bit of writing. I'm a fairly skilled writer, I think. It's a completely different skill from editing and a completely different habit of mind. It's a mental shift that I have to do, writing a document for work versus writing a Wikipedia article. I write things that I care about, and would get upset if people changed them radically. You have to drop all of that, writing for Wikipedia. I've trained myself to do that, but it is very different… I think of myself as a writer in other contexts, not necessarily Wikipedia.

SG *Can you describe any instances of resistance to the editing process? When someone just doesn't 'get' what editing is about, why it's necessary. And what response do you give to that?*

PA You're right, that happens all the time. There are often conflicts about how something should look, or how it should be phrased. It often seems that the more minute the issue, the bigger the conflict [*laughs*]. You'll see two people who both really care about a subject, going at it; you'll see these discussions that go on for pages and pages and pages. Often, as an outside third party, you have to work to find a compromise between those people; it doesn't always happen, but it can be done…it's difficult, it's difficult.

SG *Is editing creative? In what way?*

PA Oh yes, of course! Absolutely. Unquestionably, it's creative. I think from the smallest edit to the biggest act of editing. Especially in our context. We are literally creating the article, edit by edit.

SG *Is it difficult to teach editing? How can one do it?*

PA I think it is difficult. Even outside Wikipedia, in an English class, it's difficult to teach someone how to edit their own work, or somebody else's work. I like to think I'm a fairly decent editor, so I find myself editing things for people outside of Wikipedia. I'm never sure how to describe that process; the sense of fitness that you have, whether a sentence should be shorter, whether you should take something out or rearrange something, or the grammar… I feel like I know it instinctively. I can make a text better, but I find describing why you should do this thing fairly difficult. Certainly in the abstract. It's one thing to make a change and say, this should go there because then, the whole rhythm of the argument is better. It's another to say 'look at this document and make sure it's structured well'. So I think it is a mysterious, intuitive process.

The same is true on Wikipedia. We spend a lot of time worrying collectively about skills, and training new editors. It's difficult, because you can train somebody to understand the code and the technical part fairly easily, but it's more difficult to teach somebody what a good encyclopaedia article really looks like, and feels like. I'm not sure any of us know this; I'm not sure it's an obtainable ideal.

Enough information without being too much; a good summary upfront, without overwhelming the reader; well-structured references that are to the point; further reading that's to the point; appropriate illustrations—these are the things you're striving towards, in this format. It is very difficult to teach somebody that, and I think that by and large, the people who stick around and learn it are the people who have taught themselves by looking, and making judgment calls.

We try and give each other guidance—here's our best practice on Wikipedia: don't add too many links. Or, here's our best practice, try to write an appropriate summary for the article. But I'm not sure you can teach somebody how to do that well. So we rely on each other's judgment, to some extent. That's where you have to put your ego aside.

I feel I know this project; I've written a book about it; I've been teaching and writing and thinking about it for ten years. I work with literature as a profession, I work with references as a profession. I am still not going to pretend that I know the best way to write an article in any given circumstance. I think we all do our best, trying to train each other through example.

Maybe our biggest concern in the foundation is, how do you get started? How does someone new come into the project and have a good experience and become part of our community. Because we want it to be open and inclusive. A lot of that is about training. There's a lot of thinking about how to make the training better.

SG *I'm fascinated by this massive effort to train the whole world how to edit.*

PA I do think it is a massive project—no one expected us to be here ten years later. Certainly no one from Wikimedia. No one thought, 'Oh we should become the biggest reference site in the world'. That wasn't on the table. But it's happened. And so it is a massive experiment, trying to figure out what it is we're trying to do. You can take a traditional encyclopaedia as an example, but that's not quite right.

Wikipedia is something new, something different. It's not just an encyclopaedia, by any stretch of the imagination. Trying to figure out what that even looks like, and then teaching ourselves, teaching each other, teaching new people, at the same time—it is our biggest challenge. And there's a fine line, too, between innovation—a better idea about how to do something—versus teaching what we do currently as our practice. They're all open questions.

Notes

1. In a 2010 survey carried out by the Wikimedia Foundation and the Collaborative Creativity Group (CCG) at UNU-MERIT, it was found that only 12.64% of contributors were female (CCG 2010). Gardner led efforts to increase the number and proportion of women contributing to Wikipedia as editors but when she left the foundation in December 2013, she acknowledged the difficulty of the task: 'I didn't solve it. We didn't solve it. The Wikimedia Foundation didn't solve it. The solution won't come from the Wikimedia Foundation' (Huang 2013).

2. Tangible proof is provided by a 12-volume reproduction of every single Wikipedia edit made to the entry for 'The Iraq War' over five years, from December 2004 to November 2009 (Bridle 2010). In another case, several editors were banned from editing on the topic of the jailed US army private Chelsea Manning, because of controversy over using her female name following a decision to take a transsexual identity (Hern, 2013).

3. For example, the 2014 'paid to edit' scandal. See Bartlett 2014.

4. The difference between objectivity and neutrality has been referenced elsewhere in the book. 'Neutral point of view' is considered particularly problematic in cases where the weight of evidence is much stronger on one side than another. The complaint is that it ends up leading to a systematic bias against scientific validity, making Wikipedia fertile ground for the growth of conspiracy theories.

5. One example, among many, concerns a writer who sounded the alarm when she noticed that women were being moved one by one from 'American Novelists' to 'American Women Novelists'. There was no corresponding category for 'American Male Novelists'. After a public row ensued, the change was traced to a single male editor. See Filipacchi 2013, Gleick 2013.

6. The substance of the Philip Roth complaint was that his own word was not considered authoritative enough for a correction about the inspiration for one of his characters. Although there was a valid argument for the policy that any published claim should be based on statements on public record, the Roth case raises an interesting issue because the 'fact' being attributed is a belief about what was in the inventor's own mind.

Chapter 13

Evan Ratliff

Co-founder, editor and CEO, Atavist
Interview: Thursday, December 20, 2012
Brooklyn, New York

Atavist, a media and software company, launched in 2011. It produces a monthly narrative nonfiction magazine, based on original digital storytelling software called Creatavist that can be used by anyone.

Ratliff, one of the co-founders, brings a perspective strongly shaped by the new media technologies that emerged in the early years of his career. He worked at *Wired* magazine,[1] where he is still a contributing editor. He holds a multiplicity of job titles, reflecting the shape-shifting nature of the publisher's role.

The interview throws light on the way in which commercial and editorial concerns become intertwined. Even when 'good writing' is an undisputed goal, the question remains, how to make it pay? The search for new models of production, distribution and reward therefore becomes essential. The new arrangements may help in turn to create a new editorial lens through which to view work by the next generation of writers.

The publishing model described here gives a high value to editing, but operates in a wider landscape in which writers experience, and readers expect, less and less editorial intervention. In traditional magazine publishing, commercial pressure comes mainly from advertisers or proprietors. In the case of Atavist, it is more likely to come directly from readers. This raises the question, are the readers always right? It is an experiment that may change our perceptions of editing.

SG *Your website lists many job titles for you. Which is your favourite?*

ER Probably just 'writer', because that's my favourite thing to be doing at any given time. But here it's 'editor-in-chief': also 'CEO' and 'co-founder' because we're very businessy as well, like a start-up. Sometimes I just use 'co-founder'—it's easier. I'm also the 'president' according to the legal documents but I don't think it amounts to anything. I don't get paid more [for that].

SG *Is there anything in your education, training or past experience that generally informs what you're doing now?*

ER I didn't go to journalism school. I took a fairly average number of English lit-type courses [at university]. I worked on the college newspaper, so that was probably my first exposure to journalism. I wrote a couple of pieces but I was mostly a photographer. I never did any editing, for sure.

SG *Do you think of yourself as an editor? In what circumstances?*

ER Yes I do. There are two parts to it. One is the story selection process: going through pitches or soliciting writers with ideas, and then working with the copy. I feel like an editor when I have to sit down and compose the memo that goes on top of the draft. I think of that—the structural editing—as the more important part. I also line edit but a lot of other people can do that; it's much more challenging to do the wider kind of editing, which is concerned with what the piece is about, how it's structured, and how it flows.

SG *People sometimes talk about 'developmental editing'.*

ER We always use 'structural edit' and 'line edit'. First you do the structural edit, and then you do the line edit. We had a writer recently who kept insisting that the process should work the other way round—we should line edit first and then figure out what the structure is—which doesn't make any logical sense. It was hard to explain to him why it didn't make sense if he didn't already understand it.

SG *Because after a structural edit, you can end up completely rewriting it...*

ER Yes, what's the point of line editing something if you don't know whether it's in the structure you're going to keep? You don't know what the pieces of the puzzle are. Why polish these pieces to no end, potentially?

SG *How do you think you learned how to edit?*

ER The primary way of learning was by being edited myself, and watching editors. At *Wired* magazine, at first I was just an intern, around the office. Then I was a fact-checker, so I had to interact with the editor. I could see how the story evolved, I could see the interaction between the editor and the writer. That was my first exposure, but at the time I don't think I would have been able to do it myself. It wasn't until I started writing stories that I was able to see how different editors work and find ones that I worked well with.

I'd never worked as an editor myself until we started this publishing venture. I went back and looked at my own drafts, and looked at how they were treated by the editors I had liked. I mimicked their style, the way they approached a writer, trying to change something without rewriting it for them: finding that balance. I feel like I've had a lot of really good editors and a couple were good at that, in particular.

SG *Is there an example you can give?*

ER There's one technique that I use, which an editor used on me all the time. It is to take something and then rewrite it almost intentionally badly, saying, 'Not this, but give me something better than this, in your own voice'. Giving them the idea, but not making them feel you want them to use your words. Because if you just provide feedback at the abstract level—like, 'put more description here'—you just get back the same thing. But if you say, 'I want something like this, but I'm also acknowledging that I'm not trying to write this for you—I'm trying to prompt you', that can be really effective. Sometimes you have to dig in and rewrite the text, but nobody wants to feel that someone's stepping all over their work, they want to feel by the end that they own it.

SG *Any other examples you can think of? When you looked at your own work and saw what editors had done?*

ER When I wrote for *The New Yorker,* I noticed that they often aimed to minimise complexity by using simple chronology. That's one thing I go back to, a lot. People will try to set up these very complex structures. It can be wonderful if you pull it off, but it gets hard on the reader when you start mashing up the chronology; the transitions have to be effective. So it's okay to say, let's put this in chronological order and see how it feels, and more than half the time it feels right. We're doing narrative stories, and that's the way you would tell the story if you told it to someone. Jumping around only works if there's a really good reason for it, I think.

Ideally, if you stop in the middle of a story, you want the person listening to say, 'Don't stop: what happens next?' You don't want to get into a situation where that person says, 'Well, that's interesting, I've learned a lot', but you still have the second half of your story untold.

SG *Do you feel that editing your own work is different from editing someone else's?*

ER Yes. Definitely. I don't distinguish editing my own work from 'writing'. I feel that is actually part of the process of writing. I find that working on my own writing is psychologically much more difficult than editing someone else because it requires self-criticism. But editing is technically much more difficult—it requires more skill than writing, because as a writer you can rely on help from someone else, assuming you're writing for an editor who's going to help you shape it. Whereas when you're editing, you're usually without a net. You can direct the story and the writer's going to push back. Getting someone to do what you think is right, when they're immersed in something that they've spent too long on, is a much bigger challenge.

SG *In a way, you're saying that if you're the editor, you're the 'grownup'. You're in charge.*

ER Yes. It's the difference between looking at your own work and thinking, 'Wow, this is terrible. I feel so bad about myself', and looking at someone else's work and saying, 'Wow, this is terrible, I feel so bad for this person and I have to help them make it better'.

SG *What do you like most about editing, and what do you like least?*

ER The part I like most is when it works—when something comes in and you feel like you can make a positive impact on it, and the writer takes what you've suggested and makes it demonstrably better, and feels like you helped them make it better—that relationship is really fun. I really enjoy working with the writers.

I think any editor would say this, but what I like least is when a writer is really intransigent about something; you can see that it doesn't work and they can't see that it doesn't work, and they're adamant that it has to stay; and then you have to deal with that situation. Sometimes you get a draft and you think, 'it's just a pile of words'—that's a terrible feeling. I feel like someone just shovelled a bunch of words, and they've handed it to you and you're thinking, 'there must be a pattern in here, somewhere'.

SG *You've talked about how you learned to edit. How would you teach someone else?*

ER I have no idea how I would teach someone. Probably the best way would be to take a draft that went through a lot of changes and start with the beginning and show each version. You would show that by the end, what was the lead is now chapter five, for example, and here's the process by which that happened. Here's the communication that had to happen in order for that to take place. We'll have 20 versions of a story by the time we're done here. Recently, I think they closed on number ten, which is pretty good.

Line editing always seemed a little more intuitive—this is clear, this is not clear, this sentence reads strange. I can always tell people who don't read their work out loud: if you read something out loud, half of the line editing takes care of itself. You just realise, 'Wait—this doesn't make any sense; this sentence is too long; this phrase sounds trite'. I'm a big fan of reading things aloud.

SG *In the working definition, I describe editing under three headings: selecting, shaping and linking. In this interview so far, we have talked about the shaping. What about the selecting side of the work? Why put yourself in the role of someone who selects work?*

ER That's a good question. I'm not sure. Sometimes I wished I hadn't. We started doing what we're doing for a particular reason—we wanted to tell particular types of stories that were of a length that didn't often have a home, or they were cut down to be much shorter than they should be, naturally. I just really love narrative stories, so that's where we started and that's what we do.

And we had particular business reasons for wanting this. Most people aren't publishing anything long, except for books. To the extent that they are, it's something you can write without leaving your desk; it's all opinion and essay. The one place where you could out-compete everyone, especially digitally, was if you could figure out a way to send people out in the world, do reporting, and bring back stories. And then, because we were planning to sell those stories, we wanted them to be ones that we could market, stories you couldn't read anywhere else.

So that's why we don't do profiles. We don't do profiles on John McCain because we can't say to people, 'You should buy our John McCain profile for $2'. It would have to be the best John McCain profile anyone had ever written in order for us to say that. But we can say, 'We have the story of the only man who's circumnavigated the world by land and sea in the same vehicle, and you've never heard of him, and his adventure is extraordinary and you will not be able to put this story down'. That's our argument. So for better or worse, when it comes to the story selection process, that's the lens through which we see everything.

SG *How did you get to this from working at* Wired?

ER I started writing features at *Wired,* and discovered that's what I wanted to do. I had not gone to journalism school, or read a lot of nonfiction; I didn't know the history at all. So I started reading. Especially if you're a 25-year-old, the natural role model is Norman Mailer or Hunter Thompson; that sort of thing. I thought, that's what you do; these long, sprawling, first-person, re-ported narratives. At the time, I didn't realise that those were a bit of a rare bird. But when I started writing, that is what I was looking for. I was writing for *Wired*, I was writing for *The New Yorker* a little bit, I was writing for *Outside*, and other men's magazines, trying to pitch those stories.

I wrote a really long story for *Wired* called 'Vanish'—I tried to disap-pear for a month—which got a lot of attention. The person who edited it, Nicholas Thompson, is now at *The New Yorker* and he's one of the co-found-ers of Atavist. Last night was the three-year anniversary of the day we sat down, saying, 'That story was really fun: why don't we create something digitally where we could do the same thing?' He said, 'I know a guy who can help us', and that person is the other founder, Jefferson Rabb, who does all the programming.

SG *How much is your selection about commissioning from scratch, and how much is sifting through work that comes to you?*

ER It's probably 90% sifting—pitches, not completed stories. I would like to generate [more of] our own ideas, because it's always better than being reliant on pitches, but we just don't have time to do all the idea-prospecting that we would like. We get some really great pitches and we've done stories that we love and almost all of them are based on pitches. But you're relying on someone else, whereas if you have the idea yourself, it's not hard to find a writer for it.

SG *Are the pitches answering a particular brief that you set?*

ER At this point, it's known what we're looking for. People can look at what we've done. We generally say we're looking for narrative stories that are driven by plot and character. The easiest way to understand it is that almost all of our stories sound like movies, in the sense that they have characters that face conflict, and they either overcome that conflict or they don't. The stories contain surprise: we want them to read like fiction but to be true. In general, we say topic doesn't matter. Obviously we make some choices based on topics that we have already covered or which we think are overdone. We are unlikely to do a political story, even a narrative one, unless it is amazing, just because there's so much noise.

SG *Is there a rule about length?*

ER There's an outside boundary: 5,000 words is the shortest and 30,000 the longest. Magazines occasionally still run the 20,000-word article but it's incredibly rare. Everyone talks about John Hersey's *Hiroshima* [published in 1946], and stories like that which *The New Yorker* used to publish, taking up a whole issue or multiple issues. But even then, the 8,000 to 10,000-word story was more common. *The New Yorker* still runs that length but less often, and even the 5,000-word story at many magazines has been pushed down into the 3,500-word range. So 15,000 or 20,000 words is very rare. It's hard to find the space for that in a magazine, and in print, it's too short for a book.

SG *How does your length range compare with, say, Amazon Singles?*

ER It's the same, because we publish through Amazon Singles. We send them our pieces, they decide if they want to put them into Kindle Singles and for the most part they do so. We almost worked out the word limits with them, in a sense, because I started talking with them before they even launched and before we launched. We realised we had the same idea and so I sat down with the editor of Kindle Singles and talked about how we thought someone should do this.

SG *Sometimes a commercial change can drive a creative change, and sometimes it is the other way around. How does that work here?*

ER In many ways, we're positioned between magazines and books, but not really defined by either. We use elements of both but because we don't do advertising, we don't have to have the Chinese wall dividing editorial and advertising. It has never occurred to me until now, but we don't have to worry about the business side interfering with the journalism side. Our business questions concern multimedia, a big part of our work. We look for a story that might have an interesting multimedia outlet. And then there's the issue I described before, choosing stories [for which] we can make a better sales pitch, because we're selling them individually.

The only place where [commercial concerns] get tricky is that some subjects sell well, and how far do you lean into that? For example, we discovered things like memoir do really well, so how much memoir do we want to publish? How much are we going to stretch the boundary of what we mean by narrative nonfiction [to include that]?

I feel that if there's a shortage of something in the world, it's a shortage of skilful people going out and gathering other people's stories and being able to write them really well. So, we always heavily focused in that direction. Otherwise we'd just do memoir all the time. Memoir is easy to get, it's usually cheap, and it's easier to do. If you have to tell a writer, 'You didn't get enough on this part of some other guy's story—now you've got to go out and re-report it', that is much harder.

SG *Going back to the business model, can you make it pay?*

ER It depends on what you mean by 'make it pay'. We've uncovered *something* in this model. Other people are emulating it now, and the reason is that it works. Now, can it be made to work on a consistent basis for a high percentage of the writers and for the business overall?

We pay the writer a fee, and the writer gets a high royalty on the sale, usually 50%. And then we usually split with them any film or TV option that comes out of it. The fee plus decent sales gets them a nice amount of money— the same amount they would get paid to work for a magazine, which in the world of web rates is insane. If sales get into tens of thousands of copies, they're making more money than you would normally make working for a magazine.

The tricky thing is that the writer is taking on more risk. There are writers who receive a fee of $5,000; they spend $2,000 of that on expenses and sell 1,500 copies, so they make maybe $4,500. This is not a great return if they spent months on the story: you're not going to make a living doing just that. But in the landscape that writers are living in…

People always ask, is this model working? But the model never worked; it was never easy to make money as a freelance writer. Everyone's cobbling together different ways of making it work. There's no golden age when people made amazing wages by being freelance writers.

SG *Can you describe a typical day? Is there a typical day?*

ER My days are pretty variable, because I deal with a lot of business things right now. Editorially, we are in the middle of closing a story; our executive editor Charlie Homans is the person who's shepherding it, integrating the fact-checking and copy editing. I may read an early draft and then read it again after five revisions; then, weigh in on a couple of things, and then read it again at the end. Yesterday I read the final revision and we started looking at the multimedia. We have video in the story, we have photos, animated maps…So we sit down and ask, 'Okay, does this video work? Should that go here, should that go there?'

SG *When you're editing, what is your main concern and how is that resolved?*

ER I think my main concern is usually that the story should not be boring. That's my primary concern. There are a lot of things that flow from that. I like the writing to be beautiful but if the story's not boring, everything else can be fixed. If the story's boring, then nothing can be fixed. It doesn't matter how beautiful the writing is. How is that resolved? I guess through structural editing.

SG *You've talked about pushback. Can you think of examples where editing has gone wrong for some reason? And what happens when it goes right?*

ER If you do any number of stories, some of them are going to go wrong. I don't know if I want to be specific. I can talk about it in generic terms. Things go the most wrong when you have a writer who's very precious about their work. Someone who says, 'No, I had a reason that I wrote it this way. I do not want to have that changed'. Whether it's a tiny change or large-scale change, you just have to negotiate; that's part of being a good editor. If that writer is also extremely talented, then being precious about the work is just part of the process, part of what you're working with.

The problem comes when you have a writer whose level of entitlement and preciousness far exceeds their talent. So, the writer says over and over again, 'No, I did it this way for a reason' and they're putting things back in. But they don't have a good reason and what they've done is either a mess or poorly written. Everybody has to give in on some things at a certain point, but a bad writer refuses to give in on things that are destroying their own work. We've had that situation, where someone's just so sure they know how to do it, they don't want to listen to an editor. Unfortunately, those people sometimes don't have the talent to live up to that.

SG *How do you resolve that? Do you just cut the cord?*

ER Well, yeah, that's one option. With a book, the final say lies with the author. At a [traditional] magazine, it lies more with the publisher. You have a house style, and you say, 'This is our magazine, if you want this to go in the magazine it's going to read like this', or, 'We are cutting the last two paragraphs and it will end here'. And at a magazine, the author response might be 'Well, I want you to take my name off of it', but almost no one ever follows through with that.

We're in the middle—what we do feels more like books, and it *is* more like books. So we tend to fight for the things that we think are most important. We'll allow a little flat writing, in exchange for solving a huge structural problem. We say, 'You can have your paragraph of discursion that doesn't add anything as long as we can add a section here that transitions from this to this, so people aren't totally confused'. That sort of trade-off.

SG *When we read examples of a writer's published work, we're reading them* after *they've been edited. So it's hard to tell what their work is really like, if you're working with them for the first time.*

ER Oh yeah, you can't tell anything. Some drafts that arrive at a magazine are just terrible, and good editors can do amazing salvage jobs on them—to the point where, when you read it, you think, 'Wow, this person can really write'. Then you talk to the editor later and they say, 'No, I re-wrote that whole thing'. That's the classic editor complaint: 'You should have seen it when it came in.'

SG *I have a theory that one reason why editors are ignored, and even despised, is because the editor sees the raw copy, and that's somehow shameful. People use the metaphor of 'seeing the writer's dirty laundry'.*

ER Yeah, it's embarrassing. I've had the experience myself as an author. There was a story of mine—I really loved the last line. When I went back and looked at the drafts I saw that my editor wrote that line, which I had totally forgotten. I had just thought, 'Yeah, I feel pretty good about that, that's a line that I wrote'.

SG *We've talked about selecting, we've talked about shaping at the macro-level. What about shaping at the micro-level? Assuming the story is not boring, and you can fix whatever needs fixing, what matters to you at the more detailed level of style? Is it about voice or tone or rhythm or diction?*

ER Rhythm would be the closest to it. I have my own particular quirks about the things that matter to me, and probably all editors do. There's certain stylistic things that would fly somewhere else that won't fly here. I don't like echo, people repeating themselves for emphasis. That's something I'm very militant about.

SG *Is 'echo' in vogue at the moment?*

ER I don't think it's in vogue. I think it's common among younger writers who over-write; they want it to be writerly. They're a little over the top, and require paring back. I like straightforward writing. Even metaphor: if it's not done well, it's just clunky; you hear it and it's false. So if someone's going to use metaphor, it better be really smart—'Oh, I see, now you've painted a picture for me'—and not just by rote. As a writer, I almost never use it because I don't think I'm very good at it. So maybe that's why.

SG *Are there other things that young writers do? Are there any trends?*

ER We've worked with the whole spectrum: people who have been writing for three decades and people who come straight out of journalism graduate school, writing their first long story. One of the best things about younger writers is that they'll report forever, because they're worried that they're not going to have enough material, and the best reporters stay that way throughout their whole career. For all of us, if we've worked as writers for a long time, there is a financial incentive not to over-report everything because you've got to line up a certain number of stories to make a living. But when you're starting out, your attitude is, 'I'm going to learn everything there is to know about this'. And so, if you say to them, 'Hey, I think there needs to be a little more reporting about this', they will go out and get it. The downside is that people tend to want to show *in the story* that they've done the work, so sometimes they're not selective and they need reining in.

The other classic thing is wanting to show that you were *there*. So you include a scene about when you went into the jungle even when it doesn't add much to the story, because you want everyone to know that you went all the way there, and went into the jungle. Being able to scale those things back is part of working with them. But we've had a good experience with the younger writers.

Someone who started working as an editor with younger writers told me they had just realised that the writers had never been edited. They'd actually never been edited in their entire career, even after working as professional writers for years. So the idea that someone would tell them, 'You should re-structure the article like this'—they just didn't know how to deal with that.

But the writers we work with are not like that. They *want* to do this stuff; they've come out of programmes like Rob Boynton's on literary reportage, at NYU. My friend teaches magazine journalism at Berkeley; she has them write features and she edits the features, and she teaches about structure. So, the people we work with are people who are embarking on a career.

SG *Are all your contributors based in America?*

ER So far they're all American; there's one Brit but he's a resident.

SG *Is there is a particular American style?*

ER One of our first stories—which I happened to write myself—was about a big robbery in Sweden. It was international news when it happened; they had helicopters and explosives, and it was a really crazy story. And it was in the news every day in Sweden for a better part of a year. But when I got there, the guys had been sentenced and they were in prison. No one had written up the whole story; 'Here's what happened from beginning to end.' And when I talked to people there, they said the newspaper doesn't really do that, and there aren't magazines that do that. I don't know that for sure, that's just what a couple of people told me. That they don't have a tradition of telling that type of story in that way.

SG *Do you have a role model?*

ER Yes, editors I've worked with. The editor who's the co-founder of this company, Nicholas Thompson, has edited my work for years. There's a guy at *The New Yorker* named Daniel Zalewski, who's a master editor. I only got to work with him once, but he's incredibly talented. He's probably the most in-demand editor; everyone wants to work with him. There's a guy named Alex Heard who worked at *Wired*, and now he's the editorial director at *Outside*. He is the master of the magazine feature; he can look at a feature and say, 'I think this should be in five sections, this is how it should go'. There's no one better than him at doing that. I learnt a lot, watching him, about how to structure a magazine story. Also Jeff O'Brien, another long-time editor of mine at *Wired*, who used the techniques I borrowed from, to coax writers to rewrite.

SG *If things are not edited, or badly edited, are there any consequences to that?*

ER I've had this argument so many times. Partly as a result of us showing that you can do long-form things digitally, lots of places are [now] doing it; *BuzzFeed, Gawker* and tech sites. Here in our office, we share space with the guys who run *Longform.org*. But what does 'long form'[2] mean? Does it just mean that something is long?

The problem is that people are writing longer and longer on the web, but in a lot of cases it's not edited. *BuzzFeed* has a good editor who specialises in long form. But you get so many essays or opinion pieces that just pile arguments on each other, and try to overwhelm. Before, there was a feeling that everything should be shorter so [the lack of editing] didn't matter as much; someone writes a three-paragraph post saying why they think gun control is bad. But now someone writes 2,000 words on why they think gun control is bad, and it's sprawling; arguments are tossed out and not followed up; the sourcing is terrible, and the facts are dubious.

It actually degrades the value of work of a similar length. There's a danger that readers will say, 'It's great they you're running these long pieces', when they're totally unedited and they're dumbing down people's understanding of an in-depth piece. The guys from *Longform* always say that readers know the difference; either you're a discerning reader or you're not. People know the difference between a *New Yorker* feature and the story they see on a website that is unchecked and unedited. I hope they are right; there are some positive signs and they would know—they see most of the longform journalism that is being published in English.

SG *I would say that people learn how to be a discerning reader in the same way that they learn how to write or how to edit; if they are not exposed to the experience, they might not learn how. In other words, one cannot take it for granted.*

ER Right, and the question it raises in the long term is, what is the value of putting all that work into it? We put so much work into our stories, *The New Yorker* puts so much work into their stories. They will tell a writer, 'I'm sorry, you think this story's ready but you need to take another trip to Detroit because you just don't have what we need for this to be a story that's up to our standard'. You're putting so much work into that and the question is, are you doing it just for you, or are you doing it for another purpose? Are the readers going to know the difference? You hope they will, but if there's a risk that they won't, it might become harder and harder to justify putting all that effort into it. You always want to do it for your own integrity and standards, but if you're getting out-competed by people who are telling the exact same story but *not* sending the person back to Detroit again, then you have a problem.

A really good example [of that] just happened, but a heartening example. A guy who writes for *Wired*, Joshua Davis, went down to Belize months ago to write a story about the software guy John McAfee, who was on the run. [Another] story on the same topic was published on a website. Josh was worried that [even though the other version was inferior, it might] occupy the air for this story. The danger is that someone [else] writes a [short] blog post and everyone says, 'Oh, I've already read that'.

[But] in the middle of the editing and fact-checking, a murder happened.[3] It turned out that because of the murder, Josh—by virtue of having spent the time on it—became the go-to guy for that story. The magazine was going to publish it but it was going to take too long, so they put it out as a Kindle Single. But they fact-checked it and it's selling really well. I think it's the definitive story about this guy. So the hope is that by putting all that work into it, you find the audience that wants that definitive story.

Notes

1. For more details, see Ratliff's personal website <http://www.cazart.net/about/>.
2. This issue was later explored in an influential article: see Smith 2014.
3. See Malkin 2013.

Conclusion

The professional model of publishing, which designates clear roles and responsibilities, is only partly about getting things done to a consistent standard and in a timely fashion. It is also a way of managing the inevitable failure of human life in a productive way. An understanding that things can be better because of failure, not in spite of it, is a sustainable form of realism.

This book presents a set of focused conversations in a narrative form. Each encounter has its own personal qualities. At the same time, they are conceived as part of a larger study that aims to show patterns across the field. When the words of practitioners are brought into proximity, arguments become clear in a manner that cannot be achieved by analysis alone, no matter how well supported.

Overall, one gets a sense of the professional identity of editing practitioners. They tend to be people who are able to see things from different points of view and who see editing as an opening up of possibilities, rather than closing things down; a collaborative conversation rather than hierarchical control; judgment as action rather than criticism. They come across as being driven not just by the ulterior motive of meeting a practical target, but also by an ultimate motive, love for the work.

This counterintuitive picture brings more nuance and complexity to our understanding of an important practice. Some key themes are explored as follows:

Naming and metaphors

The uncertainty that practitioners show about what to call their work is a recurring theme. Mary Hockaday at the BBC and Adam Moss at *New York* describe multiple editorial identities on the executive floor. Johnny Grimond of *The Economist* describes the versatility demanded at a weekly publication where 'pretty much everybody is a jack of all trades'. Freelance book editor

Constance Hale uses the portmanteau 'scribe'. The publisher Peter Binfield states upfront: 'What I do isn't editing, but I facilitate others to do editing.'

As a literary agent, Carole Blake's work involves a significant amount of editing, but it is not her declared identity. Instead, she defines herself as someone who reads, 'engaging the critical faculties' while doing so. Ileene Smith at Farrar, Straus and Giroux also describes herself primarily as a reader: 'To explain what I do, I say that I read and I decide. I read in order to figure out what we might publish.' Can one describe the editor as an 'embodied reader'? Jerome McGann of the University of Virginia thinks so: 'I definitely respond positively to that. The most embodied reader. There are other embodied readers—reviewers, for example—but no one is more an embodied reader than an editor, that's for sure.'

Contemporary synonyms such as 'curating' are fast-changing. In contrast, the midwife metaphor has been in use for centuries. A 1663 dictionary citation of the word's use, for example, conjures up the world as a 'great Volume' that has needed no amendment since the 'first edition' was produced by God (OED 1989d). Nearly 300 years later, T.S. Eliot's introduction to *The Waste Land* praises Ezra Pound's 'maieutic skill' (Eliot 1971: xxii)—a reference to the Greek *maia* for 'midwife' (OED 2000). Hale considers it apt because '[y]ou're helping the delivery but it's really not your baby'. However she also evokes the expert waiter, dispensing elegant attention: 'Your glass is always full; the waiter is never there.'

Editing also evokes the imagery of cleaning and repair. Newspaperman John McIntyre offers the metaphor of 'Surgeon. I open up the patient, examine what is healthy and what is unhealthy, and excise diseased tissue'. Phoebe Ayers of Wikimedia volunteers: 'We sometimes half-jokingly refer to the administrators as 'janitors', and there's some truth to that.' This imagery can have a shadow meaning, in which the 'badness' being removed from the text is projected onto the person removing it, evoking a sense of shame about the work.

Defining editorial principles

To reflect on core editing principles, all interviewees are asked, 'What is your main concern when editing?' Despite differences of emphasis, a significant overlap of core concerns emerges. It can be summed up in the trio: clarity, interest and accuracy. As Moss says: 'I would say I have two main concerns. Is it interesting? Which is also to say, what ideas are we throwing into the world? The second part is, is it clear?'

A concern for clarity and accuracy cannot be reduced to concern for 'correct' facts or language. It stands in for wider concerns about meaning and relevance. For Blake, the ultimate purpose of seeking clarity is to ensure the translation of meaning from author to reader and 'make sure the author is telling the reader what the author thinks they're telling the reader'. And both meaning and relevance depend on interest. 'I think my main concern is usually that the story should not be boring,' says digital publisher Evan Ratliff. 'There are a lot of things that flow from that. I like the writing to be beautiful but if the story's not boring, everything else can be fixed. If the story's boring, then nothing can be fixed.'

A recurring concern is the desire to 'make things better'. This has a normative, ulterior sense of correcting something that is 'wrong', if only aesthetically. But there is also an ultimate motive; the desire to do something that is 'good' on some level, for its own sake. Smith, working with book authors, describes it as trying 'very hard to encourage the best possible version of the book, without ever imposing my will on the author... pushing every aspect of the book in the direction of an ideal'. In magazines, Moss talks about 'trying to understand [the staff's] issues, making it easier for them to do good work'. And for Wikipedia, Ayers describes an emphasis on '[h]ow do we process better, more efficient, easier, less contentious'.

Making the text better is experienced as a creative process, even in a commercial context. The question 'Is editing ever creative?' prompts delight. But for those working in more 'literary' contexts, sensitivities about the editor-author relationship make it more difficult to answer. Smith says, for example, 'there isn't a constant sense of creativity because of the constraints, because you want to be sure that in the end it's the author's book'. Blake also says: 'I think [editing is creative], but you have to put your own ego to one side and remember that it is always the author's book. Their name goes on the spine, they're the ones who are going to be criticised.'

Just as the notion of 'better' requires close attention, the concept of judgment also needs unpicking. Judgment can have a negative association with criticism and the imposition of rules. But it also has a positive meaning. The 'neutral point of view' rule provides a fixed point of principle and helps to guard against unwarranted bias. But at some point—if one is to advance knowledge, or just get things done—decisions are needed about what is relevant, salient, or 'good'. When the criteria for decisions are explicit, judgment can help support ethical rules that protect the weak. How editors navigate these decisions is one of the main themes running through the book.

Because editing is an act that calls for the exercise of human judgment, those deeply involved in the practice tend to be highly aware of the possibility of error and failure. McIntyre captures this when he says: 'Any editor makes thousands of judgments, most of them minor, in the course of a day, and any change an editor makes can be detrimental…It is particularly important for editors to identify and learn from their mistaken judgments.'

The importance of collaboration is a strong recurring concern. In public debate, collaboration is often associated with new media and defined against more hierarchical legacy structures. Differences certainly exist between these media, but in the interviews it is the similarities that are striking. Editing is consistently described as being 'the work of many hands', negotiated rather than arbitrary, carried out by people who work hard to keep their ego in check. Collaboration extends to the reader: as McIntyre puts it, 'The greatest service that an editor can provide is to approach the text the way the reader would, to identify difficulties or inadequacies in the text'. The relationship between editor and reader is not a simple one of service; there is a mix of tough love and courtship. 'I think it's a mistake to prejudge your readers' interests and curiosities,' says Grimond.

Finally, there is a shared concern captured by the question, 'Do you know when you are finished?' Digital texts are sometimes described as perpetually unfinished, compared to the 'finality' of print media. However the interviews illustrate the problematic nature of this simple binary. A scenario emerges of infinite tinkering, and the arbitrariness of a final version is keenly felt—even in projects lasting for many years. You're finished, says McGann, 'when the publisher is on your back asking "Where's Volume Four?" and there's all those deadlines that are effectively laid upon you. So, you're finished when you're finished'.

The idea of completion, however imperfect, is still a useful one because it allows for failures to be absorbed and something new to be born. For McGann, there's a 'terrible error, a theoretical error' in the idea of making a virtue out of infinity. 'OK, you can continue to add,' he says. 'But once you see the structural limits of what you're doing, then adding is brainless. What you really need is a whole new system.'

Giving value to practice

One of the research questions driving the larger research project asks, 'Is there a way of identifying the difference made by editing, or its absence?' This question is hard to separate from another: 'Does editing have a value and if so, how is it articulated and shared with others?' It turns out that a head-on approach to the question has limited usefulness, and assessments of value emerge in other, more indirect ways.

An obvious proof of value lies in the financial rewards given to a practice; its 'capital' on a literal, economic level. Bourdieu's model of cultural fields allows us to identify more intangible forms of cultural capital. But what comes first? Does a lack of investment create low status, or does a lack of visibility result in low monetary rewards? The interview responses help to tease out perceptions.

In the interviews, a sense of value comes across in unprompted expressions of affinity for the work. By the same token, questions about examples of resistance to editing, or editing gone wrong, prompt anguish about the ways in which the practice can be misunderstood, and delight when it is met with appreciation and enthusiasm.

Interviewees are understandably cautious about identifying specific examples of failure or conflict, which might betray client confidences, and they stick to generic illustrations. Ratliff, for example, describe how things go wrong 'when you have a writer whose level of entitlement and preciousness far exceeds their talent'. Appreciation for the editor's contribution is an important source of professional satisfaction. Says Hale: 'When there's something that bothers me about a piece, [I'm able to] persuade the writer to come my way...Most good writers will see if something's better, and they want it to be better.'

It's one thing for editors to believe in the value of what they do. But in a fight for scarce resources, others may ask: 'Or else, what?' If things are not edited or they are badly edited, are there any consequences? This is a hard thing to demonstrate, and the answer depends on the values brought to the discussion.

Ratliff, for example, is in the business of publishing long-form nonfiction. But he asks, 'What does "long-form" mean? Does it just mean that something is long?' The problem is that 'people are writing longer and longer on the web, but in a lot of cases it's not edited'. The question this raises in the long term is: 'What is the value of putting all that work into it?...Are the readers going to know the difference?'

For some of the interviewees, editing's low capital is a persistent puzzle. One explanation is that it reflects (incorrect) assumptions about the difficulty of producing a text to a high standard, and the level of skills and qualities needed to do that. 'There's this sense of writing not having the same value as painting, or other arts,' says Hale. 'We can all draw but none of us equate ourselves with Rembrandt [yet] somehow we don't have the same sense of how difficult it is to get from A to Z when it comes to language.'[1] Ayers, a different kind of editor, uses similar language: 'Writing and editing is not easy. I'm probably as much of a professional as you can be [in this work] and I still find it incredibly difficult.'

Similar concerns arise about how to pass those skills and qualities on to others. Not one of the people interviewed here received formal training in editing, and opinions differ about how that could, or should, be approached. All practitioners agree that learning by example, over time, is vital. Accounts stress the importance of constant, 'conscious conversation' between practitioners, and with readers or listeners. Examples are also given of circumstances that can prevent the formation or survival of a successful editing culture.

Overall, the consensus in the interviews is for on-the-job learning. But the question arises, is an aversion to formal teaching a reflection of its inherent difficulty, or could more be done to explore what that might look like? The wide range of learning models described in these 13 accounts may provide the basis for future research.

Responding to digital challenges

An attempt to answer the question 'Who pays for editing and why?' is likely to reckon with the impact of technological change. In the interviews, this was acknowledged directly in the question, 'What particular challenges and opportunities arise from digital publishing?' and indirectly, when asking, 'How has your work changed over time?' But in conversation, the subject needed elaboration: in one direction, towards a discussion about 'What is specific about digital editing compared to other kinds of editing practice?' and in another, towards an exploration of business models.

Digital media's claim to distinction dominates the discussion about Wikipedia. In other conversations, the potential similarities of editing practice across old and new media are more warmly embraced. *Nature* editor Campbell says, for example, that despite a difference in the degree of selectivity, the editorial processes used by open access publications are very similar and use 'exactly the same mindset'.

The possibility that textual mediation has simply moved to a new position on the communications circuit is addressed in the interview question, 'If publishers do not edit, who will do it, or should do it?' While all respondents understood that devolution is now a fact of life, it is a cause for concern for some.

When it comes to business models, technological disruption has affected authors as well as editors. For an agent like Blake, 'getting the author paid properly is the biggest challenge at the moment'. Ratliff has set an entire new business model in an attempt to meet the challenge. He cautions: 'People always ask, is this model working? But the model never worked…Everyone's cobbling together different ways of making it work. There's no golden age when people made amazing wages by being free-lance writers.'

Both Binfield and Campbell argue that a decision to use open access is distinct from a decision about the type of editing intervention that will be used. They also agree, however, that editing adds an extra layer of cost, and so far it can only be sustained by either subscriptions or institutional support. As Binfield sums up, 'The problem is that the traditional open access model doesn't work in a very highly selective environment because if you're rejecting 99% of your submissions and only publishing 1%, the fees that you charge authors for that 1% can never cover the work'. They both remain hopeful that something new will emerge, but accept that there is still, as Ratliff puts it, a lot of 'cobbling together' going on.

A number of general observations stand out about the practice of editing. The first is that *attention* is important: not just the attention the editor brings to bear on a text, but the attention that scholars and readers can give to accounts of practice. It is not unusual to enjoy talking about one's own ex-perience. But in these conversations, there is a palpable excitement; it is as if interviewees have been given a chance to admit to a secret passion. McGann says in his own interview that editing equals attention, and attention equals memory. One can add here, that attention equals value.

Another observation is that *identity* is important. Names are not just de-scriptive; they also reflect value, both cultural and monetary. Editing is also defined by what happens when it does not take place. The recurring imagery of 'janitor', 'dirty laundry' or 'naked' copy are reminders of the act's liminal-ity, and associations with shame. But that can be part of the fascination.

A good theory is important: Practice is important to theory, because it provides a level of attention to detail that is otherwise lost. In return, our conceptual frameworks influence the value we give to a practice.

And finally, *culture* is important: editing practice is part of a working cul-ture, whose features are often tacit rather than explicit. Culture does not exist solely in legacy institutions: it arises the moment a single person writes for an audience. And that culture stretches into the past and future.

Note

1. A similar point is made by novelist Celia Brayfield, who notes: 'Writers have been learning, teaching and sharing their experiences for millennia but, because language is our medium, and language is mastered, at a basic level, by almost all human beings, great achievement in this art seems accessible...It's said that everyone has a book in them, but not a symphony, a digital installation or a pickled shark' (2009: 176).

Appendix

All the interviews in this book cover the same themes, but the selection of questions from the full set—and the precise wording of each question— are varied to suit each encounter. This approach falls in the category of the 'semi-structured interview', a form of fieldwork found in naturalistic enquiry in which the discussion is guided by a common set of questions, but the exchange is not as formally structured as a structured questionnaire.

Your own practice

1. Do you think of yourself as an editor? If not, what do you call what you do?
2. What do you *do*? Describe a typical day
3. What do you like most/least about editing?
4. What is your main concern when editing and how is it resolved? Is there a particular example of editing that illustrates this concern?
5. At the more detailed level of style, what matters?
6. Do you think of your reader? How? On what level?
7. How do you know when you are finished?
8. How important is 'judgment'?
9. Is editing creative? In what way?
10. What examples of resistance to editing, or criticism of it, have you encountered?
11. What are consequences of bad/good/absent editing?
12. How is writing different from editing? Is it more/less difficult?
13. How did you *learn* the practice of editing? Is it difficult to *teach*?

General editing practice

14. Should editing receive more public recognition? Is it valued in your own organisation? Does value depend on *type* of editing?
15. What particular challenges and opportunities arise from digital publishing? How is digital editing different from print?
16. If publishers do not edit, who will/should do it?
17. Do you agree/disagree with the following statement by Amazon executive Russell Grandinetto: 'The only really necessary people in the publishing process now are the writer and reader.'

About yourself

18. Personal: Age, m/f, x yrs overall experience
19. Work: Type of publisher, job title; x yrs at this place
20. What did you study? Any connection to your work? Formal qualifications? Anything else in your background, education, that informs your work?
21. What drew you to this type of work?
22. Do you see yourself as part of any particular tradition? Do you have a role model?

Afterwards

1. Is it unusual to be asked questions about editing?
2. Does being in a formal interview on the subject prompt any new thoughts for you about editing practice?
3. Does being a writer or editor yourself change the way you respond to questions?
4. [When you look at the transcript of your own interview] Is there anything particularly funny/silly/interesting about editing a text about editing?

References

Atavist. 'People.' <https://atavist.com/team/> accessed 7 August 2014.

Athill, Diana. *Stet: An Editor's Life*. London: Granta, 2000.

Ayers, Phoebe, Matthews, Charles, and Yates, Ben. *How Wikipedia Works and How You Can Be a Part of It*. San Francisco: No Starch Press, 2008.

Babbage. 'SXSW blog, day two: Journalistic nuclear physics.' *Economist*, 14 March 2011 <http://www.economist.com/blogs/babbage/2011/03/sxsw_blog_day_two> accessed 14 August 2014.

Ball, Philip. 'Scientists, not editors, are distorting science publishing.' *Prospect*, 10 January, 2014 < http://www.prospectmagazine.co.uk/blogs/philip-ball/why-science-journals-still-matter> accessed 7 August 2014.

Bardoel, Jo, and Deuze, Mark. '"Network journalism": Converging competencies of old and new media professionals.' *Australian Journalism Review* 23.3 (December 2001): 91–103.

Bartlett, Jaime. 'Wikiwashing: How paid professionals are using Wikipedia as a PR tool.' *The Daily Telegraph*, 11 July 2014 <http://blogs.telegraph.co.uk/technology/jamiebartlett/100013979/wikiwashing-how-paid-professionals-are-using-wikipedia-as-a-pr-tool/> accessed 17 August 2014.

Berg, A. Scott. *Max Perkins, Editor of Genius*. New York: E.P. Dutton, 1978.

Berger, Peter L., and Luckmann, Thomas. *The Social Construction of Reality: A Treatise in the Sociology of Knowledge*. New York: Anchor Books, 1990.

Blake, Carole. *From Pitch to Publication: Everything You Need to Know to Get Your Novel Published*. London: Macmillan, 1999.

Blake Friedmann. 'The agency' < http://blakefriedmann.co.uk/the-agency/> accessed 7 August 2014.

Bourdieu, Pierre. *The Field of Cultural Production*. Cambridge: Polity Press, 1993.

Boynton, Robert, ed. *The New New Journalism*. New York: Vintage Books, 2005.

Bradley, Sue, ed. *The British Book Trade: An Oral History*. London: British Library, 2008.

Brayfield, Celia. 'Creative writing: The frequently asked question.' *New Writing: International Journal for the Practice and Theory of Creative Writing* 6.3 (2009): 175–186.

Bridle, James, ed. *'The Iraq war,'* 6 September 2010. <http://booktwo.org/notebook/wikipedia-historiography/> accessed 6 October 2012.

Bruns, Axel. *Gatewatching: Collaborative Online News Production.* New York: Peter Lang, 2005.

Burke, Kenneth. *A Rhetoric of Motives.* Berkeley: University of California Press, 1969.

Carr, David. 'A gamble on a weekly that paid off.' *The New York Times,* 9 August 2010 <http://www.nytimes.com/2010/08/09/business/09carr.html?pagewanted=1&sq=adam%20moss&st=cse&scp=1&_r=0> retrieved 7 August 2014.

Clayman, Steven, and Reisner, Ann. 'Gatekeeping in action: Editorial conferences and assessments of newsworthiness.' *American Sociological Review* 63.2 (April 1998): 178–199.

Cohen, Philip, ed. *Devils and Angels: Textual Editing and Literary Theory.* Charlottesville: University of Virginia Press, 1991.

Collaborative Creativity Group. 'Reports Wikipedia survey available.' *Way Back Machine,* 24 March 2010 <https://web.archive.org/web/20130718220145/http:/wikipediasurvey.org/> accessed 14 October 2012.

Conroy, Frank, ed. *The Eleventh Draft: Craft and the Writing Life from the Iowa Writers' Workshop.* New York: Harper Collins, 1999.

Coser, Lewis A. 'Publishers as gatekeepers of ideas.' *Annals of the American Academy of Political and Social Science* 421 (September 1975): 14–22.

Crowley, S., and Hawhee, Sharon. *Ancient Rhetorics for Contemporary Students,* Fifth edition. New York: Macmillan, 2012.

Darnton, Robert. 'What is the history of books?' In Darnton, Robert, *The Kiss of Lamourette: Reflections in Cultural History.* New York: W. W. Norton & Co, 1990: 107–135.

Donohew, Lewis. 'Newspaper gatekeeper and forces in the news channel.' *The Public Opinion Quarterly* 31.1 (1967): 61–68.

Doughty, Louise. *Apple Tree Yard.* London: Faber & Faber, 2014.

Doughty, Louise. *A Novel in a Year: A Novelist's Guide to Being a Novelist.* London: Simon & Schuster, 2007.

Economist, The. *The Economist Style Guide,* London: Economist Books, 2012.

Edemariam, Ade. 'White teeth and enthusiasm.' *The Guardian,* 2 December 2006 <http://www.guardian.co.uk/books/2006/dec/02/news.comment> accessed 2 December 2006.

Eliot, Valerie, ed. *The Waste Land: A Facsimile and Transcript of the Original Drafts Including the Annotations of Ezra Pound.* London: Faber & Faber, 1971.

Faber, Geoffrey. *A Publisher Speaking.* London: Faber & Faber, 1934.

Filipacchi, Amanda. 'Wikipedia's sexism toward female novelists.' *The New York Times,* 24 April 2013.

Finkelstein, David, and McCleery, Alistair. *An Introduction to Book History*. London: Routledge, 2005.

Finkelstein, David, and Patten, Robert. 'Editing Blackwood's or, what do editors do?' In Finkelstein, David, ed., *Print Culture and the Blackwood Tradition, 1805–1930*. Toronto: University of Toronto Press, 2006: 146–183.

Forde, Kathy Roberts. *Literary Journalism on Trial:* Masson v. New Yorker *and the First Amendment*. Amherst: University of Massachusetts Press, 2008.

Gabler, Hans Walter, ed. *Ulysses: A Critical and Synoptic Edition*. London: Routledge, 1984.

Gibney, Elizabeth. 'Research paper "sloppiness" on the increase, warns publisher.' *Times Higher Education*. 12 May 2013.

Gleick, James. 'Wikipedia's women problem.' *New York Review of Books*, 29 April 2013. <http://www.nybooks.com/blogs/nyrblog/2013/apr/29/wikipedia-women-problem/> accessed 14 August 2014.

Gorman, G.E., and Clayton, Peter. *Qualitative Research for the Information Professional*. London: Facet, 2005.

Gourevitch, Philip, ed. *The Paris Review Interviews, Vol 4*. Edinburgh: Canongate Books, 2009.

Gowers, Sir Ernest. *The Complete Plain Words*. London: Penguin, 1987.

Greenberg, Susan. 'Editorial roles and practices: Exploring the creative enterprise.' In Abrahamson, David, and Prior-Miller, Marcia, eds., *The Handbook of Magazine Research: The Future of the Magazine Form*. London: Routledge, forthcoming.

Greenberg, Susan. 'The ethics of narrative: A return to the source.' *Journalism: Theory, Practice, Criticism*, 15.5 (July 2014): 517–532.

Greenberg, Susan. 'Slow journalism in the digital fast lane.' In Keeble, Richard Lance, and Tulloch, John, eds., *Global Literary Journalism: Exploring the Journalistic Imagination*. New York: Peter Lang, 2012: 381–393.

Greenberg, Susan. 'Personal experience, turned outward.' *Free Associations* 62 (September 2011): 151–174.

Greenberg, Susan. 'When the editor disappears, does editing disappear?' *Convergence: The International Journal of Research into New Media Technologies*. 16.1 (February 2010): 7–21.

Gross, George, ed. *Editors on Editing: What Writers Need to Know About What Editors Do*. New York: Grove Press, 1993.

Hale, Constance. *Sin and Syntax: How to Craft Wicked Good Prose*. New York: Three Rivers Press, 2013.

Hale, Constance. *Vex, Hex, Smash, Smooch: Let Verbs Power Your Writing*. New York: W.W. Norton & Co, 2012.

Hale, Constance. *Wired Style: Principles of English Usage in the Digital Age*. New York: Broadway Books, 1999.

Hamilton, James F., and Heflin, Kristen. 'User production reconsidered: From convergence, to autonomia and cultural materialism.' *New Media & Society* 13.7 (2011): 1050–1066.

Hartsock, John C. *A History of American Literary Journalism: The Emergence of a Modern Narrative Form.* Amherst: University of Massachusetts Press, 2000.

Hemingway, Ernest. *A Moveable Feast.* New York: Scribner, 2010.

Hern, Alex. 'Chelsea Manning name row: Wikipedia editors banned from trans pages.' *The Guardian,* 24 October 2013 < http://www.theguardian.com/technology/2013/oct/24/chelsea-manning-name-row-wikipedia-editors-banned-from-trans-pages> accessed 14 December 2014.

Hockaday, Mary. *Kafka, Love and Courage: The Life of Milena Jesenská,* London: André Deutsch, 1995.

Huang, Keira. 'Wikipedia fails to bridge gender gap.' *South China Morning Post,* 11 August 2013.<http://www.scmp.com/news/hong-kong/article/1295872/wikipedia-fails-bridge-gender-gap> accessed 6 August 2014.

Jeffries, Stuart. 'Lawrence Norfolk: A life in writing.' *The Guardian,* 7 September 2012 <http://www.theguardian.com/books/2012/sep/07/lawrence-norfolk-life-in-writing> accessed 15 August 2014.

Jolliffe, Lee. 'Research review: Magazine editors and editing practices.' In Abrahamson, David, ed., *The American Magazine: Research Perspectives and Prospects.* Ames: Iowa State University Press, 1995: 51–71.

Keeble, Richard. 'Intimate portraits: The profiles of Kenneth Tynan.' In *Journalism: Theory, Practice, Criticism,* 15.5 (July 2014): 548–560.

King, Stephen. *On Writing.* London: Hodder & Stoughton, 2000.

Latham, Harold S. *My Life in Publishing.* London: Sidgwick & Jackson, 1965.

Lerner, Betsy. *The Forest for the Trees: An Editor's Advice to Writers.* London: Pan Macmillan, 2002.

Lewin, Kurt. *Field Theory in Social Science: Selected Theoretical Papers.* New York: Harper, 1951.

Lincoln, Yvonna S., and Guba, Egon G. *Naturalistic Inquiry.* London: Sage, 1985.

Litz, A. Walton. 'Maxwell Perkins: The editor as critic.' In Howard, W.J., ed., *Editor, Author, and Publisher.* Toronto: University of Toronto Press, 1969: 96–112.

MacFarquhar, Larissa. 'Robert Gottlieb, the art of editing no 1.' *The Paris Review* 132 (Fall 1994): 182–223.

Malkin, Bonnie, ed. 'John McAfee says he will testify about murder in Belize.' *The Daily Telegraph,* 13 November 2013 < http://www.telegraph.co.uk/news/worldnews/northamerica/usa/10448351/John-McAfee-says-he-will-testify-about-murder-in-Belize.html> accessed 7 August 2014.

Maynes, Mary Jo, Pierce, Jennifer L., and Laslett, Barbara. *Telling Stories: The Use of Personal Narratives in the Social Sciences and History.* Ithaca, NY: Cornell University Press, 2008.

Mays, J.C.C., ed. *The Collected Works of Samuel Taylor Coleridge*, 6 vols. Princeton, NJ: Princeton University Press, 2001.

McCormack, Thomas. *The Fiction Editor.* London: St Martin's Press, 1988.

McGann, Jerome. Fenimore Cooper and the American World, ed. with Ryan Cordell (NINES, in progress). Collaborative work being developed under the auspices of University of Virginia's Speclab (Speculative Computing Laboratory) and ARP (Applied Research in 'Patacriticism).

McGann, Jerome. The Complete Writings and Pictures of Dante Gabriel Rossetti. A Hypermedia Research Archive [2000–present]. Charlottesville: Institute for Advanced Technology in the Humanities. NINES (Networked Infrastructure for Nineteenth-Century Electronic Scholarship).

McGann, Jerome. *A New Republic of Letters: Memory and Scholarship in the Age of Digital Reproduction.* Cambridge, MA: Harvard University Press, 2014.

McGann, Jerome. *The Textual Condition.* Princeton, NJ: Princeton University Press, 1991.

McGann, Jerome J. *A Critique of Modern Textual Criticism.* Chicago: University of Chicago Press, 1983.

McGann, Jerome. *Byron: The Complete Poetical Works, ed. with Introduction, Apparatus, and Commentaries.* The Oxford English Texts series. Vol. I (1980); Vols. II and III (1981); Vols. IV and V (1986); Vol. VI (1991); Vol. VII (1993). Oxford: Clarendon Press.

McIntyre, John E. 'My editor, my oppressor.' *The Baltimore Sun*, 8 August 2014 <http://articles.baltimoresun.com/2014-08-28/news/bal-my-editor-my-oppressor-20140828_1_editors-writer-media> accessed 8 August 2014.

McIntyre, John E. 'Day one.' *The Baltimore Sun*, 3 September 2013a <http://touch.baltimoresun.com/#section/-1/article/p2p-77255034/> accessed 3 September 2013.

McIntyre, John E. *The Old Editor Says: Maxims for Writing and Editing.* Baltimore, MD: Apprentice House, 2013b.

McKenzie, D.F., ed. *The Works of William Congreve.* New York: Oxford University Press, 2011.

Morozov, Evgeny. *To Save Everything, Click Here: The Folly of Technological Solutionism.* New York: Public Affairs Books, 2013a.

Morozov, Evgeny. 'To Save Everything, Click Here: A Breakfast with Evgeny Morozov.' Nesta, London, 22 March 2013b <http://www.nesta.org.uk/assets/events/to_save_everything_click_here_a_breakfast_with_evgeny_morozov> [Personal notes from recording].

Morrison, Blake. 'Black day for the blue pencil.' *The Guardian*, 6 August 2005, 4.

Murray, Padmini Ray, and Squires, Claire. "The digital publishing communications circuit" in Book 2.0. 3.1. (June 2013): 3–23.

Nature. 'History of the journal *Nature*' <http://www.nature.com/nature/history/timeline_1860s.html> accessed 7 August 2014.

New York. 'Media Kit.' <http://mediakit.nymag.com/> accessed 7 August 2014.

Norton, Scott. *Developmental Editing: A Handbook for Freelancers, Authors and Publishers.* Chicago: University of Chicago Press, 2009.

Orwell, George. *Politics and the English Language.* London: Penguin, 2013.

Oxford English Dictionary. 'Maieutic.' Third Print Edition, June 2000. [Online version June 2012] <http://www.oed.com/view/Entry/112474?redirectedFrom=maieutic#eid> accessed 24 May 2013.

Oxford English Dictionary. 'Editing.' Second Print Edition, 1989a. [Online version June 2012] <http://www.oed.com/view/Entry/59547?redirectedFrom=editing#eid> accessed 10 January 2011.

Oxford English Dictionary. 'Edit.' Second Print Edition, 1989b. [Online version March 2013] <http://www.oed.com/view/Entry/59546#eid5739815> accessed 10 January 2011.

Oxford English Dictionary. 'Editor.' Second Print Edition, 1989c. [Online version September 2013] <http://www.oed.com/viewdictionaryentry/Entry/59553> accessed 10 January 2011.

Oxford English Dictionary. 'Edition.' Second Print Edition, 1989d. [Online version September 2012] <http://www.oed.com/view/Entry/59548#eid5740123> accessed 10 January 2011.

Oxford English Dictionary, 'Epigones.' Second Print Edition, 1989e. [Online Version March 2013] accessed 18 August 2014.

Pickard, A.J. *Research Methods in Information.* London: Facet Publishing, 2013.

Polis. 'Trust in the BBC.' <http://www.youtube.com/watch?feature=player_embedded&v=bBW-Iq6ySd4> accessed 15 May 2013.

Potter, Clarkson N. *Who Does What and Why in Book Publishing.* New York: Birch Lane Press, 1990.

Quinlan, Mary Kay. 'The dynamics of interviewing.' In Ritchie, Donald A., ed., *The Oxford Handbook of Oral History.* Oxford: Oxford University Press, 2011: 25–31.

Rabinowitz, Peter J. 'Truth in fiction: A reexamination of audiences.' *Critical Inquiry* 4 (Autumn 1977): 121–141.

Saller, Carol. *The Subversive Copy Editor: Advice from Chicago.* Chicago: University of Chicago Press, 2009.

Schekman, Randy. 'Randy Schekman answers questions on his stance against #luxuryjournals.' eLife, 13 December 2013. <http://elifesciences.org/elife-news/randy-schekman-answers-questions-on-his-stance-against-luxuryjournals> accessed 7 August 2014.

Shirky, Clay. 'How we will read: Clay Shirky.' *Findings,* 5 April 2012 <http://blog.findings.com/post/ 20527246081/how-we-will-read-clay-shirky> accessed 8 April 2012.

Shirky, Clay. *Here Comes Everybody: How Change Happens When People Come Together.* London: Penguin, 2008.

Simon, Rita J., and Fyfe, James J., eds. *Editors as Gatekeepers: Getting Published in the Social Sciences.* London: Rowman & Littlefield, 1994.

Sims, Norman. 'The problem and the promise of literary journalism studies.' *Literary Journalism Studies* 1.1 (Spring 2009): 7–16.

Singer, Jane B. 'Online journalists: Foundations for research into their changing roles.' *Journal for Computer Mediated Communication* 4.1 (September, 1998).

Smith, Ben. 'What the longform backlash is all about.' *Medium*, 26 January 2014. <https://medium.com/journalism-deliberated/958f4e7691f5> accessed 20 March 2014.

Spencer-Brown, George. *Laws of Form*. Leipzig: Bohmeier Verlag, 2011.

Streitfeld, David. 'Amazon signs up authors, writing publishers out of deal.' *The New York Times*, 16 October 2011 < http://www.nytimes.com/2011/10/17/technology/amazon-rewrites-the-rules-of-book-publishing.html?_r=0 > accessed 6 May 2014.

Sullivan, Hannah. *The Work of Revision*. Cambridge, MA: Harvard University Press, 2013.

Tennis, Joseph T. 'Epistemology, theory and methodology in knowledge organization: Towards a classification, metatheory and research framework.' *Knowledge Organization* 25.2/3 (2008): 102–112.

Thompson, John B. *Merchants of Culture: The Publishing Business in the Twenty-First Century*, Cambridge: Polity, 2010.

Thomson, Alistair. 'Memory and remembering in oral history.' In Ritchie, Donald A., ed., *The Oxford Handbook of Oral History*, Oxford: Oxford University Press, 2011: 88–91.

Tompkins, Jane. 'Masterpiece theater: The politics of Hawthorne's literary reputation.' In Tompkins, Jane, *Sensational Designs: The Cultural Work of American Fiction 1790–1860*. New York: Oxford University Press, 1985: 20–34.

Unsworth, John. 'Documenting the reinvention of text: The importance of failure.' *Journal of Electronic Publishing* 3.2 (December 1997).

Vida, Vendela. *The Believer Book of Writers Talking to Writers*. San Francisco: Believer Books, 2005.

Waldman, Simon. 'Who knows?' *The Guardian*, 26 October 2004.

White, David Manning. 'The "gatekeeper": A case study in the selection of news.' *Journalism Quarterly* 27.4 (1950): 383–390.

Wikipedia. 'Neutral point of view.' <http://en.wikipedia.org/wiki/Wikipedia:Neutral_point_of_view> accessed 7 August 2014.

Wilmsen, Carl. 'For the record: Editing and the production of meaning in oral history.' *The Oral History Review* 28.1 (Winter–Spring 2001): 65–85.

Zinsser, William. *On Writing Well*. New York: Quill/HarperCollins, 2001.

Further Reading

Alvarez, Al. *The Writer's Voice*. London: Bloomsbury, 2005.

Baker, Barbara, ed. *The Way We Write: Interviews with Award-Winning Writers*. London: Continuum, 2007.

Bhaskar, Michael. *The Content Machine: Towards a Theory of Publishing, from the Printing Press to the Digital Network*. London: Anthem Press, 2013.

Bisaillon, Jocelyne. Professional editing strategies used by six editors.' *Written Communication* 24.4 (2007): 295–322.

Booth, Wayne C. *The Rhetoric of Fiction*. London: Penguin, 1983.

Bourdieu, Pierre. *Distinction: A Social Critique of the Judgment of Taste*. London: Routledge, 2010.

Bourdieu, Pierre. *Language and Symbolic Power*. Cambridge: Polity Press, 1992.

Bridge, Marie, ed. *On the Way Home: Conversations between Writers and Psychoanalysts*, London: Karnac, 2008.

Bruccoli, Matthew. *The Sons of Maxwell Perkins: Letters of F. Scott Fitzgerald, Ernest Hemingway, Thomas Wolfe, and Their Editor*. Columbia: University of South Carolina Press, 2004.

Bruchler, Birgit, and Posthill, John, eds. *Theorising Media and Practice*. Oxford and NY: Berghahn, 2010.

Bryman, Alan, and Burgess, Robert G., eds. *Analyzing Qualitative Data*. London: Routledge, 2001.

Burdick, Anne, Drucker, Joanna, Lunenfeld, Peter, Presner, Todd, and Schnapp, Jeffrey. *Digital Humanities*. Cambridge, MA: The MIT Press, 2012.

Burns, Carole, ed. *Off the Page: Writers Talk About Beginnings, Endings, and Everything in Between*. London: Norton, 2008.

Butcher, Judith, Drake, Caroline, and Leach, Maureen. *Butcher's Copy-editing: The Cambridge Handbook for Editors, Copy-editors and Proofreaders*. Cambridge: Cambridge University Press, 2006.

Carter, Rebecca. 'A world of editing.' *Words Without Borders*, January 2011 <http://wordswithoutborders.org/article/a-world-of-editing> accessed 4 January 2011.

Charmaz, Kathy. 'Grounded theory: Objectivist and constructivist methods.' In Denzin, Norman K., and Lincoln, Yvonne S., eds., *Handbook of qualitative research*. Thousand Oaks, CA: Sage, 2000: 509–535.

Chartier, Roger. *Forms and Meanings: Texts, Performances and Audiences from Codex to Computer*. Philadelphia: University of Pennsylvania Press, 1995.

Chartier, Roger, and Cochrane, Lydia G. *The Order of Books: Readers, Authors, and Libraries in Europe Between the Fourteenth and Eighteenth Centuries*. Cambridge: Polity Press, 1994.

Chartier, Roger. 'Labourers and voyagers: From the text to the reader.' *Diacritics* 22.2 (1992): 49–61.

Chartier, Roger. 'Texts, printing, readings.' In Hunt, Lynn, ed., *The New Cultural History*. Berkeley: University of California Press, 1989: 154–175.

Clark, Roy Peter. *How to Write Short: Word Craft for Fast Times*. New York: Little, Brown, 2013.

Creswell, J.W. *Qualitative Inquiry and Research Design: Choosing Among Five Approaches*. London: Sage, 2007.

Darnton, Robert. 'Google and the future of books.' *New York Review of Books*, 14 February 2009.

Denzin, Norman K., and Lincoln, Yvonne S., eds. *Handbook of Qualitative Research*, Thousand Oaks, CA: Sage, 2000.

Edwards, Rosalind, and Holland, Janet. *What Is Qualitative Interviewing?* London: Bloomsbury Academic, 2013.

Ehrlich, Kate. 'The invisible world of intermediaries: A cautionary tale.' *Computer Supported Cooperative Work*, 8.1/2 (1999): 147–167.

Ellis, David. 'The information seeking patterns of academic researchers: A grounded theory approach.' *Library Quarterly* 63.4 (1993): 469–486.

Epstein, Jason. *Book Business: Publishing Past, Present and Future*. New York: W.W. Norton, 2012.

Evans, Michael Robert. *The Layers of Magazine Editing*. New York: Columbia University Press, 2004.

Finkelstein, David, and McCleery, Alistair, eds., *The Book History Reader*. London: Routledge, 2006.

Franklin, Dan. 'The role of the editor.' In Owen, Peter, ed., *Publishing Now*. London: Peter Owen, 1996.

Franklyn, Jon. *Writing for Story*. New York: Penguin Books, 1986.

Frisch, Michael. *A Shared Authority: Essays on the Craft and Meaning of Oral and Public History*. Albany: SUNY Press, 1990.

Fylan, Fiona. 'Semi-structured interviewing.' In Miles, Jeremy, and Gilbert, Paul, eds., *A Handbook of Research Methods for Clinical and Health Psychologists*. New York: Oxford University Press, 2005: 65–78.

Gerard, Philip. *Writing A Book That Makes a Difference*. Cincinnati, OH: Story Press, 2000.

Gill, Brendan. *Here at the New Yorker*. New York: Random House, 1975.

Glaser, Barney. *Basics of Grounded Theory Analysis*. Mill Valley, CA: Sociology Press, 1992.

Glaser, Barney, and Strauss, Anselm. *The Discovery of Grounded Theory: Strategies for Qualitative Research*. Mill Valley, CA: Sociology Press, 1967.

Goldberg, Natalie. *Writing Down the Bones: Freeing the Writer Within*. Boston: Shambhala, 2005.

Gornick, Vivian. *The Situation and the Story: The Art of Personal Narrative*. New York: Farrar, Straus and Giroux, 2002.

Greenberg, Susan. 'Knowing what you don't know.' In Hillson, David, ed., *The Failure Files: Perspectives on Failure*. London: Triarchy Press, 2011: 57–65.

Greenberg, Susan. 'Is curating the new editing?' *Oddfish*, 17 August 2010 <http://odd-fish.co.uk/2010/ 08/17/is-curating-the-new-editing/> accessed 10 August 2010.

Grunwald, Edgar A. *The Business Press Editor*. New York: New York University Press, 1988.

Guba, Egon G. 'Criteria for assessing the trustworthiness of naturalistic inquiries.' *Educational Communication and Technology Journal* 29 (1981): 75–91.

Harris, Sharon M., ed. *Blue Pencils and Hidden Hands*. Boston: Northeastern University Press, 2004.

Hunt, Celia, and Sampson, Fiona. *Writing, Self and Reflexivity*. London: Palgrave, 2006.

Jefferson, George. *Edward Garnett: A Life in Literature*. London: Cape, 1982.

Johanson, Katya. 'Dead, done for and dangerous: Teaching editing students what not to do.' *New Writing: International Journal for the Practice and Theory of Creative Writing* 3.1 (2006): 47–55.

Jones, John. 'Patterns of revision in online writing: A study of Wikipedia's featured articles.' *Written Communication* 25.2 (2008): 262–289.

Kachka, Boris. *Hothouse: The Art of Survival and the Survival of Art at America's Most Celebrated Publishing House, Farrar, Straus and Giroux*. New York: Simon & Schuster, 2013.

Kaplan, David M. *Revision: A Creative Approach to Writing and Rewriting Fiction*. Cincinnati: Story Press, 1997.

Knott, William C. *The Craft of Fiction*. Menlo Park, CA: Askmar Publishing, 2012 [e-book].

Kramer, Mark, ed. *Telling True Stories: A Nonfiction Writers' Guide*. Cambridge: Nieman Foundation at Harvard University, 2007.

Kunkel, Thomas, ed. *Letters from the Editor: The New Yorker's Harold Ross*. New York: Modern Library, 2001.

Lanham, Richard A. *The Economics of Attention: Style and Substance in the Age of Information*. Chicago: University of Chicago Press, 2006.

Leonard, M. *Dear Genius: The Letters of Ursula Nordstrom*. New York: Harper Collins, 1998.

Liddle, Dallas. *The Dynamics of Genre: Journalism and the Practice of Literature in Mid-Victorian Britain*. Charlottesville, VA: University of Virginia Press, 2009.

Mariyani-Squire, Edward. 'Social constructivism: A flawed debate over conceptual foundations.' *Capitalism, Nature, Socialism* 10:4 (1999): 97–125.

McIntyre, John E. 'Maybe they could try to teach editing.' *The Baltimore Sun*, 20 June 2012 <http://articles.baltimoresun.com/2012-06-20/news/bal-maybe-they-could-try-to-teach-editing-20120620_1_editing-grammar-journalism-education> accessed 20 June 2012.

McKay, Jenny. *The Magazines Handbook*. London: Routledge, 2006.

McKee, Robert. *Story*. London: Methuen, 1998.

McKenzie, Donald F. *Bibliography and the Sociology of Texts: The Panizzi Lectures 1985*. Cambridge: Cambridge University Press, 1999.

Mehta, Ved. *Remembering Mr Shawn's New Yorker: The Invisible Art of Editing*. Woodstock and New York: The Overlook Press, 1998.

Moss, Paul. 'Is modern fiction just not up to scratch?' *BBC News Magazine*, 29 October 2010 <http:// www.bbc.co.uk/news/magazine-11648471> accessed 29 October 2010.

Mossop, Brian. *Revising and Editing for Translators*. Manchester: St Jerome, 2001.

Murch, Walter. *In The Blink of An Eye: A Perspective on Film Editing*. Los Angeles: Silman-James Press, 2001.

Navasky, Victor S., and Cornog, Evan. *The Art of Making Magazines: On Being an Editor and Other Views from the Industry*. New York: Columbia Journalism Review Books, 2012.

Nielsen, Jakob. 'Usability 101: Introduction to usability.' *Alertbox*, 4 January 2012 <http://www. nngroup.com/articles/usability-101-introduction-to-usability/> accessed 18 July 2013.

Page, Walter H. *A Publisher's Confession*. London: Heinemann, 1905.

Perks, Robert, and Thompson, Alistair, eds. *The Oral History Reader*. London: Routledge, 2006.

Plotnik, Arthur. *The Elements of Editing: A Modern Guide for Editors and Journalists*. New York: Macmillan, 1982.

Prose, Francine. *Reading Like a Writer*. New York: HarperCollins, 2006.

Rabiner, Susan, and Fortunato, Alfred. *Thinking Like Your Editor: How to Write Great Serious Nonfiction and Get It Published*. New York: W.W. Norton, 2002.

Roth, Philip. 'An open letter to Wikipedia.' *The New Yorker*, 7 September 2012 <http:// www.newyorker.com/online/blogs/books/2012/09/an-open-letter-to-wikipedia. html> accessed 1 October 2012.

Speck, Bruce W., Hinnen, Dean A., and Hinnen, Kathleen. *Teaching Revising and Editing: An Annotated Bibliography*. Westport, CT: Greenwood Press, 2003.

Speck, Bruce W. *Editing: An Annotated Bibliography*. Westport, CT: Greenwood Press, 1991.

Squires, Claire. *Marketing Literature: The Making of Contemporary Writing in Britain*. London: Palgrave Macmillan, 2009.

Stephen, Leslie. 'The evolution of editors.' In *Studies of a Biographer, Vol 1*. New York: G. P. Putnam's Sons, 1907: 35–68.

Stevenson, Iain. *Book Makers: British Publishing in the Twentieth Century*. London: British Library, 2010.

Strauss, Anselm L., and Corbin, Juliet. *Basics of Qualitative Research: Grounded Theory Procedures and Techniques*. London: Sage, 2008.

Strauss, Anselm L., and Corbin, Juliet. 'Grounded theory methodology: An overview.' In Denzin, Norman K., and Lincoln, Yvonne S., eds., *Handbook of Qualitative Research*, Thousand Oaks, CA: Sage, 1994: 273–285.

Surma, Anne. *Public and Professional Writing: Ethics, Imagination and Rhetoric*. London: Palgrave Macmillan, 2005.

Wendig, Chuck. *500 Ways to Be a Better Writer*. Terrible Minds, 2011 [e-book]. <http://www.amazon.com/500-Ways-Better-Writer-ebook/dp/B0062A7QHW> accessed 14 September 2013.

Wiener, Joel H. *Innovators and Preachers: The Role of the Editor in Victorian England*. Westport, CT: Greenwood Press, 1985.

Index

A

absence of editing 41, 70, 80, 107–108
   See also failures
abstract languages 65
academics
   as authors 92, 98, 135, 146, 153, 154
   as editors 97–98, 146, 147, 151
accuracy 30, 60, 77, 79, 85, 120, 187
   See also clarity
advertising 27, 38, 177
aesthetics 4, 26–27, 187
agents 8, 49–50, 108–109, 113–125
Amazon
   gatekeeping 16n14
   Kindle publications 52, 125, 177
   writers and readers (Grandinetti quote)
     50, 90, 109, 125, 155
Amis, Kingsley 46
anonymity of authors 25
   See also collective voices
Aristotle 65
Athill, Diana 3
attention
   to accounts of practice 191
   to design 48
   to language 27–28, 50
   of scholars 54, 57, 58, 70
authorial intention 65–66
authors
   academics as 92, 98, 135, 146, 153,
     154

and agents 8, 49–50, 108–109,
   113–125
and editors 1, 5, 48–49, 51, 116–118,
   130, 134
and readers 4, 7, 106
awareness of readers
   authors 4, 7, 106
   blogs 100
   book editors 106, 129, 135, 137
   journals 93–94, 98–99, 147, 149
   magazines 21–22, 23–24, 27, 28, 39,
   171
   news media 76, 77, 78–79, 80, 81,
   82, 88
   nineteenth century periodicals 64
   scholarly editing 57, 62

B

backgrounds. *See* career paths
Ball, Philip 92
Baltimore Sun, The 83–90
BBC 23, 75–82, 185
bibliography 3, 53, 59, 62–63, 68
biographies 48, 55
blogs 85–86, 88, 100, 132, 133
book editors 45–52, 103–139
   awareness of readers 106, 129, 135,
   137
   career paths 45–48, 52, 113–115, 130
   collaboration 134, 136
   creativity 48, 99–100, 107, 128
   daily routines 49–50, 104, 120

editing own work 40–41, 104, 107, 117–118
ego, suppression of 118, 122, 137
imagery of editing 51, 134, 136
impact of editing 48
job satisfaction 137
judgment 51, 106–107, 123
making text better 48, 49
processes 48–49
proofreading 135, 137
recognition of 108, 123
relationships 48–49, 106, 115–116
resistance to 49, 107, 137, 189
roles 45, 51
shaping 131, 132
training 46, 108, 122
book fairs 114, 115, 120
book history 54, 59, 70
book list-building 4, 45, 48, 49
books 45–52, 103–139
buying 116–117
clarity 105, 119
cover designs 48, 49, 134–135
failures in 107–108, 123
illustrations 133
layout 48, 133
selection 48, 49
sub-editing 116, 128, 135
titles 5, 49, 129
typefaces 63, 133
writing styles 122
booksellers 119, 123
See also Amazon
Bourdieu, Pierre 7, 8, 189
Bowers, Fredson 55, 57, 69
Boynton, Robert 181
brand value 93, 99
British Broadcasting Corporation (BBC) 23, 75–82, 185
broadcasting codes 78
Burnet, Alistair 20, 26
business models 96, 144–146, 152, 171, 178, 191
See also costs of editing
BuzzFeed 182
Byron, Lord 54, 55, 59, 61, 65, 66, 70

C

Calder, Liz 46
career paths
books 45–48, 52, 113–115, 130
journals 94–95, 153–154
magazines 20–21, 130, 172, 175–176
news media 75, 83–84
scholarly editing 55–56
Wikipedia 162–163, 163–164
Carr, David 33
Chadwick, Elizabeth 117–118
Cincinnati Enquirer, The 83–84, 87
citizen journalism 78
clarity
books 105, 119
editorial principles 186–187
magazines 25, 27, 39
news media 77, 81, 85, 88, 89
scholarly editing 60, 61
See also accuracy
coaching 29–30, 55, 130
Coleridge, Ernest Hartley 54
collaboration
books 134, 136
editorial principles 188
magazines 21, 35–36, 40–41
news media 88, 89
scholarly editing 61–62, 63–64
Wikipedia 159, 164
collective voices 19, 24–25, 35–36, 40
commercial fiction 119
communication circuits 7, 8, 101, 103, 127, 190
communities
open access journals 149, 151, 155
scientific journals 96, 98, 99, 146
Wikipedia 158–159, 168
completion of work 67, 85, 106, 121, 136, 188
conciseness 25
context. See linking
Cooper, James Fenimore 56–57, 58, 63, 66
copy editing. See sub-editing
copyright 64, 152, 164
costs of editing 135, 138
See also business models

courses. *See* teaching, courses; writing
    courses
cover designs
    books 48, 49, 134–135
    magazines 26, 36, 38, 39, 40
creativity
    constraints on 50–51, 122–123, 187
    in editing 48, 99–100, 107, 128, 167
Crime Writers' Association 117
criticism
    books 49, 107, 137
    journals 92, 97, 155
    magazines 41, 174, 179, 180
    scholarly editing 69
    Wikipedia 167
cultural production 7, 8, 189
curation. *See* selection

D

daily routines
    books 49–50, 104, 120
    magazines 29–31, 38–39, 178
    news media 77, 84–85
    scholarly editing 66
    Wikipedia 164–166
    See also music; rituals
Darnton, Robert 7
Davis, Joshua 183
deadlines. *See* completion of work
decision-making 4, 8, 98, 150–151, 157,
    160–161
    See also selection
definition of editing 3–6
design
    book covers 48, 49, 134–135
    digital media 67
    layout 26–27, 38, 48, 133
    magazine covers 26, 36, 38, 39, 40
    typefaces 63, 133
developmental editing 92, 105–106,
    116, 127, 135, 172
    See also shaping in editing; sub-editing
Dickens, Charles 64, 132
digital media
    business models 96, 144–146, 152,
        171, 178, 191
    challenges 89–90, 125, 190–191

design 67
linking 5, 67, 93, 147, 148, 165
news media 79
processes 88, 96
tools 59, 67, 147
voices 36
See also absence of editing; new media;
    open access journals; Wikipedia
dislikes about editing 51, 86, 105, 122,
    174

E

ebooks 52, 125, 177
echoes 116, 180
eclectic editing 55, 57
Economist, The 19–31, 185
editing, definition 3–6
editing own work 40–41, 68, 85–86,
    104, 107, 117–118, 174
    See also writers editing own work
editorial boards 92, 146, 147, 149–151
editorials 22, 93, 99, 100
education 20, 55, 83, 94–95, 109, 153
    See also teaching; training
ego, suppression of 118, 122, 137, 158,
    159, 168, 188
electronic books 52, 125, 177
eLife 92, 144, 145, 152
Eliot, T.S. 52n3, 90, 186
encyclopaedias. *See* Wikipedia
Erskine, Barbara 115
Esquire 33, 35
ethical standards 4, 5, 146, 154, 187
experience 20, 45–46, 52, 75–76, 83–84,
    109, 113–114

F

Faber, Geoffrey 64
failures
    books 107–108, 123
    magazines 28, 41, 134, 179, 182, 183
    news media 87, 89
    scholarly editing 59–60
    value of 185, 188, 189
    See also absence of editing
female editors 157, 160

Fenwick, Liz 116–117
fiction 46, 50, 117, 119–120
foreign languages 30, 114, 115, 121, 124–125, 158, 165
frameworks for editing 7–9, 78, 191
freelance editors 47, 116, 124, 127–138
freelance writers 26, 178
Friedmann, Julian 122

G

Gabler, Hans Walter 57
Galassi, Jonathan 50
gaming in open access publishing 147–149
Gardner, Sue 160
gatekeeping 4, 8, 9, 16n14, 109, 147, 151
    See also selection
gender of editors 157, 160
ghostwriting 135
Gowers, Ernest 27
Grandinetti, Russell 50, 90, 109, 125, 155
Greg-Bowers eclectic editing 55, 57
Gross, Gerald 3
Gross, John 28–29

H

Habermas, Jürgen 54
Hamill, Pete 36
headlines 21, 39, 84
Heard, Alex 182
Hennessy, Peter 24
Hewitt, David 54–55, 70
historical texts 54, 55, 58, 61–62, 65
Homans, Charlie 178
Hoyt, Jason 143–144
humour 26, 27
Hurricane Sandy 34, 40

I

identities 19, 24–25, 35–36, 40, 185
    See also imagery of editing; naming of editor role
illustrations 26–27, 133, 168, 178

imagery of editing 51, 84, 134, 135, 136, 151, 164, 186
    See also identities; naming of editor role
impact of editing 48, 94, 96–97, 99, 160–161, 174
impartiality in news media 77, 79, 81–82
    See also neutral point of view
information architecture 67
interest 39, 178, 186, 187
interviews 3, 6–7, 9–12, 13–14
invisibility. *See* visibility

J

Jackson, Laura Riding 60
James, Henry 132
jargon 28, 88, 137
job satisfaction 84, 86, 137, 166, 189
journalists as editors 20–21, 88, 131, 136, 137
journals. *See* open access journals; scientific journals
judgment in editing
    books 51, 106–107, 123
    concept of 187–188
    journals 92, 94–95, 96
    magazines 22, 41
    news media 77, 78–79, 81–82, 84, 86–87, 88

K

Kelly, Kevin 136
Kindle publications 52, 125, 177
Kruger, Kobie 124–125

L

Lang, Cecil 55
language 26, 27–28, 50, 88, 129, 137, 138–139
languages, foreign 30, 114, 115, 121, 124–125, 158, 165
Latham, Harold 3
Laws of Form (Spencer-Brown) 65
layout 26–27, 38, 48, 133
Leaves of Grass (Whitman) 63
Lewin, Kurt 8

line editing. *See* sub-editing
linking
   book list-building 4, 45, 48, 49
   digital media 5
   journals 93, 147, 148
   magazines 22
   news media 77, 80
   scholarly editing 67
   Wikipedia 165
   See also metadata
list-building, books 4, 45, 48, 49
literary agents 113–125
literary consultancies 117, 124
literary criticism 55
literary festivals 111
literary fiction 46, 119–120
Longform.org 182
Lonsdale, Roger 56

M

Macmillan 125
macro-editing. *See* selection
magazine editors 19–31, 33–41,
    171–183
   awareness of readers 21–22, 23–24,
     27, 28, 39, 171
   career paths 20–21, 130, 172,
     175–176
   collaboration 21, 35–36, 40–41
   daily routines 29–31, 38–39, 178
   editing own work 174
   impact of editing 174
   judgment in editing 22, 41
   making text better 35
   processes 29–31, 173
   proofreading 21
   recognition of 24
   relationships in editing 30, 37–38
   resistance to editing 41, 174,
     179, 180
   roles 17, 19, 27, 35, 175
   selection 22–23, 35, 41, 136, 172,
     175, 176
   shaping in editing 35, 133–134,
     172–174, 178–179, 181
   training 28–29, 37, 41, 172–173,
     175–176

magazines 19–31, 33–41, 171–183
   business models 171, 178
   clarity 25, 27, 39
   cover designs 26, 36, 38, 39, 40
   failures 28, 41, 179, 182, 183
   failures in 134
   illustrations 26–27, 178
   layout 26–27, 38, 133
   linking 22
   as metaphor for design 132,
     133–134
   neutral point of view 23
   opinions 23, 25
   sub-editing 20, 30, 172, 175
   tone 25, 26, 27
   voices 36
   writing styles 19, 25, 27–28, 29, 179,
     180, 181
making text better 35, 48, 49,
    158, 187
Malcolm, Janet 48
managerial role of editor 35, 38, 77
marked text 65
Maschler, Tom 46
Mayer, Peter 46
Mayes, J.C.C. 57
McAfee, John 183
McCloud, Randall 62
McCormack, Thomas 1
McKenzie, Don 57, 62
memoirs 3, 177
memories 58, 61, 70, 191
mentoring 29–30, 55, 130
metadata 5, 16n14, 93
   See also linking
metaphors for editing 51, 84, 134, 135,
    136, 151, 164, 186
metrics in open access publishing
    147–149
micro-editing. *See* shaping in editing
midwife as metaphor of editor 51, 136,
    151, 186
Mills, Kate 116–117
multimedia 81, 177, 178
Murray, John 'Jock' 61
music 51, 85
   See also daily routines; rituals

N

naming of editor role
  facilitators 144
  multiple identities 24, 35, 76
  readers 51, 62, 118
  scribes 136
  summary 185–186
  See also identities; imagery of editing
Nature 91–100, 146, 151–152, 152–153
neutral point of view 7, 23, 157–158,
    162, 163
  See also impartiality in news media
new media 8, 70, 111, 132, 191
  See also digital media
news media 75–82, 83–90
  awareness of readers 88
  clarity 77, 81, 85, 88, 89
  digital media 79
  failures 87, 89
  linking 77, 80
  tone 77, 81
  writing styles 85, 88
news media editors 75–82, 83–90
  awareness of readers 76, 77, 78–79,
    80, 81, 82
  career paths 75, 83–84
  collaboration 88, 89
  daily routines 77, 84–85
  editing own work 85–86
  imagery of editing 84
  job satisfaction 84, 86
  judgment in editing 77, 78–79,
    81–82, 84, 86–87, 88
  opinions in editing 77, 82
  proofreading 84
  recognition of editors 89
  relationships in editing 77, 78–79
  roles of editors 75, 76, 81, 84
  standards in editing 76, 77, 78
  training 80–81, 88, 89
New York 33–41
New Yorker, The
  editors 136, 176, 182
  production values 21, 36, 40, 173,
    177, 183
New York Public Library 58
nineteenth-century editing 2–3, 54

non-fiction 50, 128–130, 131, 132
Norfolk, Lawrence 115–116
novelists 103–104, 108, 110

O

objectivity. *See* impartiality in news media;
    neutral point of view
O'Brien, Jeff 182
Ofcom broadcasting code 78
open access journals 143–155
  awareness of readers 147, 149
  business models 96, 144–146, 152
  career paths 153–154
  challenges to traditional media 91–92,
    95–96
  communities 149, 151, 155
  decision-making 150–151
  imagery of editing 151
  linking 147, 148
  metrics 147–149
  relationships in editing 147
  resistance to editing 155
  roles of editors 147
  selection 144–145, 146–147, 148,
    149
  shaping in editing 147, 150
  standards in editing 149–150
  training 150–151
  See also scholarly editing
opinions in editing 23, 25, 77, 82
O'Reilly Media 143–144
Orion 116
Orwell, George 27, 29
Outside 176, 182

P

paper choices 26
PeerJ 143–144, 144–145, 146, 150
peer reviews 30–31, 94, 128, 146, 147,
    154
periodicals 2–3, 56, 63–64, 91
Perkins, Maxwell 15n5, 133
philology 54, 59, 70
PLoS Biology 95, 96, 152
PLoS Medicine 95, 152
PLoS ONE 95, 146, 147, 150, 153, 154

PNAS 151–152
Poe, Edgar Allan 56, 63–64
point of view. *See* neutral point of view
Potter, Clarkson 1
Pound, Ezra 90, 186
*Proceedings of the National Academy of
    Sciences* 151–152
processes 4, 29–31, 48–49, 88, 158,
    159, 173
    See also decision-making; selection
Progress of Stories (Jackson) 60
proofreading 21, 66, 84, 135, 137, 158
Public Library of Science 91–92, 95, 143
    See also PLoS titles
publishers and editing 64, 93, 116–117,
    124, 147
publishers lists 4, 45, 48, 49

Q

qualifications
    education 20, 55, 83, 94–95, 109,
        153
    experience 20, 45–46, 52, 75–76,
        83–84, 109, 113–114
    See also teaching; training

R

Rabb, Jefferson 176
Random House 47
recognition of editors 24, 89, 100, 108,
    123
recruitment process 94–95
referees 92, 95, 96, 97
relationships in editing
    authors, editors and texts 5
    books 48–49, 106, 115–116
    journals 92, 147
    magazines 30, 37–38
    news media 77, 78–79
    scholarly editing 60–61
    Wikipedia 158–160
repeated words and phrases (echoes) 180
reporting 22–23, 77, 82, 131, 152, 175,
    181
resistance to editing
    books 49, 107, 137, 189

journals 92, 97, 155
    magazines 41, 174, 179
    scholarly editing 69
    Wikipedia 167
re-writing obsession 104
rituals 51, 85, 165
    See also daily routines; music
role models 88, 109–110, 176, 181–182
roles of editors
    books 45, 51
    journals 147
    magazines 17, 19, 27, 35, 175
    news media 75, 76, 81, 84
    scholarly editing 57
    See also freelance editors
Romantic Novelists' Association 117
Rossetti, Dante Gabriel 54, 59, 66, 67
Roth, Philip 163, 169n6
routines, daily. *See* daily routines
royalties 115, 125, 178

S

Sage Publications 153–154
Schekman, Randy 91–92
Schell, Orville 130
scholarly editing 53–70
    attention 54, 57, 58, 70
    awareness of readers 57, 62
    career paths 55–56
    clarity 60, 61
    collaboration 61–62, 63–64
    daily routines 66
    editing own work 68
    failures 59–60
    linking 67
    proofreading 66
    relationships in editing 60–61
    resistance to editing 69
    roles of editors 57
    training 55, 56, 68
    See also open access journals
Science 92, 146, 151–152, 152–153
scientific journals 91–100
    awareness of readers 93–94, 98–99
    career paths 94–95
    communities 96, 98, 99, 146
    decision-making 98

impact of editing 94, 96–97, 99
judgment in editing 92, 94–95, 96
linking 93
recognition of editors 100
relationships in editing 92
resistance to editing 92, 97
selection 92–93, 94, 98, 149
shaping in editing 97
sub-editing 93, 97
training 94–95, 97–98, 100
Scott, Sir Walter 54–55, 61, 70
selection
　books 48, 49
　definition of 4
　magazines 22–23, 35, 41, 136, 172,
　　175, 176
　open access journals 144–145,
　　146–147, 148
　scientific journals 92–93, 94, 98, 149
　Wikipedia 160–161
　See also decision-making; gatekeeping
self-publishing 78, 109
shaping in editing
　books 131, 132
　definition of 4–5
　journals 97, 147, 150
　literary agents 116, 123
　magazines 35, 133–134, 172–174,
　　178–179, 181
　See also developmental editing; editing
　　own work; sub-editing; writers
　　editing own work
Silberman, Jim 46
Simon & Schuster 45, 46, 47
social constructivism 7, 9, 10, 12
social media 2, 8
Spencer-Brown, George 65
Sphere 114
Spitzer, Elliot 36, 37
standards in editing
　ethical 4, 5, 146, 154, 187
　journals 149–150
　news media 76, 77, 78
Stewart, Tom 46
styles. See writing styles
sub-editing
　books 116, 128, 135
　journals 93, 97

magazines 20, 30, 172, 175
Wikipedia 158
See also developmental editing; shaping
　in editing
Summit Books 46, 47

T

teaching
　courses 89, 130–131, 167–168
　on-the-job 41, 69, 108,
　　174–175, 190
　See also qualifications; training
Tennis, Joseph 14
theories of editing 55, 57–59, 62
Thompson 114
Thompson, Nicholas 176, 182
titles, books 5, 49, 129
Tompkins, Jane 8
tone 25, 26, 27, 77, 81
tools for digital media 59, 67, 147
trade publishing 47, 57
training
　books 46, 108, 122
　journals 94–95, 97–98, 100,
　　150–151
　magazines 28–29, 37, 41, 172–173,
　　175–176
　news media 80–81, 88, 89
　scholarly editing 55, 56, 68
　Wikipedia 158, 159, 168
　See also qualifications; teaching
Trenhaile, John 118
typefaces 63, 133

U

unediting theory 62
university presses 47–48, 50
Unsworth, John 59

V

Valery, Paul 106
value of editing 87, 182, 188–190
Victorian editing 2–3, 54
visibility 3, 24, 28–29, 89, 138, 189
Vulture 36

W

Wales, Jimmy 157
Waste Land, The (Eliot) 52n3, 90, 186
website editing 36, 38, 132
W.H. Allen 114
Whitman, Walt 63
Wikipedia 157–169
  career paths 162–163, 163–164
  collaboration 159, 164
  communities 158–159, 168
  creativity in editing 167
  daily routines 164–166
  decision-making 157, 160–161
  editing own work 167
  ego, suppression of 158, 159, 168
  female editors 157, 160
  illustrations 168
  imagery of editing 164
  impact of editing 160–161
  job satisfaction 166
  linking 165
  making text better 158
  neutral point of view 157–158, 162, 163
  processes 158, 159
  proofreading 158
  relationships in editing 158–160
  resistance to editing 167
  selection 160–161
  sub-editing 158
  training 158, 159, 168
  writing and editing 166–167
  writing styles 159
Wired 127, 136, 171, 172–173, 175–176, 182, 183
wit 26, 27
Wolfe, Tom 36
women editors 157, 160
workload 49, 51–52
writers editing own work 109, 110, 121
  See also editing own work
writing courses 89, 107, 108, 117, 124
writing styles
  books 122
  magazines 19, 25, 27–28, 29, 179, 180, 181
  news media 85, 88

Wikipedia 159
Wroe, Anne 27

Y

Yale University Press 47–48, 50

Z

Zalewski, Daniel 182

Lee B. Becker, *General Editor*

The Mass Communication and Journalism series focuses on broad issues in mass communication, giving particular attention to those in which journalism is prominent. Volumes in the series examine the product of the full range of media organizations as well as individuals engaged in various types of communication activities.

Each commissioned book deals in depth with a selected topic, raises new issues about that topic, and provides a fuller understanding of it through the new evidence provided. The series contains both single-authored and edited works. For more information and submissions, please contact:

Lee B. Becker, Series Editor | *lbbecker@uga.edu*
Mary Savigar, Acquisitions Editor | *mary.savigar@plang.com*

To order other books in this series, please contact our Customer Service Department at:

(800) 770-LANG (within the U.S.)
(212) 647-7706 (outside the U.S.)
(212) 647-7707 FAX

Or browse online by series at www.peterlang.com